Twayne's United States Authors Series

Sylvia E. Bowman, *Editor*

INDIANA UNIVERSITY

William Vaughn Moody

WILLIAM VAUGHN MOODY

by Martin Halpern
University of Massachusetts

 64

Twayne Publishers, Inc.   ::   New York c 1964

Preface

IN KEEPING with the general policy of the Twayne's United States Authors Series, the aim of this book has been to describe, interpret, and evaluate the whole body of William Vaughn Moody's published work in poetry and the drama. My critical focus throughout has been on the work itself; I have included in the text-proper only such biographical information and comments on literary, social, or intellectual background as seemed necessary to an understanding of the poems and plays and of the general progress of Moody's career. Additional information and commentary, when it seemed important but not indispensable, I have relegated to footnotes or to the chronological outline which precedes Chapter One; and I have simply resisted the temptation to include other matter which, however relevant it may be historically, did not appear directly pertinent to the main business of the book.

Though I have taken pains to say something about every item in Moody's collected *Poems and Plays*, and about most of the uncollected pieces published in magazines and newspapers, it has not, of course, been possible or advisable to discuss all his works in anything near equal detail. My emphases have been largely dictated by three considerations: the degree of a work's importance, either in itself or in terms of the author's artistic development; the degree of complexity, difficulty, or my own sense of the need for explication; and the degree to which I have something to say that has not been said before or that runs contrary to the views of earlier commentators. But these emphases are subjectively conditioned, and can only be checked and corrected by an activity which the entire book endeavors to provoke: confrontation with the texts of Moody's neglected—and, as I have argued, often unjustly neglected—poems and plays.

All references to and quotations from Moody's writings for which no citation is given are taken from the standard collected edition, the two-volume *Poems and Plays* edited by John M. Manly and published by Houghton Mifflin in 1912. I have omitted citations to this edition in order to avoid constantly encumbering the text with distracting page references or swelling the already oversized bulk of the footnotes at the rear. Wherever possible, however, I have tried to give sufficient indication of context so that quotations and references may be located by simply consulting the table of contents. Writings of Moody not included in the 1912 edition have been cited in the footnotes, as have all secondary materials which are referred to directly or to which my own commentary may owe a particular debt not acknowledged in the text. The most useful of these secondary materials, both for the present study and for anyone seeking to penetrate further into previous Moody criticism, are listed with brief annotations in the bibliographical appendix following the footnotes.

Most of the time spent in writing this book was provided by a George and Eliza Gardner Howard Foundation fellowship for the academic year 1962-63. I should like to thank Professor Sylvia E. Bowman, Editor of the Twayne's United States Authors Series, for some perceptive and helpful, but undogmatic, editorial suggestions; and Professor Josephine Miles for the original impetus to the entire undertaking.

MARTIN HALPERN

Berkeley, California

Contents

Chronology

1869 William Vaughn Moody born July 8 in Spencer, Indiana. Father, a former steamboat captain, now in business, had migrated from central New York about 1852; mother descended from one of the oldest pioneering families of southern Indiana. William Vaughn the third son and sixth child of seven.

1871 Family moves to New Albany, Indiana, where Moody attends grammar school and high school, edits high school newspapers, excels in painting and outdoor sports, and attends church and Sunday School regularly.

1884 Death of Moody's mother.

1885 Moody graduates from high school; enters Pritchett Institute of Design in Louisville, Kentucky, to study painting.

1886 Death of his father. Moody becomes teacher in district school near New Albany.

1887 Enters Riverview Academy, Poughkeepsie, New York, for college preparation with special training in the classics.

1889 Enters Harvard College. Becomes frequent contributor of poems and articles to the *Harvard Monthly*; later an editor. Friendships with Daniel Gregory Mason, George Santayana, Bliss Carman, George Pierce Baker, Robert Herrick, Robert Morss Lovett, and other contributors to the *Monthly*.

1892-
1893 Having completed graduation requirements in three years, spends senior year traveling in Germany, Switzerland, England, Italy, Greece, and Turkey.

1893 Graduates from Harvard; second in his class and class poet.

1893-
1894 Graduate student in English at Harvard; M.A., 1894.

1894-
1895 Member of Harvard English Faculty. Friendships with Trumbull Stickney and Josephine Preston Peabody.

1895   Spends summer traveling in France. In September joins English faculty of the University of Chicago.

1896   While teaching full year, edits Bunyan's *Pilgrim's Progress* for Houghton Mifflin; also composes several of the lyric poems collected in *Poems,* 1901. Colleagues and friends include Herrick, Lovett, Ferdinand Schevill, John M. Manly, Hamlin Garland, Henry Fuller.

1897   Spends spring and summer on bicycle trip through Italy and Austria, with Schevill and later Lovett. Composes "Good Friday Night" and other poems, and begins *The Masque of Judgment.* Returns to Chicago in September; teaches through March, 1898. Edits Coleridge's *The Ancient Mariner* and Lowell's *The Vision of Sir Launfal* for Lake English Classics series. Begins work on edition of Milton for Houghton Mifflin.

1898   April to July, in New York, finishing edition of Milton and working on *Masque.* "Good Friday Night" published in May *Atlantic Monthly,* his first major magazine publication. July to December, teaching at University of Chicago.

1899   January to June, in New York, then London, working on *Masque* and first version of *The Faith Healer.* In New York, friendship begins with Edwin Arlington Robinson. Milton edition published. July to December, teaching at Chicago. Edits various works of Scott and co-edits selections from Pope's *Iliad* for Lake series. Meets Harriet Tilden Brainerd.

1900   Spends entire year in the East, chiefly in Boston, Gloucester, and New York. Completes *Masque* in January. New poems—including "An Ode in Time of Hesitation" and "Gloucester Moors"—published in *Atlantic, Scribner's,* and other leading journals. Finishes first version of *The Faith Healer.* Begins work on *A History of English Literature* in collaboration with Lovett. *Masque of Judgment* published by Small, Maynard, & Co. in November.

1901   January to July, teaching at Chicago; working on *A History of English Literature. Poems* published in May by Houghton Mifflin. In May, begins correspondence with Harriet Brainerd. In summer, travels on horseback through

Rocky Mountains with Hamlin Garland. Spends fall and winter in East, mainly Boston.

1902 Completes work on *A History of English Literature*, published later in the year by Scribner's. Withdraws from teaching. April to June, travels in Greece; begins *The Fire-Bringer*. Spends July and August in Paris, reading all of Greek tragedy with Stickney. September to November, travels through Austrian and Italian Tyrol. Returns to America in November.

1903 Lives in New York, Chicago, and Mackinac Island, Michigan. Friendship begins with Ridgely Torrence. Works on *The Fire-Bringer* and writes various poems, including "Second Coming," "Thammuz," first version of narrative "The Death of Eve."

1904 *Fire-Bringer*, completed in January, published by Houghton Mifflin. In spring, travels in Arizona desert with Schevill. Spends fall and winter in New York. Writes various poems, including "Old Pourquoi," "The Fountain," "I Am the Woman," and second version of narrative "The Death of Eve." Begins "The Sabine Woman" (first version and original title of *The Great Divide*). Collaborates with Lovett on *A First View of English Literature*. Friendship begins with Percy MacKaye.

1905 *A First View of English Literature* published by Scribner's. In April, undergoes serious operation for growth on leg, probably a result of a fall on Mount Parnassus during 1902 trip to Greece. Slow recuperation in New York and then Chicago through the summer. Returns to New York in November. Works on "The Sabine Woman."

1906 Completes "The Sabine Woman" early in the year. "Sabine Woman" produced in Chicago in April, with Moody present. Spends summer in New Hampshire, revising play for New York production. Play opens, with title *The Great Divide*, in October, and runs for two years, a large commercial and critical success. Moody remains in New York until March, 1907. Begins play *The Death of Eve*.

1907 Spends spring in Tangiers, Spain, Italy, and England with Torrence. Spends summer in Chicago and Mackinac Island. Works on *The Death of Eve*. In fall, back in New York, working on second version of *The Faith Healer*.

1908   In March, attack of typhoid fever; recuperates in New York until June. Elected to National Academy of Arts and Letters, and receives honorary D. Litt. at Yale. Spends summer on Mackinac Island, working on *The Faith Healer*. Returns to New York in November. Production of *The Faith Healer* postponed; returns to Chicago in December, his health failing.

1909   In February, makes recuperative trip to California with painter William Wendt. In March, travels to St. Louis for tryout of *The Faith Healer*. Second version of *The Faith Healer* (four acts) published by Houghton Mifflin. In May, marries Harriet Brainerd in Quebec. Honeymoon in England until September. Becomes seriously ill in England, with beginnings of blindness. In December, settles in southern California with Harriet, his health broken. Edition of DeQuincey, largely distilled from *A History of English Literature,* published in Lake Classics series.

1910   *The Faith Healer* opens in New York in January. Final version (three acts), based on revisions made after St. Louis tryout, published by Macmillan. Spends summer in Chicago. In October, moves with Harriet to Colorado Springs in last desperate attempt to recover health. Dies of a brain tumor on October 17, 1910.

1911   *The Great Divide* published by Macmillan.

1912   Manly's edition of the two-volume *Poems and Plays* published by Houghton Mifflin.

William Vaughn Moody

CHAPTER 1

Introductory

DURING THE FIRST QUARTER of the twentieth century, William Vaughn Moody's reputation ranked near the highest in American literature. Before his death in 1910 at the age of forty-one, he had been celebrated in some quarters as the man-most-likely-to-succeed in realizing America's hope for a major renaissance in both poetry and the drama.[1] Though his early death partly confounded such prophecies, even the relatively small body of writing collected in the 1912 edition of his *Poems and Plays* led reviewers in prominent journals to describe him in such phrases as "one of the great poets of our day," "a great American poet," "one not unworthy to walk in paths first trod by the feet of Milton and of Shelley," and "such a poet as had not been raised up before him in America—or even in the English-speaking world — since the eclipse of the great line of the older singers."[2] In a critical anthology of American poetry published in 1918, Moody was the latest poet represented; and the editor predicted that "we may look forward with confidence to a final estimate that will put him among the greatest of American poets, and among the leading singers in the world choir of his day."[3] As late as 1922, a critic strongly committed to the new poetry of his time and able to find almost nothing to admire in most American poetry from the Civil War to 1910, could still speak of Moody's poems and verse dramas as "a great ocean with thousand-league currents and wide treasure caves of gold" and as "a splendid fruition after which young American poets might well turn to revolt and experiment."[4]

Since then, Moody's reputation has steadily declined. Though his two prose plays — especially *The Great Divide*, which had been hailed in the author's own time as "the present high water mark in American drama" and evidence that Moody would be "the great American playwright"[5]—still hold a fairly prominent place in histories of the twentieth-century drama, his other work has fallen increasingly into neglect[6] and, with some critics, into contempt. The one book written about him—David D. Henry's informative but critically unassuming *William Vaughn Moody: A Study* (1934)—did little to stem the decline; and by 1946, Horace Gregory and Marya Zaturenska could sum up their sense of contemporary attitudes toward the poems and verse dramas with observations like, "The present reader of William Vaughn Moody's verse is almost certain to be faced with embarrassment."[7] Despite occasional expressions of dissent,[8] this kind of view has generally prevailed until today, as is perhaps most clearly shown by the fact that Moody's work has turned up less and less frequently in anthologies of the last fifteen years.[9] And by 1961, Roy Harvey Pearce, in his large-scale study *The Continuity of American Poetry,* could dispose of Moody with only a passing reference to him as one name on the "depressing list" of minor poets operating in America at the turn of the century.[10]

This decline of a once major reputation is explicable enough in terms of literary history. Moody's death occurred just before the poetic revolution of the 1910's and 1920's; and in many outward and some inward respects, the bulk of his dramatic and non-dramatic verse reflected characteristics of its age against which poets and critics began to react soon after his death, and have in a sense been reacting ever since. But what is explicable in terms of the actions and reactions of literary history is not therefore true in terms of absolute literary values. Distinctions must be made, for Moody as for any writer, between what is intrinsically spurious, independent of time and historical context, and what may only seem so to the reader brought up on different standards of taste and unwilling or unable to make the simple imaginative leap necessary to comprehend any artistic expression of another age. At the same time, of course, historically based criteria can have only limited relevance for readers who seek in the literature of the past experiences that are more than merely archaeological. Once the necessary historical leap is made, a poet must still speak meaningfully to our own age if his work is to be valued not as document but as living literature.

It is the constant assumption, and sometimes the explicit contention, of this book that a good part of the value which

Moody's own age discerned in his poetry, and especially in his plays, is still discernible today and still capable of reaching us as living experience. Only by confronting his work from a perspective broader than that afforded by transient literary fashion can we distinguish the enduringly genuine from the spurious; and by so distinguishing, we can see how, over the past four decades, Moody's reputation has suffered more than most from the vicissitudes of literary history.

Such a confrontation will readily reveal characteristics which appear, *prima facie,* to alienate Moody from the contemporary literary mentality. For one thing, there is his general approach to poetic language and verse technique. Like most of his American contemporaries, Moody was a conservative in prosodic matters; even a profound admiration for Whitman did not prevent him from rejecting the "Whitmanic verse-mode" as such[11] and from adhering in all his own work to traditionally sanctioned forms and meters. This alone, of course, would hardly cut him off from the subsequent development of twentieth-century poetry, since some of the greatest talents associated with that development—for instance, Yeats, Frost, and Stevens—have usually been just as conservative. But for Moody, formal and metrical conservatism was part of a larger conservatism which often permeated his diction, syntax, and rhetorical techniques and lent much of his verse an air of studied artificiality. Moreover, his verse dramas and the more ambitious non-dramatic poems of his adult years were animated by an unabashedly self-conscious wish to be a "big" poet, a singer of grand themes in the grand manner. For Moody this sometimes meant a diction, syntax, and rhetoric that were artificial in a very special sense, keyed as they were to what had been taken since the late seventeenth century as the appropriate English version of the "sublime" mode. And though some widely admired twentieth-century poets, like Hart Crane,[12] have attempted with some success to revivify this mode, it is not one that has been generally congenial to our age's temper and taste.

We must, however, constantly look behind the surface manner of Moody's verse to the ideas and emotions that inform it, in order to make meaningful judgments on his language and verse technique. At his best—especially in the mature verse dramas—the "sublime" mode proves a legitimate vehicle for honestly intense emotions and honestly high-serious ideas. Only when his substance is unequal to its expression—when, as one of his most intelligently sympathetic early critics remarked, he closes "the gaps in his inspiration with a rubble-work of very clever rhetoric"[13]—does Moody lapse into the two vices most common in this mode: bathos and bombast. And such lapses, as we shall see, decrease as his artistry and philosophical vision mature.

Nor was Moody always confined in his diction, syntax, and rhetoric to traditional artifices. Considering the prevailing poetic climate in America during the time he wrote, some of his linguistic techniques—as in the best dialogue of his plays and those poems like "Song-Flower and Poppy," "The Menagerie," and "Old Pourquoi," which experiment with contemporary colloquial speech idioms—were notably unorthodox and ahead of their time. Even when committed to traditional modes, Moody was far from slavish in his orthodoxy; and within those modes his personal gifts found far more natural and effective expression than did those of any of his American contemporaries who made the same stylistic commitment.[14]

Besides their frequent adherence to a now rejected style, Moody's poems and verse dramas have also found disfavor with later critics for their downright eclecticism—their echoings of, and sometimes their direct borrowings from, earlier authors from the Greeks to the English Victorians. Moody was a well-educated man. He is, in fact, of rather special interest today as the forerunner of a long and growing line of twentieth-century American poets who are also scholars and university teachers. After a thorough prep-school training in the classics, he took his Bachelor's and Master's degrees at Harvard in English, concentrating in medieval literature but also furthering his classical studies and acquiring a good acquaintance with Continental literatures. Then, from his twenty-fifth to thirty-second year, he earned his livelihood as a member of the English faculty first at Harvard and later at the University of Chicago. He was editor of several scholarly and popular editions of classic English writers (see Bibliography), and was co-author, with Robert Morss Lovett, of A History of English Literature, which is still a standard college textbook.[15]

Though the profits from the latter enterprise allowed Moody to withdraw from university teaching at thirty-two, the scholarly habit remained with him throughout his adult life and exerted a tangible influence on much of his imaginative writing. His friend Edwin Arlington Robinson, who admired and sometimes rather envied Moody for his early achievements and critical success, once felt compelled to remark; "Perhaps Moody's greatest trouble lies in the fact that he has so many things to unlearn."[16] And several later critics, even among his devotees, have commented on what Gregory and Zaturenska condemned as a quality of "fatal . . . literary reminiscence" in some of Moody's work.[17]

Here, too, however, the critic must look behind surfaces. T. S. Eliot has argued, partly in justification of his own eclecticism (one far more pervasive than Moody's), that

> One of the surest of tests is the way in which a poet borrows. Immature poets imitate; mature poets steal; bad poets deface what they take, and good poets make it into something better, or at least something different. The good poet welds his theft into a whole of feeling which is unique, utterly different from that from which it was torn; the bad poet throws it into something which has no cohesion.[18]

In much of his early poetry, Moody simply imitated, with unimpressive results. But as he matured, his borrowings tended to become more and more—to use Eliot's term—"thefts," or, in other words, conscious and purposeful literary allusions. Moody's use of the allusive method differs from Eliot's, of course, in that its intent is not usually ironic and the language of the allusion is not usually as distinct stylistically from the author's own. But in his case as well as Eliot's, the sanction for the method is in the belief in a general "community" of poetry, a kind of common storehouse into which all important poetry goes and from which later writers may draw for the enrichment of their own work by literary and historical association. The only real test of a poet's success in using the method is, as Eliot says, the extent to which the borrower makes the allusion his own, integrates it into the new context in such a way that it becomes transformed while still retaining the associative values of the original context. Moody's maturer eclectic practices must be judged, no less than Eliot's, or Ezra Pound's, in terms of their effectiveness in fulfilling the author's personal purpose.

As will be seen in the following chapters, neither these eclectic practices nor his general technical conservatism prevented Moody from being regarded by his contemporaries as a vitally individual talent and as a much-needed antidote to the genteel timidities of most turn-of-the-century American poetry. Yet even in his own time, Moody was criticized by some for substantive elements in his work which have given increasing discomfort to later commentators. Especially in the verse dramas, but also in the prose dramas and in certain of the lyric and narrative poems, he set his sights extremely high. His themes were often cosmic, either directly or, as in the prose dramas, obliquely; and cosmic themes, perhaps in this age more than any other, leave an author vulnerable to charges of overreaching or pretentiousness. Furthermore, in the verse dramas themselves, Moody based his subject matter on various Greek, Hebraic, and Christian mythologies remote from his own time and place; and the consequence, for several commentators both during and after his own lifetime, was an effect of abstractness and escapism, as though in attempting to universalize his ideas by embodying them in timeless mythological structures, he had only dehumanized them or reduced them to the merely ornamental.

Finally, those ideas themselves have seemed to some critics invalid or outmoded when submitted to empirical tests based on twentieth-century knowledge and experience. This last criticism has been aimed chiefly at the optimism regarding the problem of evil and at the acceptance of nineteenth-century beliefs in the doctrine of progress and the ultimate perfectibility of man, which appear both on and below the surface of Moody's poems and plays. For instance, one recent critic, in comparing the verse drama *The Fire-Bringer* with dramas on comparable subjects by Moody's lesser contemporaries Trumbull Stickney and George Cabot Lodge, relegates Moody to a weak third place in the trio almost entirely on the grounds of what he considers the play's "facile" affirmativeness and hence its "lack of serious tension at the core."[19]

Evaluation of these substantive kinds of criticism will occur both explicitly and implicitly throughout this study. All that can be said here is that such criticism is just only in inverse proportion to the maturity and imaginative strength of Moody's writings. As the following chapters will try to demonstrate, when his intellect and imagination operated at their fullest powers, Moody was a man adequate to his own ambitious themes; when successful, his use of Greek, Hebraic, and Christian myth is authentically applicable to situations and issues of this epoch; and his affirmations, far from being those of a complacent man telling himself and others what they want to hear, actually reflect a sensibility which could not rest in negations but which did move open-eyed through such negations in its quest for the difficult kind of belief that may lie beyond them.

Generally speaking, Moody's writing career may be divided into two periods. During the first—extending from the early imitative verse he wrote in college through the publication of his first two volumes, *The Masque of Judgment* (1900) and *Poems* (1901)—he was predominantly a lyric poet. Though the form of *The Masque of Judgment* is ostensibly dramatic, this first *magnum opus* was fully in the tradition of the nineteenth-century closet drama, utterly unproducible and perhaps better referred to as a dramatic poem than a verse play. Of the twenty-three poems that made up the 1901 volume, the majority are either lyrics or narratives and dramatic monologues with a decidedly lyrical bent. The rest are the more famous "public" utterances—poems dealing directly with social and political issues of turn-of-the-century America. These are the latest contributions to the volume, all of them having been written in 1900; and with them Moody gained his first large critical and popular acclaim. Poems like the much-anthologized (until recently) "An Ode in Time of Hesitation" and "Gloucester Moors," first published in important journals like the *Atlantic Monthly* and *Scribner's,* put Moody on the map of American poetry; and at the time of the 1901 collection he was already a known poet whose work had a ready market in the journals and whose name had begun to figure prominently in critical reviews and articles.

The second period begins after the publication of the 1901 volume and extends until Moody's death—or, to be more accurate, until the spring of 1909, since, in the last year-and-a-half of his life, the rapid development of the illness that was to cause his death made him incapable of serious literary labor. This period is separable from the first on several counts. First, it was in 1902 that Moody's and Lovett's *A History of English Literature* was completed and published; thereafter, though he did maintain a nominal connection with the University of Chicago until 1907, Moody did no more teaching. Secondly, this was the period of Moody's intimate friendship with Mrs. Harriet Tilden Brainerd, a Chicago divorcee some eleven years his senior, whom he was eventually to marry in 1909. Moody had met Mrs. Brainerd in 1899, but it was not until the spring of 1901 that their relationship became the central one in his life. Her home in Chicago became a regular haven for him, as well as for other writers of the time;[20] and from May, 1901, to the time of their marriage, they carried on a steady correspondence, of which Moody's part has been published in the informative and eloquent *Letters to Harriet,* edited by Percy MacKaye in 1935.

But the chief reason for dividing his career at 1902 is that from this year on—though he continued to produce poems, some of them among the most interesting of his career—Moody's creative energies were directed primarily at the drama. With the extremely successful New York production of *The Great Divide,* which opened in 1906, and with the much less successful but even more attention-getting New York production of his second prose play *The Faith Healer* in 1910, Moody became the first American poet of any stature to make a significant incursion into the commercial theater. Yet it is not only, or even primarily, by virtue of these prose plays that Moody earned an important place in modern drama. Unlike the earlier *Masque of Judgment,* the two verse dramas he produced in this period—*The Fire-Bringer* and the unfinished *The Death of Eve*—were conceived not as dramatic poems but as producible plays, and the considerable theatrical value of both works has still to be fully recognized. Perhaps largely because Moody himself referred to them as parts of a trilogy of which the *Masque* formed the second member, many of his critics have simply lumped the three works together and treated them as a single creation in a single genre. The fact is, however, that the idea of considering them a trilogy did not occur to Moody until he was writing *The Fire-Bringer* in 1903; and by that time his approach to the verse drama had changed radically enough so that the *Masque* is comparable to the other two members mainly in general thematic terms—and hardly at all in terms of structure or dramatic technique.

Despite the view common in his age that poetry and the practical theater were now incompatible, Moody had been interested from nearly the start of his adult career in the possibility of rescuing dramatic verse from the "closet" and applying it to the revitalization of the theater itself; and during the first decade of this century, he was something of a spiritual mentor to several poets—including Robinson, Josephine Preston Peabody, and later Ridgely Torrence and Percy MacKaye—dedicated to the establishment of a new verse-drama movement in the American theater. Among the productions of these poets, Moody's emerge as the most considerable realizations of their dramatic aims, even though it was the lesser creations of Mac-

Kaye and Miss Peabody which actually made their way onto the stage, while Moody was reaching audiences only through his prose plays. Important as those prose plays were, Moody's highest dramatic and literary achievements were the verse plays *The Fire-Bringer* and *The Death of Eve*—works which are not only significant for the time in which they were written, but still are significant today as lasting specimens of theatrical excellence at a level beyond the timorous standards of the commercial stage.

CHAPTER 2

The Poet of the 1890's

THE TERM "interregnum," as coined in 1885 by the then leading American critic E. C. Stedman, has since become a standard critical epithet for the state of poetry in the United States at the time Moody began writing. With Whitman and the New England Brahmin poets either dead or near death and well past their important creative periods, with Emily Dickinson as yet unrecognized and nearly unpublished, the literary scene was populated by a profusion of barely individualized and studiously minor poets who only occasionally afforded that "promise of a stronger utterance than ever" which allowed Stedman to predict the imminent termination of the interregnum in a major imaginative revival.[1] Nor did it appear to young poets of Moody's own generation, like Robinson, that the revival had made much headway in the decade following Stedman's prediction. By the mid-1890's, Robinson was still complaining of "this changeless glimmer of dead gray," "this barren age of ours" in which poetry was largely the province of "little sonnet-men" who

> fashion, in a shrewd mechanic way
> Songs without souls, that flicker for a day
> To vanish in irrevocable night.[2]

After the turn of the century, both the young and still obscure Robinson and the old, venerable Stedman were to share a belief that American poetry had at last found in Moody one of those large, bold voices capable of declaring the end of the now rather extended interregnum.[3] Yet the judgments of both men were based chiefly on Moody's writings after 1896. Before then, his work represented, as much as that of any of the poets discussed by Stedman in 1885, all the "minor" literary qualities the critic had described: narrow limitations of "breadth and interest," remoteness and "over-refinement," addiction to mere formal and technical exercises at the expense of vital substance, and a pervasive derivativeness.

I *Student Poems*

It is perhaps unjust to say that the verse Moody composed during his student years, from 1889 to 1894, bore no relation to his personal experience. The Harvard curriculum, as well as the densely literary atmosphere of the extracurricular circles he frequented, would have exerted a powerful influence on any young man of intellectual and esthetic leanings recently transplanted from a provincial Midwestern town; and it was natural enough that the intensive reading and discussion of literature should itself have been for Moody the most poignantly personal experience at the time. Though he carried on the classical studies begun at preparatory school, his main field of concentration in both college and graduate school was medieval English literature; and his absorption in that literature, along with his enthusiastic study of romantic medievalists from Keats to the Pre-Raphaelites, is evidenced everywhere in his student verse.

Of the twenty-odd poems he contributed to the *Harvard Monthly* during these years, the majority are narratives and dramatic monologues set in the Middle Ages and inhabited by knights, monks, minstrels, serfs, cloistered maidens, and mysterious *femmes fatales*—all bearing family likenesses to the inhabitants of the romances of Keats, Browning, and William Morris. Even the more strictly lyrical pieces, drawing constantly as they do on imagery of minstrels, harps, lyres, and court pages "on bended knee,"[4] seem to be intentionally projected out of a personal and contemporary frame of reference into an impersonally archaic one, usually medieval. The dominant mood of the poems is a kind of wistful nostalgia, in the fashion of much Pre-Raphaelite verse and that of the English "Decadent" poets of the late 1880's and early 1890's. All that is colorful and imaginatively stimulating is associated with the remote in time and place; and the few suggestions of Moody's poetic stance toward the here-and-now are perhaps best summarized in the lines from the sonnet "We Dying Hail Thee, Caesar": "The world is gray; the twilight of her days/Draws on."[5]

Moody retained only three poems from his student work in the 1901 volume of *Poems,* and the reasons for his suppressions are not hard to see: the poems are for the most part clearly exercises. Though their actual subject matter often grew out of his own medieval studies, his manner of treatment reflects an undisguised attempt to apprentice himself to certain admired predecessors. In the lyrics, the dominant stylistic influence is Rossetti. Narratives like that of the progress to sainthood of the art-loving Alberic in "The Picture and the Bird" emulate Browning in both matter and manner,[6] as does the multiple dramatic monologue "Angelle," with its four points of view successively illuminating the tragic *amour* of the fallen heroine and the knightly Count Bertram.[7] Other narratives, especially the Arthurian moral romance of Sir Owain and "The Lady of the Fountain," frequently recall Morris' medieval reconstructions.[8] And such a poem as "The Amber Witch" is not only modeled on the *femme fatale* motif and the plot pattern of Keats's "La Belle Dame Sans Merci," but also employs exactly the same stanza form and, in stanzas like the following, echoes the very phrasing of the Keats poem:

> Her body swayed into a tune,
>   Her lips were writhen as with pain,
> Her eyes swam dim while she did croon
>   A dim, dim strain.[9]

The three poems which Moody did republish—"Harmonics," "The Departure," and "How the Mead-Slave Was Set Free"— share many of the characteristics of the rejected poems, including their rather skillful management of tonal and rhythmic nuance within tight stanzaic forms. The first is a sonnet and the second a double sonnet, both in the manner of Rossetti; the third is a short dramatic monologue reminiscent of Morris in style and setting, and cast in the five-line tetrameter stanzas which seem to have been a favorite of Moody's at this time. Though written in the first-person, the two lyrics have almost as much the quality of a dramatic monologue as the "Mead-Slave" poem. Yet, for all their apparent impersonality, each of the poems does deal with a theme that probably meant a good deal to Moody personally: the need for human love as an inspiration to artistic creation. And his decision to include them in the 1901 volume may well have reflected—in addition to his justified opinion that they were simply better performances than the other student poems—a feeling that what they had to say was still relevant to his situation as a poet and a man in 1901.

The speaker in "Harmonics" is a musician, representative of the artist in general. A certain vagueness in setting the scene, and a Rossettian use of abrupt associative transitions in place of logical development, make it a difficult poem to paraphrase. In essence, though, the old man who, in the octave, bends over the younger musician to bring sudden supernal music from his harp-string—a music which, like Jacob's ladder, suddenly spans earth and heaven—seems to embody the eternal youthfulness and miraculous transforming power of love, capable of inspiring even his aged and "untaught hand" to timeless creation. The harp would then represent something like the potentiality for such creation, latent and only dimly apprehended ("harmonics") until, as the sestet suggests, it is incarnated through the experience of love:

> O vibrant heart! so metely tuned and strung
> That any untaught hand can draw from thee
> One clear gold note that makes the tired years young—
> What of the time when Love had whispered me
> Where slept thy nodes, and my hand pausefully
> Gave to the dim harmonics voice and tongue?

The mead-slave's reminiscent monologue is more explicit in its expression of the same theme. Before the lady he is addressing rescued him from death at the hands of his outraged Anglo-Saxon masters, this rebellious slave from a Southern land had possessed only an unrecognized potentiality for artistic creation; weary of his exile in the "hateful North" and of his bondage to "drunken sea-thieves," he welcomed the quick death that his masters threatened as punishment for his disobedience. But the lady, seeing in him one who has "hearkened Odin sing" and whose "heart is thralled/To music," intervened and led him to the minstrel "old Skagi" to prove his bardic calling. With the harp thrust in his hands, his love for his rescuer suddenly inspired him to song and, his latent creativity now manifested, he succeeded to the bardic title which he still possesses at the time of his reminiscence:

> All grew a blur before my sight,
> As when the stealthy white fog slips
> At noonday on the staggering ships;
> I saw one single spot of light,
> Your white face, with its eager lips—

And so I sang to that. O thou
Who liftedst me from out my shame!
Wert thou content when Skagi came,
Put his own chaplet on my brow,
And bent and kissed his own harp-frame?

In "The Departure" (originally titled "By the Evening Sea" when published in the *Harvard Monthly* of January, 1893), the theme recurs once more, only now with a negative turn. Again the speaker is a bard or minstrel, sitting beside the evening sea in some vaguely located landscape with his once potent lyre beside him, silent and unregarded, as he watches the fêted embarkation of a ship filled with beautiful women such as he has once loved and possessed. But the beauty they embody is no longer his: love has departed from his heart as the ship is departing from the shore; and, with it, his own creative powers have left him. The poem ends on a note of heavy desolation as the ship sails off with its burden of beauty and with intimations of a destination in death, leaving the speaker

alone in my great need,
One foot upon the thin horn of my lyre
And all its strings crushed in the dripping weed.

II *Early Chicago Years*

His removal to Chicago in the fall of 1895 was a major event in Moody's life, and many of his letters during the first two years after his appointment at the University of Chicago record the radical effects which he felt his new environment was having on him. In a letter of September 22, 1895, for instance, he remarked:

I begin to believe . . . that all my life there in the east was a sort of tragi-farce, more or less consciously composed, so rudely awake and in earnest is everything here. . . . I do not know what this place is going to do for me, but I am sure of its potency—its alchemical power to change and transmute. It is appallingly ugly for one thing—so ugly that the double curtain of night and sleep does not screen the aching sense. For another thing it is absorbing—crude juice of life—intellectual and social proto-plasm. Far aloft hovers phantom Poetry, no longer my delicate familiar. But I dream of another coming of hers, a new companionship more valorous and simple-hearted.[10]

The transmutation was, however, a gradual one, and several of the poems Moody wrote during this period clearly hark back in subject and treatment to the work of his Harvard years. For instance, the poems "The Ride Back" and "The Golden Journey"—which may be regarded as companion pieces contrasting positive and negative views of a single theme in the manner of "Harmonics" and "The Departure"—retain the medieval setting and atmosphere and much of the derivative quality of the earlier narratives. Though both contain strong suggestions of personal allegorical meanings, and are despite their narrative form essentially lyrical in mood and effect, they seem to be designed more as objective exercises in the manner of the Pre-Raphaelites or 1890's poets than as expressions of urgently personal emotions and ideas. Yet the poems are worth lingering over not only for their crystallization of certain typical qualities of Moody's apprentice work, but also for their minor foreshadowings of thematic concerns that were to become increasingly central in his mature poems and dramas.

"The Ride Back" takes up a subject adumbrated in the earlier "The Briar Rose" (*Harvard Monthly*, May, 1893): the arduous journey of a protagonist to reunion with an idealized lady—a conventional medieval-romance subject probably intended as an allegory of the individual soul's estrangement from and quest for the divine. An italicized blank-verse stanza which precedes the narrative-proper rather pointedly suggests this intent:

> *Before the coming of the dark, he dreamed*
> *An old-world faded story: of a knight,*
> *Much like in need to him, who was no knight!*
> *And of a road, much like the road his soul*
> *Groped over, desperate to meet Her soul.*
> *Beside the bed Death waited. And he dreamed.*

The "old-world faded story," cast again in Moody's favorite five-line tetrameter stanzas, recalls the narrative manner of Morris throughout; and in its descriptive details it often resembles Browning's "Childe Harold to the Dark Tower Came." Bound on his horse with a cross tied to his breast, the knight rides out of battle weak and wounded; and the dark landscape he journeys over on his way to the lady is crowded with grotesque images that would frighten or distract him from his quest and mock its purpose. The "scrawny hands" of "haggard" trees grasp at him; the moon laughs at his feebleness; overhead,

petals shake in the moonlight "Lewd as the palsied lips of hags";
and the snow on the mountain heights around him and the
shadows of the mountain passes seem to prophesy his failure to
complete the journey. Then, at the point where his spirit,
"sealed ... up with pain," is about to succumb to defeat, morning comes and various images of thriving life, probably representing divine grace, give him new strength to persist. At last
the knight arrives at his destination and, ushered to the lady
by an unearthly nuptial music, he embraces her and dies,
giving the lie to those who had told him the quest was hopeless.
Though Moody does not recur to the dream-frame at the end,
the implication is that, for the troubled latterday dreamer, the
conclusion provides a vision of hope that his own "need" for
spiritual reunion before death is a possibility.

"The Golden Journey" explores the opposite allegorical resources of the medieval-journey motif. In it the lady appears
to be associated with the several *femmes fatales* of the earlier
poems, especially with the speaker in "The Picture."[11] A kind
of priestess in the service of a god with "sweet cruel eyes"
(presumably Eros in his more sinister aspect), she weaves spells
which lure the hapless mariner-protagonist across sea and land
to her enchanted altar. Throughout the description of his journey, the imagery stands in direct contrast to that in "The Ride
Back": instead of threatening and mocking landscapes, we find
attractive images of bird, flower, olive dell, and dawn breeze
which make human existence on earth seem "Too sweet to
leave for such a dream." The quest itself has all the appear-
ances of a dangerously specious fantasy; and the lady, like certain supernatural females of Irish mythology who perform similar functions in several of Yeats's poems, succeeds in blinding
the protagonist to the value of things of this world by tempting
him to an unattainable desire for a love beyond the human. In
the end, the completion of his journey brings him not to redemption nor to transcendence of his humanity in divine love,
but only to death:

> . . . grown faint with thirst of her,
> He shall bow down his face and sink
> Breathless beneath the eddying brink.
> Then a swift music will begin,
> And as the brazen doors shut slow,
> There will be hurrying to and fro,

> And lights and calls and silver din,
> While through the star-freaked swirl of air
> The god's sweet cruel eyes will stare.

If the poem has a moral implication, it would seem to be a rejection of false dreams of ideality in favor of commitment to the
imperfections and attainable fulfillments of human existence on
earth.

For all their interest as projections of the poet's own philosophical gropings at the time, however, poems like "The Ride
Back" and "The Golden Journey," as well as the three poems
Moody retained from his Harvard years, tend to diminish the
seriousness of their themes by their remotely literary settings
and *personae,* and their general conventionality of style. In
many places, Moody's sensitive—if sometimes overly impressionable—ear for subtle verse music is evident. Now and then
—as in the Jacob's ladder image in the octave of "Harmonics"
and as in the vivid simile comparing the enthralled protagonist
to a lark soaring through sunbeams toward the sun's own heart
in the seventh stanza of "The Golden Journey"—we find ink-
lings of a talent for unusual, striking figures of speech. But for
the most part the imagery is stock Victorian and Pre-Raphaelite,
and the allegorical meanings of the poems are submerged in
a sense of the merely fanciful and decorative. As important as
his speculations on art and human and divine love may have
appeared to the young poet, they remain merely speculations,
embodied in imaginative forms whose origins are too clearly
in secondhand rather than firsthand experience to sustain more
than a lightweight significance.

On the other hand, the letters of the early Chicago period,
a few of the small lyrics, and particularly the long poem "Jetsam" show a growing absorption in realities outside of books and
a growing concern to work those realities into his writing. In
May, 1896, Moody sent the first version of the lyric "Heart's
Wild-Flower" to Daniel Gregory Mason with this comment:
"it is almost the first thing I have done which has been a direct
impulse from 'real' life, and you know I have theories about
that."[12] Though the original poem was an immaturely senti-
mental and overwrought attempt to capture his personal emotions during a briefly rapturous love affair with a Chicago
girl,[13] and though the much foreshortened final version seems
a somewhat distilled specimen of what Moody had called in

his earlier letter the "crude juice of life," the lyric does at least cast off the medieval trappings of his work until then, and does make some attempt to cope with his own experience in the here-and-now. So do the slight but poignant lyric "On the River" and the more substantial "The Bracelet of Grass," which takes up the theme of erotic unfulfillment treated so remotely in "The Departure" and in "The Golden Journey" and gives it moving personal application via the effective image of a sudden storm that interrupts and finally dispels an illusion of shared love with a girl now lost to the poet.[14] Though the manner of poems like these still shows signs of derivativeness (one reviewer of the 1901 *Poems* justly pointed out the rhythmic correspondence between the first stanza of "The Bracelet of Grass" and that of Francis Thompson's "Dream-Tryst"),[15] the matter is largely Moody's own. In their small way, and within the limitations of their tight lyric forms and traditional diction, they reflect something of that excited awakening to immediate and "simple-hearted" human feeling which is perhaps most fully expressed in a letter of February 16, 1896 to Mason, in which Moody describes his delight at meeting and skating together one evening with a poor and charmingly awkward fifteen-year-old Irish girl:

> I have had few sensations in life that I would exchange for the warmth of her hand through the ragged glove, and the pathetic curve of her half-formed breast where the back of my wrist touched her body. I came away mystically shaken and elate. . . . She was something absolutely authentic, new and inexpressible. . . . With a world offering such rencontres, such aery strifes and adventures, who would not live a thousand years stone dumb? I would, for one—until my mood changes and I come to think on the shut lid and granite lip of him who has done away with sunsets and skating, and has turned away his face from all manner of Irish. I am supported by a conviction that at an auction on the steps of the great white Throne, I should bring more in the first mood than the second—by several harps and a stray dulcimer.[16]

III *"Jetsam"*

In the 226-line blank-verse meditation "Jetsam"—begun after an "unforgettable night in the fields of Chartres" during his trip through France in the summer of 1895, and probably completed in late 1896 or early 1897—Moody wrote the most ambitious and intensely personal poem of his career to date.[17] It is not an easy poem to comprehend, largely because Moody was evidently trying to apply certain techniques derived from French Symbolist poetry which were then being given currency in America by poets like Richard Hovey. In 1894 Hovey had published a translation of some plays of Maeterlinck, and in his introduction he had set forth his views on the nature of the new poetic method:

> The symbolism of to-day . . . by no means of necessity involves a complete and consistent allegory. Its events, its personages, its sentences rather imply than definitely state an esoteric meaning. . . . behind every incident, almost behind every phrase, one is aware of a lurking universality, the adumbration of greater things. One is given an impression of the thing symbolized rather than a formulation. . . . But these correspondences must not be pursued too curiously. They are intended to appeal to the imagination and the emotions, not to the mere ingenuity of the intellect.[18]

Of course Hovey was not saying anything particularly new, and Moody himself—under the influence of Rossetti, among others— had already written poems (for example, "Harmonics") that fit this description without necessarily any direct recourse to the French Symbolists. Yet it is more than probable that by 1896 he had become acquainted with their work, either on his own or via his friend Hovey; and an intensification of his concern for non-rational, evocative means of reaching beyond the apprehensions of normal experience is obvious enough in certain poems of the period to indicate that Moody may have come more directly under the influence of the Symbolists' method than heretofore. As an example, we may consider the odd syntactical distortions and the attempt to suggest an inexpressible emotional state through disjointed exclamation in the last five lines of "The Bracelet of Grass":

> We gazed from shelter on the storm,
> And through our hearts swept ghostly pain
> To see the shards of day sweep past,
> Broken, and none might mend again.
> Broken, that none shall ever mend;
> Loosened, that none shall ever tie.
> O the wind and the wind, will it never end?
> O the sweeping past of the ruined sky!

But it is in "Jetsam" and in certain passages from the later poems and dramas that Moody makes his most extensive use of

Symbolist techniques. Unlike earlier narratives such as "The Ride Back" and "The Golden Journey," the poem is not a simple and readily paraphrasable allegory. The narrative transitions are frequently abrupt and impressionistic, and the symbols around which the narrative revolves are clearly intended to suggest more than is or can be stated about them. To be sure, in "Jetsam" as elsewhere Moody goes only part way toward adopting the pure Symbolist method of a poet like Mallarmé; he retains a recognizable if sometimes tenuous narrative and meditative thread, and a rationally perceivable set of ideas does operate throughout the poem. Yet beyond these elements lies a a residue of indefinable meanings which are the real substance of the poem; in fact, Moody's central intention throughout seems to be a demonstration that such meanings, unavailable to the rational mind or to ordinary perceptual experience, are the only ultimate ones. Though neither "Jetsam" nor any other work of his shows any direct substantive indebtedness to the Symbolists, it is Moody who probably comes closest of any American poet before the 1910's to assimilating the spirit of the movement.[19]

"Jetsam" begins normally enough, except that for Moody the imagery is notably contemporary and realistic:

> I wonder can this be the world it was
> At sunset? I remember the sky fell
> Green as pale meadows, at the long street-ends,
> But overhead the smoke-wrack hugged the roofs
> As if to shut the city from God's eyes
> Till dawn should quench the laughter and the lights.

In a mood of deep depression, feeling his life lying "waste about me," the poet has wandered through a city dusk (presumably in Chicago) described in terms comparable to those of Eliot's *Prufrock* or the "violet hour" of *The Waste Land*. In his wandering, he has been haunted by an image of his own sense of blighted promise in the shape of a "thrice-virginal" female apparition singing "lost verses from my youth's gold canticle." But the apparition has quickly vanished, and he has "stumbled on" alone, cursing God for the sordidness of his surroundings and state of mind, to where "The river lay/Coiled in its factory filth and few lean trees." There, a sudden vision of the risen moon has transfigured everything around him, and in the unearthly beauty of the scene his spirit has been visited with "Insufferable ecstasy of peace." Now, though in his bravado he claims the strength to sustain such a vision, he is beset by hallucinations that reflect his fear of a too-total surrender to these feelings of supernatural blessedness:

> I dare not look again; another gaze
> Might drive me to the wavering coppice there,
> Where bat-winged madness brushed me, the wild laugh
> Of naked nature crashed across my blood.

This is the basic "situation" of the poem. All the rest is an elaborate fabric of reminiscence and introspection, as the force of the present experience calls up associations from other times and other places in which the same tension between desire for and dread of some ultimate illumination is examined in multiple perspective. The poet's immediate surroundings blend inexplicably into similar ones from his past, including a scene apparently drawn from the original experience at Chartres which first inspired the poem:

> Bright rivers tacit; low hills prone and dumb;
> Forests that hushed their tiniest voice to hear;
> Skies for the unutterable advent robed
> In purple like the opening iris buds;
> And by some lone expectant pool, one tree
> Whose grey boughs shivered with excess of awe,—
> As with preluding gush of amber light,
> And herald trumpets softly lifted through,
> Across the palpitant horizon marge
> Crocus-filleted came the singing moon.

Similarly, the dazzling moonlight which pervades many of the descriptive passages becomes increasingly identified with the female apparition who had haunted the poet earlier, thus provoking recurrent assaults of guilt at the wastage of his powers. His mood shifts constantly from the ecstatic to the agonized as the imagery moves back and forth from the transfiguring moon to the untransfigured facts of his normal existence. But, in the final section, as he imagines his return to that existence—"Tomorrow, when the fishers come at dawn/Upon that shell of me the sea has tossed/To land, as fit for earth to use again" (lines which clarify the poem's title)—he realizes that it too must

somehow be partly transfigured by memory of the experience
he is now undergoing. He therefore rejects the temptation to
ascetic denial of life held out by those who "work your soul's
redemption" through

> Increase of wisdom, and acquaintance held
> With the heart's austerities; still governance,
> And ripening of the blood in the weekday sun
> To make the full-orbed consecrated fruit
> At life's end for the Sabbath supper meet.

Instead, he chooses the artist's commitment to the world, sustained by the memory of experiences beyond time, like the
present one, which can consecrate the life of the flesh:

> I shall not sit beside you at that feast,
>
> . . . .
>
> For I of old am beauty's votarist,
> Long recreant, often foiled and led astray,
> But resolute at last to seek her there
> Where most she does abide, and crave with tears
> That she assoil me of my blemishment.

This paraphrase of the poem's general ideological contents
goes only a short way toward indicating its abundance of
suggestive imaginative detail, whose total effect more than
compensates for the obvious faults—occasional bombast, structural
diffuseness, and obscurities that cannot always be explained
away as a necessary function of the Symbolist method. In its
best moments, the poem's imagery and verse music evoke
a sense of the ineffable, in both terror and rapture, worthy of
comparison with the best Symbolist verse. There is, for instance,
this passage describing the poet's first hallucination after arriv-
ing at the moonlit river bank:

> The rocks and clods
> Dissemble, feign a busy intercourse;
> The bushes deal in shadowy subterfuge,
> Lurk dull, dart spiteful out, make heartless signs,
> Utter awestricken purpose of no sense,—
> But I walk quiet, crush aside the hands
> Stretched furtively to drag me madmen's ways.
> I know the thing they suffer, and the tricks
> They must be at to help themselves endure.

Or there is this daring conceit—pure Shelley for one line but after that unique—suggesting the opposite kind of supernatural apprehension:

> . . . spirit reaches of the strenuous vast,
> Where stalwart stars reap grain to make the bread
> God breaketh at his tables and is glad.

With a poem like "Jetsam," uneven and sometimes immature as it is, Moody is starting to force his way out of the interregnum.

IV *Recollections of Europe*

His bicycle trip through Italy and Austria in the spring and summer of 1897 provided Moody not only with the original inspiration for *The Masque of Judgment,* but also with raw materials for at least three poems completed during the next couple of years. "Good Friday Night," based on an actual Eastertide procession he watched in Sorrento,[20] became Moody's first work to reach a wide audience when it was published in the *Atlantic Monthly* for May, 1898, and it has remained one of the most praised poems of the 1901 volume.[21] One reason for the poem's cordial reception was probably a quality of clarity and restraint such as friends like Mason, and later Robinson, often tried to instill into Moody, with only occasional success.[22] Compared with the lush and syntactically complex blank verse of "Jetsam," the tight quatrains of "Good Friday Night" (all containing a tetrameter followed by a trimeter couplet) seem a model of restraint and simple directness; yet in this poem too the literal contents lead off into open-ended ambiguities which suggest that its intentions are not quite so clear-cut as may at first appear.

The poet, having watched the solemn procession of the crucifix go past, and having failed, perhaps because of "too much youth," to feel any emotional participation in the ceremony, turns to a fellow stranger standing in the shadows to complain of the emptiness he feels in the presence of these literal images of Christ's passion:

> "Why do they make this mummery?
> Would not a brave man gladly die
> For a much smaller thing
> Than to be Christ and king?"

The stranger's only response is to kneel when the crucifix is followed by a statue of the Madonna. Then the poet, abashed at this display of piety and struck by a resemblance between the Madonna's face and that of his own dead mother, suddenly feels constrained to kneel himself. After the procession has vanished, he and the stranger walk silently together through the dark and emptied streets until a sudden burst of moonlight reveals, in the "anguish of his eyes," the stranger's own re--semblance to Christ. The enigmas latent in the figure of the stranger and his relation to the poet then come full force in the poem's conclusion:

> "Friend! Master!" I cried falteringly,
> "Thou seest the thing they make of thee.
> Oh, by the light divine
> My mother shares with thine,
>
> "I beg that I may lay my head
> Upon thy shoulder and be fed
> With thoughts of brotherhood!"
> So through the odorous wood,
>
> More silently than friends new-found
> We walked. At the first meadow bound
> His figure ashen-stoled
> Sank in the moon's broad gold.

A question that naturally emerges is: to what extent does the poem transcribe or at least epitomize an actual experience beyond that of simply having watched an Eastertide procession at Sorrento? David Henry, following the lead of earlier commentators,[23] takes the events of the poem quite literally—as one of several indications in Moody's work that "Blake-like, he believed that Jesus appeared to him on several occasions." There is, of course, no way of verifying the biographical truthfulness of the encounters described here, in the later poem "Second Coming," or in one of the reminiscent passages from "Jetsam" which states: "Once at a simple turning of the way/I met God walking." Nor does it suffice to dispose of the question as irrelevant to the meanings of the poems themselves. Whether or not Moody actually had, or thought he had, Blakean visions of supernatural presences makes a considerable difference to our understanding of his poems; and it is not an easy matter to accept his own references to such visions at face value as Henry does, or to dismiss them as wholly metaphorical or conventional allegorical devices.

Yet, in the absence of any conceivably convincing evidence one way or the other, one is obliged simply to suspend judgment and try to interpret what the poems are saying about the kinds of experience they deal with, whether real or imaginary. In the case of "Good Friday Night," the experience is set throughout in a purposefully ambiguous light. Is the stranger Christ, or merely a man whom the poet, in his need for religious self-identification, takes for Christ on the basis of accidental likenesses to the figure on the crucifix? Does the stranger kneel before the Madonna because she is his mother, or because, like the poet, he is reminded by her of his real mother? Is his silence a rebuke to the Catholic procession, with its pagan undertones, or to the poet himself for his blasphemy? Or, if it is not a rebuke at all, but a sign of communion beyond the power of words between the stranger and the poet, does his abrupt disappearance mean that the "thoughts of brotherhood" envisioned by the poet have been rendered futile by the corruption of the original Christian ethos, or simply that the communion, though genuine, is necessarily transitory?

These may seem overly conceptional questions with which to burden a simple lyrical narrative; but the very simplicity of the poem, its lack of external commentary and concentration on the bare "facts" of the experience, makes it all the more open to multiple ideological applications. For what Moody is depicting is not an ideology but a complex state of mind in which conflicting and even contradictory attitudes occur together. As in "Jetsam" and *The Masque of Judgment*, both the blasphemy and the piety, the disillusion and the hope, reflect Moody's own ambivalent religious position. Reared in an evangelical Protestant environment, but possessed of a strongly pagan and anti-ascetic temperament, he craved religious illumination and security while at the same time suspecting any sort of theological dualism which would suppress or deny the claims of the flesh or the joys of natural existence. Through the rest of his career his writings show an obsessive search for means of reconciling the conflicts suggested in "Good Friday Night."

The "Road Hymn for the Start," written in commemoration of a morning when Moody and Ferdinand Schevill bicycled together out of Orvieto on their way north,[24] is a more forthright expression of the same idea that informs the earlier "The Ride

Back" and passages in "Jetsam": the value of striving for its own sake, though the destination of one's quest be hidden and the route difficult. Composed in romping trochaics apparently imitative of horse hooves, the poem's rhythms remind one of Kipling's; and its mood is strongly reminiscent not only of Browning's more heartily affirmative utterances but also, as several commentators have remarked, of Whitman's "Song of the Open Road" and of Hovey and Carman's *Songs of Vagabondia*. The poem is, in fact, Moody's chief contribution to the literature of the Rooseveltian "robust age." The keynote is the command "Wander!"—a rejection of the sorts of comfortable but confining domesticity represented in the first stanza by "the forms of sons and fathers" and "the sounds of mothers":

> Unto them a part is given; we will strive to see the whole.
> Dear shall be the banquet table where their singing spirits press;
> Dearer be our sacred hunger, and our pilgrim loneliness.

In contrast to "Good Friday Night," the poem concludes with a cheerful and fairly uncharacteristic affirmation of uncertainty as the necessary human condition and of the superiority of simple action to even the loveliest productions of the introverted sensibility, as represented by the song of a hidden bird described in the next-to-last stanza and commented on in the last:

> Leave him still to ease in song
> Half his little heart's unrest:
> Speech is his, but we may journey toward the life for
> which we long.
> God, who gives the bird its anguish, maketh nothing manifest,
> But upon our lifted foreheads pours the boon of endless quest.

During his first extended residence in New York in the winter and early spring of 1899, Moody composed the two-part lyrical meditation "Song-Flower and Poppy," in which images from his immediate surroundings stimulate associations from the 1897 journey through Italy. Thematically, the poem is the antithesis of "Road Hymn for the Start," for its central motif affirms the artistic imagination as the sole force capable of transforming the drab facts of human existence into something endurable. The first section, which describes a young Italian street-singer performing under Moody's apartment window, is noteworthy for being the first instance of openly colloquial diction in his verse,

though to an American ear the speaker's voice may seem somewhat Anglicized:

> He plays the deuce with my writing time,
> For the penny my sixth-floor neighbor throws;
> He finds me proud of my pondered rhyme,
> And he leaves me—well, God knows
> It takes the shine from a tunester's line
> When a little mate of the deathless Nine
> Pipes up under your nose.

The tone of whimsical humor (also something rather new in the
poems) soon disappears as the poet contemplates his ugly and
sterile surroundings: "this gray gulch of a street," the dismal
sky over the city's rooftops where "A rag of sunset crumbles
grey," the shrill cries of newsboys proclaiming "The worst of
the city's infamy/For one more sordid day." But the street-
singer's performance calls up the more genial atmosphere of
contemporary and ancient Italy; and the poet's imagination is
lifted beyond the lusts and profit-seeking vulgarities of New York
into an apprehension of timeless beauty that becomes more
immediately real than his literal environs. He is, therefore, inspired to exclaim:

> Heart, we have chosen the better part!
> Save sacred love and sacred art
> Nothing is good for long.

The second section is set entirely in Italy; and here the theme
shifts from a contrast between the lesser reality of modern urban
ugliness and the higher reality of imaginative beauty, to one
between the ascetic way of salvation—represented by the presence of St. Francis among remembered scenes at Assisi—and the
way of the artist committed to the fullness of physical life—represented by a freely blown poppy-bell on the countryside near
Assisi whose vital earthly beauty "laughs down" the saint's aus-
terer creed. The closing stanza recalls the more recondite expression of an anti-dualistic attitude in Moody's rejection of
asceticism at the close of "Jetsam":

> How long, old builder Time, wilt bide
> Till at thy thrilling word
> Life's crimson pride shall have to bride
> The spirit's white accord,

Within that gate of good estate
Which thou must build us soon or late,
Hoar workman of the Lord?

The whole poem, in fact, by implicitly identifying both material-
ism and asceticism with the same essential denial of life, and by
setting up the creative imagination as the antithesis of both,
reflects the highly Blakean moral position of *The Masque of
Judgment,* on which Moody was hard at work at the time he
wrote "Song-Flower and Poppy."

V "The Daguerreotype"

Next to the famous poems of political and social protest composed after the turn of the century, the piece in the 1901 volume
which was most highly regarded by Moody's friends and by his
early critics was the elaborate ode entitled "The Daguerreotype" on the memory of his mother.[25] The subject of the ode
is not, of course, one calculated to succeed so easily with readers
reared in the shadow of Mencken's and Philip Wylie's satires on
American "mom" worship and familiar with popularizations of
Freudian Oedipal theories; and "The Daguerreotype" has, in
fact, been singled out for special damnation by Gregory and
Zaturenska, who find it a notable example of Moody's "lack of
sensibility and taste."[26] Yet the earlier commentators were probably much more just in their evaluations of this complex, sometimes uncommonly candid, and largely unsentimental study of
the poet's emotions on contemplating a picture of his dead
mother in her premarital adolescence.

Mrs. Moody had died when her son was fifteen, and the extent of Moody's attachment to her memory can be seen in a
poem like "Good Friday Night," as well, perhaps, as in the
strange female apparition of "Jetsam," whose association with the
unfulfilled promise of the poet's youth resembles the more overt
identification in the later ode. But to quote one of the twentieth-
century critics most given to Freudian speculation, Moody always reacted to his "powerful mother fixation" "creatively and
not neurotically."[27] Indeed, the very candor of "The Daguerreotype" indicates how fully Moody himself recognized that fixation, and also how capable he was of sublimating his very real
sense of guilt and loss while still remaining faithful to the psychological actualities of the original experience.

Perhaps the most daring thing about the poem—and apparently the main cause of later critics' discomfort—is the openly erotic quality of several passages. Like "Song-Flower and Poppy," the ode begins rather casually and rises in a slow crescendo to intense utterance. But even in the simple, expository opening lines we have a hint of the erotically based tensions of later passages:

> This, then, is she,
> My mother as she looked at seventeen,
> When she first met my father. Young incredibly,
> Younger than spring, without the faintest trace
> Of disappointment, weariness, or tean
> Upon the childlike earnestness and grace
> Of the waiting face.
> These close-wound ropes of pearl
> (Or common beads made precious by their use)
> Seem heavy for so slight a throat to wear;
> But the low bodice leaves the shoulders bare
> And half the glad swell of the breast, for news
> That now the woman stirs within the girl.

As his eye moves to her earrings, associated in their "matron-sober" color and shape with the austerities of Sunday worship, they seem ill-fitted to her girlishly sensuous features and to the suggestions in her cheeks of "passions forest-shy and forest-wild,/ And delicate delirious merriments." Despite his efforts not to, the poet lingers irresistibly before the attractions of her hair and lips, until his mounting sense of anguish is released in tears as he focuses, less sensually now, on "The unforgettable, the unforgotten eyes." With this, his thought shifts from the adolescent girl in the picture to remembrance of her as an older woman on her death-bed; and finally to the actual day of her death, and the contrast between his father's noble sorrow and his own impotent fury as—in lines reminiscent of the opening section of "Jetsam" —he

> Fled from the horrible roof
> Into the alien sunshine merciless,
> The shrill satiric fields ghastly with day,
> Raging to front God in his pride of sway. . . .

Only the eyes persist in counteracting the impression that the girl in the picture might be someone the poet himself could desire and woo; and so powerful is this impression that he actually begins to see her, not as the woman who bore him and whom he knew after time had defaced her beauty, but as

> . . . a girl I never saw before,
> A little thing to flatter and make weep,
> To tease until her heart is sore,
> Then kiss and clear the score;
> A gypsy run-the-fields,
> A little liberal daughter of the earth,
> Good for what hour of truancy and mirth
> The careless season yields
> Hither-side the flood of the year and yonder of the neap;
> Then thank you, thanks again, and twenty light good-byes.

But the cynical cavalier pose, compounded by the overtly incestuous suggestions of the image, suddenly revolts the poet. He vehemently apologizes for his lapse by claiming that he has imposed this image on that of the picture only to protect himself against the anguished memory of his mother and the knowledge of his failure to live up to her own idealized vision of him. There follows a passage of bitter self-condemnation, centering on a sustained conceit comparing his life to the drippings of a wine-press, which have turned sour and whose containing vessels have been emptied and thrown aside. The poet begs forgiveness for his unfulfilled promise and his sinful wastage of the powers inherited from his mother; and he pleads with her to turn from him the "looks of rejoicing love, of pride, of happy trust" which he now reads into the picture. But the eyes finally triumph, both over the erotic suggestions driven out by his guilty confession and over the guilt itself. By the end of the poem, the face in the picture is no longer arousing forbidden desires nor rebuking the poet for his sinfulness. Instead, its look becomes a stimulus to rebirth of his spirit from the morbid dejection into which it has driven him:

> See how the shriveled heart, that long has lain
> Dead to delight and pain,
> Stirs, and begins again
> To utter pleasant life, as if it knew
> The wintry days were through;
> As if in its awakening boughs it heard
> The quick, sweet-spoken bird.
> Strong eyes and brave,
> Inexorable to save!

Like "Jetsam," "The Daguerreotype" is a young man's poem
of confession and dedication—or perhaps rededication—built on
an intensely felt experience of emergence from a mood of guilt-
ridden negation under the influence of a benign external force.
Like "Jetsam," the ode has certain weaknesses identifiable with
the poet's youthfulness: it is prolix and bombastic in places, and
now and then oddly flat in its diction and rhythm. But the
concrete dramatic situation and the sustained development of
certain focal images (details in the picture itself, the winepress
metaphor, etc.) give it a more recognizable unity than the
earlier poem; and Moody shows throughout a decided gain in
clarity and tonal variety. The ode form itself—influenced, as
critics have shown, by the pseudo-Pindaric odes of Francis
Thompson[28]—works to good effect in providing contrasts between
the structural freedom of the lines (nearly always iambic, but
ranging in length from one to seven feet) and the tight discipline
of the elaborate rhyme schemes, with their effect of rapid re-
currence when the lines are short and of leisurely expansiveness
when they are long. These formal contrasts enhance, in turn,
the substantive contrasts which are the real triumph of the
ode: its persuasive delineation of the dramatic shifts and turns,
actions and reactions, of a complex sensibility confronting a
significant and honestly described experience. If the intimacy
of the subject and uninhibitedness of the treatment have em-
barrassed some readers, the same qualities have impressed others
as indicating Moody's willingness to forego delicate decorums
and to lay bare depths of psychic experience which a lesser poet
would pull up well short of. It was some such recognition of
Moody's healthy ambition to be a major poet, for whom no theme
was unmanageable, which prompted Robinson to tell Moody
in 1901 that he had it in him to give American literature "a
new meaning for the new century," because "You know what
life means to you and it is not likely that you will spend your
days in the making of [a] book that will leave the souls of your
readers unfed. The final note of hope and faith in the Daguerreotype—which is a great poem—makes me sure of all this."[29]

VI *"Until The Troubling of The Waters"*

In the longest poem of the 1901 volume, the 323-line blank-
verse dramatic monologue "Until the Troubling of the Waters,"
Moody again explored the psychological complexities of a

mother-child relationship, only now in an objective context. The poem was inspired by the same fascination with the faith-healing activities of a contemporary itinerant evangelist named Schlatter, which Moody was already laboring to make into a play during the late years of the 1890's; for all we know, passages in the monologue may have been intended as parts of the dialogue in Moody's first abortive attempt to write *The Faith Healer* in blank verse.[30] Like earlier dramatic monologues such as "Angelle" and "How the Mead-Slave Was Set Free," "Until the Troubling of the Waters" seems an objectification of certain of the poet's own religious and philosophical struggles. But unlike them, the poem is entirely contemporary and American in setting; relatively naturalistic in idiom; and directly expressive of social, psychological, and theological problems indigenous to the time and place in which Moody lived. In it we see for the first time in his work a sustained expression of the sense of economic injustice which was to become central to some of the best-known 1900 poems. We also see Moody experimenting with a mode quite different from that of the nineteenth-century poets whom he had formerly emulated—one which anticipates, and quite possibly influenced, one important mode of twentieth-century American poetry. Ludwig Lewisohn was quite right in claiming that the dramatic-monologue techniques in this poem are "far closer in method to the narratives of Robert Frost or Mark Van Doren" (and, we might add, Robert Lowell) "than to the British examples," such as Wordsworth's "Michael" or Browning's simpler monologues, by which the basic technique may have been suggested.[31]

The title of "Until the Troubling of the Waters" is derived from the passage in John 5:2-4 which tells of the pool at Bethesda whose waters, having been "troubled" by an angel, were possessed of miraculous powers to heal the sick, and beside which Jesus was to perform an important act of faith-healing. The speaker is a poor workingwoman, presumably unmarried, who has brought her defective infant son to the place where the contemporary faith-healer is to arrive in two hours. Her monologue is largely taken up with a troubled account of her own vaguely defined guilt in causing the child's illness (perhaps an attempted abortion?), of the awakenings of hope, and of her struggles against the doubts and the reluctances which have beset her since she first learned about the healer's coming. In one passage describing a mood of almost manic rapture at the anticipation of her child's recovery, Moody has her describe the mill where she works in terms that foreshadow the optimistic sentiments of his later poem on the machine, "The Brute":

> . . . all day long the noises of the mill
> Were spun upon a core of golden sound,
> Half-spoken words and interrupted songs
> Of blessed promise, meant for all the world,
> But most for me, because I suffered most.
> The shooting spindles, the smooth-humming wheels,
> The rocking webs, seemed toiling to some end
> Beneficent and human known to them,
> And duly brought to pass in power and love.

But the mood soon gives way to recurring doubts and, more pointedly, to a confession of a guilty possessiveness and jealousy at the thought that the healed child might no longer wholly belong to her. This, coupled with a subtler suggestion of fear that the success of the miracle would necessitate a spiritual transformation in her and a loss of the misery and self-pity to which she has become morbidly attached, creates a psychological conflict similar to the personal one depicted in "Jetsam" between the poet's own opposed reactions to the thought of ultimate religious commitment:

> After the change, would my boy be the same
> As this one? Would he be my boy at all,
> And not another's—his who gave the life
> I could not give, or did not anyhow?
> How could I look in his new eyes to claim
> The whole of him, the body and the breath,
> When someone not his mother, a strange man,
> Had clothed him in that beauty of the flesh—
> Perhaps (for who could know?), perhaps, by some
> Hateful disfiguring miracle, had even
> Transformed his spirit to a better one,
> Better, but not the same I prayed for him
> Down out of Heaven through the sleepless nights,—
> The best that God would send to such as me.

The psychological, but not the moral conflict is temporarily resolved when she hits upon the device of carrying the child herself the whole long and difficult way to the place where the faith-healer is to come, thereby assuring herself that in future years she will share in the child's gratitude (". . . he should have no one to thank/But me for that") and, like the faith-healer, be looked on as one who has performed a superhuman act of strength and sacrifice. All this is, of course, seen in retrospect, for the immediate setting of the entire poem is before the steps to which the mother has arrived after her arduous journey to join the multitude hopefully awaiting the miracle. At the end, having conquered her jealousy and reluctance by the act of carrying the child all the way herself, she feels strengthened in hope and better able to bear the possible spiritual demands which the miracle, if it occurs, may make on her. Yet her last words still temper the hope with a strong element of doubt and fear of her own unworthiness:

> In two hours He will come, they say, will stand
> There on the steps, above the waiting crowd,
> And touch with healing hands whoever asks
> Believingly, in spirit and in truth.
> Can such a mercy be, in these hard days?
> Is help still sent in such a way as that?
> Christ, I believe; pity my unbelief![32]

On this note the poem concludes. There is no attempt to carry the "plot" through to the appearance of the healer and the testing of his powers. Either because his own attitude toward latter-day faith-healers like Schlatter was at best ambivalent (as his various earlier versions of the play *The Faith Healer*, discussed in Chapter 8, suggest), or because he felt incapable of the artistic challenge involved in depicting the actual miracle, or its failure (a challenge which, as will be seen in Chapter 8, he never did quite meet, even in the final version of the play), Moody contents himself with a psychological portrait of the speaker prior to the awaited event, and leaves the general religious issues which the poem raises in a state of deliberate irresolution. The portrait itself does, however, stand up fairly well as a self-contained and self-justified dramatic creation. In several places its effectiveness is weakened by real sentimentality and a disturbing inconsistency of idiom: in passages like the one about the mill quoted above, for instance, we hear Moody's own voice and sentiments imposing themselves on the speaker's; neither the elaborate imagery and rhetoric nor the rather sophisticated speculation on the future social role of the machine sits well with the simplicity of her mind, and the dramatic effect of the poet's impositions is one of bathos. Elsewhere, on the other hand, the monologue is very persuasive, both dramatically and psychologically, in its revelations of pathetic egocentricity and the degrading effects which poverty, social isolation, and the dehumanized routine of mechanized labor have on the speaker's character. Indeed, taken as a whole, "Until the Troubling of the Waters" stands as something of a landmark in Moody's transition from a minor, imitative, and generally escapist lyric poet of the 1890's to an authentic voice of early twentieth-century America—and one whose most important and original contributions to twentieth-century literature would be in the drama.

This is not to say that Moody's early poetic manner had completely vanished by 1900. The 1901 volume does contain poems written near the end of the decade with passages that are just as imitative or remote in style and substance as anything in the Harvard poems. There is, for instance, the rather delicately wistful meditation on the still brilliant eyes of an otherwise decayed old portrait in "Faded Pictures," which emulates Browning (e.g., "Old Pictures in Florence") throughout.[33] Or there is "A Dialogue in Purgatory," where Moody reverts to his early medieval manner by taking a passage from the fifth canto of Dante's *Purgatorio* (the "*Siena me fe, disfecemi Maremma*" passage which has since passed into popular currency with its ironic use by both Pound and Eliot in *Mauberley* and *The Waste Land*) as a text on which to base a set of conventionally melancholy reflections by La Pia and Buonconte on requited and unrequited love. But such instances are not nearly so typical as they had been before 1897; and, in most of Moody's work from "Jetsam" on, the use of literarily derived materials becomes increasingly personalized. He continues to echo the literary past throughout the rest of his career; but, except for occasional lapses of judgment, his borrowings from here on are transmuted by their contexts into vehicles for Moody's own ideas and perceptions, which gain solidity and coherence as his maturing talent comes more and more to dominate, rather than be dominated by, his adopted literary ancestry.

CHAPTER 3

Cosmic Satire

I The Masque of Judgment: *Origins, Sources, Genre*

IN A LETTER TO Daniel Gregory Mason from Venice dated
June 8, 1897, Moody, after mentioning his recent completion
of a draft of "Good Friday Night," went on to announce:

> I am at work now on a rather hopelessly fantastic thing, I fear,
> half-lyric, half-dramatic; I shall try to excuse the wilfulness of
> the form by calling it a Masque. The subject is the Judgment-
> day—no less—a kind of sketchy modern working over of the
> theme, from the point of view of the accusing human. God
> Almighty promises to be an engaging figure, with proper fore-
> shortening. The protagonist is the archangel Raphael, a staunch
> humanist (his enemies—Heaven confound their counsels!—
> would say a sentimentalist), and principal rôles are sustained
> by such pleasing characters as the Seventh Lamp of the Throne,
> the Angel of the Pale Horse, the Lion of the Throne, and the
> Spirit of the Morning-star. I foresee great possibilities,—a kind of
> Hebrew Götterdammerung, with a chance for some real speaking-
> out-in-meeting—hoop-la!—Excuse my barbaric yawp; it is merely
> meant to express enthusiasm.[1]

Despite the tone of playful self-deprecation, rather frequent
in Moody's accounts of his own literary endeavors, it is clear
enough from the end of this passage and from all his subsequent remarks about the work-in-progress that he took *The
Masque of Judgment* very seriously. Over the next two-and-a-
half years he devoted the greater part of his creative time and
energy to writing and rewriting this first *magnum opus;* and,
when it was finally completed in January, 1900, its prelude and
five acts comprised not only his most ambitious performance to
date, but the longest single work in verse he was ever to produce. The *Masque* became Moody's first published volume of
poetry when it was brought out in November of the same year
by Small, Maynard, and Company of Boston.

At the time, of course, Moody had not yet conceived the *Masque* to be what it eventually became: the second member of a trilogy of which the later verse dramas *The Fire-Bringer* and *The Death of Eve* were the first and third. The *Masque* was written, and will therefore be considered in this chapter, as a self-contained work. Indeed, though ideologically it came to fit quite neatly into the scheme of the trilogy, and though some of its more tenuously abstract philosophical gropings gain solidity by being seen in the context of the whole, in structure and technique the earlier member represents a different order of composition from the other two. For one thing, it makes no pretense at being what the later members decidedly aim to be —plays. In calling his work a "masque," Moody was placing it in a genre which had attracted several late-nineteenth-century American poets who were concerned not with any notion of creating a new verse idiom for the theater but simply with finding a form capable of communicating large philosophical ideas with greater vividness and flexibility than was possible in the direct discursive poem. Less indebted technically to the Renaissance masque than to the Romantic closet drama of Goethe, Shelley, and Byron, the genre is perhaps best represented in the work of Moody's contemporaries by Hovey's two masques *The Quest of Merlin* (1891) and *Taliesin* (1899) and by George Santayana's first long poetic endeavor *Lucifer, or the Heavenly Truce* (1899).

But the work which seems to have had the most direct influence on Moody's masque was the earlier religious allegory *The Masque of the Gods* (1872) by the genteel poet Bayard Taylor—a fairly short and rather mechanical and poetically uninteresting effort from which Moody may nevertheless have derived both the idea for the general subject of his own work— a critical revaluation of man's erring theological doctrines—and the central device of personifying certain abstract religious ideas and having them act out their own implications by way of objectifying the poet's personal attitudes toward them.[2] A glance at Moody's cast of personifications—made up largely of Miltonic archangels and an assortment of less substantial celestial "Spirits" and emblematic creatures out of the Book of Revelation—or at several of his "stage directions"—such as those that call for long soliloquies or intricate choral lyrics to be delivered while *"Flying"*—will suffice to show that the idea of theatrical

production was as far from his thoughts as it had been from
Taylor's.

Even apart from questions of practical staging, however, *The
Masque of Judgment* is in a broader sense non-dramatic. Though
there is a plot of sorts, the basic structural principle is not a
steadily developing linear action but a kind of elaborate theme-
and-variations pattern. Somewhat like the typical opening para-
graph of an Emersonian essay, the two scenes of the Prelude
comprise a microcosm of the whole work, stating in brief the
various motifs that are then examined in fuller detail and with
widening ramifications through the ensuing five acts. Almost
no real action occurs "onstage"; and the behind-the-scenes plot
line, mostly related via blocks of expository narrative, is broadly
abstract and for long stretches wholly static. It serves as a kind
of minimal horizontal thread on which are hung the vertical
interplays of soliloquy, debate, and song that are the real substance of the work.

According to Lovett, who was with the poet in Venice when he
began writing the *Masque,* its immediate inspiration had come
from a triptych of the Last Judgment which had particularly
fascinated and shocked Moody during a visit to an exhibition
of modern Venetian art: "in the center, the Deity in his wrath,
and on the sides the contorted bodies of the damned."[3] The
effect of that experience, a heightened sense of revulsion against
traditional apocalyptic myths and their corresponding theological and moral doctrines, was to crystallize in Moody's mind
a set of attitudes which had been germinating in his early
poems and which were to become increasingly central to his
work from then on.

We have seen in poems like "Jetsam" and "Song-Flower and
Poppy" an impulse toward rejection of asceticism and simple du-
alistic solutions to the problem of evil. Along with this rejection
went a growing distrust of the Puritan mentality, associated in
some measure with the poet's own upbringing—though to Moody
the specific phenomenon of Calvinism was only representative
of all theological or philosophical outlooks rooted in what he
considered an essentially negative approach to salvation and a
consequent suppression of the free development of human
personality. Throughout the introduction to his edition of Milton, which he was writing at the same time as the *Masque,* we
find Moody virtually going out of his way to attack the "fanat-
icism" of the seventeenth-century Puritans who had "crushed

out the joy and poetry of life in England" or to criticize Milton's own excessive "passion of purification."[4] His discussion of *Paradise Lost* likewise shows a strong inclination toward Blake's position that "The reason Milton wrote in fetters when he wrote of Angels and God, and at liberty when of Devils and Hell, is because he was a true Poet, and of the Devil's own party without knowing it."[5] In the *Masque*, then, Moody set out to create his first full-scale poetic formulation of such attitudes, taking the image of the vindictive Hebraic-Christian Judge in the Venetian triptych as an archetypal expression of the general mentality he had come to reject.

II *Götterdammerung*

The half-jocular description Moody had given Mason of the projected subject of the *Masque* turned out to be remarkably consistent with the finished product. The bare offstage plot which provides the backdrop for his "modern working over" of the Judgment-Day myth is indeed a kind of Wagnerian *Götterdammerung* transferred to a Hebraic-Christian context,[6] with the destruction of an unsubmissive humanity depicted as ultimately and irresistibly recoiling back on the Creator himself. Moody's "properly foreshortened" God of the Venetian triptych never appears as an actual *persona*, but a fairly full characterization is achieved through the narration of his actions and the reflections made on those actions by the members of the speaking cast. Early in the Prelude, the essentials of that characterization appear in a dialogue between the two chief *personae*, the archangels Raphael and Uriel, during which the latter—partly by way of cautioning his companion against his excessive addiction to mankind and to temporal things—delivers an extended account of the origins of celestial and earthly life. The main part of his account, as Professor Shorey has pointed out, is clearly influenced by Moody's acquaintance with old gnostic myths of creation and neo-Platonic cosmogonies.[7] Its style, like that of many passages in the *Masque*, is just as clearly influenced by Milton's blank verse:

> Of old the mind of God, coiled on itself
> In contemplation single and eterne,
> Felt suddenly a stealing wistfulness
> Sully the essence of his old content
> With pangs of dim division. Long He strove

Against his bosom's deep necessity,
Then, groping for surcease, put forth the orbs
Of Paradise, with all their imagery,
And the ordered hierarchies where we stand;

. . . .

Demand of joy, hardly to be gainsaid,
And vast necessity of grief, still worked
Compulsive in his breast: our essence calm,
Those lucid orbs accordant, could not bring
Nepenthe long. His hand He still withheld
Ages of ages, fearing the event,
Till, bathed in brighter urge and wistfulness
He put forth suddenly this vine of Time
And hung the hollow dark with passionate change.

It is, however, a far cry from Milton's calmly and confidently omnipotent Father to this imperfect and unstable Deity driven by forces beyond his control—though significantly located within rather than without his being—to an act of creation motivated in large part by a rather masochistic compulsion to satisfy his "vast necessity of grief." No wonder, then, that the final product of this compulsion, man, should appear to the rational Uriel a finite reflection of his Creator's own "disquietude" and ambiguity of purpose:

At last! At last! O shaken Breast, nowhere
Couldst thou find quiet save in putting forth
This last imagination? Could no form
Of being stanch thee in thy groping thought
Save this of Man? Puny and terrible;
Apt to imagine powers beyond himself
In wind and lightning; cunning to evoke
From mould and flint-stone the surprising fire,
And carve the heavy hills to spiritual shapes
Of town and temple; nursing in his veins
More restlessness than called him from the void,
Perfidies, hungers, dreams, idolatries,
Pain, laughter, wonder, anger, sex, and song!

Having been made in the image of the imperfect Deity, man bears within him the necessity of that very evil for which the Deity will decree his punishment. During the second scene of the Prelude, we see this necessity manifesting itself as man's irrepressible but uncharted natural energies drive him to rebel against, and finally to deny, his supernatural origins. In an episode whose Greek setting and *personae* are unique in the general Hebraic-Christian mythology of the *Masque*, Raphael is led by a shepherd and his boy to watch a distant group of frenzied Bacchantes bewitch, then murder, and finally dismember an Orpheus-like youth who had shunned their orgies to sing "in lonesome places piercing lonesome songs/Of other lives and other gods than theirs."[8] Moody's depiction of the scene is not without its attractiveness; and the action of the Bacchantes, especially as described in the racy archaic vernacular of the shepherd's boy—Moody's attempt to evoke the atmosphere of Greek pastoral poetry in its most familiar English equivalent—has in it something of that primal energy that the poet celebrates elsewhere in the *Masque*.

> Coney, how passed the hailstorm o'er, quotha!
> Patter! patter! 't was sung beneath i' the dark.
> I lost a birch cup full of whortleberries
> Scrambling to cover when I heard their songs.
>
> . . . .
>
> No more thou'lt shun their orgies in the wood,
> Throat of the hermit-thrush and ring-dove eyes!
> Throat of the mourning thrush, thy songs are done;
> Sad ring-dove eyes, the lids have shut you in!

Hence, though the episode does obviously symbolize the abuse of human freedom in a self-sufficing and brutish naturalism on the one hand and in an overreaching pride on the other, our own reactions are meant to be at least ambivalent. Not so the reaction of Moody's Puritan God. The evil represented by the Bacchantes only compels him to repent his bestowal of freedom on his finite creation; and with the entrance midway through the scene of the ominous Angel of the Pale Horse, bearing "the scourge of the wrath of God," we are introduced to the Judgment-motif itself. To this agent of retribution and death, the only way to deal with human animality and human pride is to deprive man of his freedom or, failing that, to annihilate him; and in such temper he arrives with tidings of God's own projected intention: "Those who consent/To render up their clamorous wills to Him,/...He will accept: the rest He will destroy."

On this note the Prelude concludes. In its two apparently inconclusive scenes, the whole moral issue of the *Masque* has been presented in capsule form. The plot action of the five acts simply draws out the implications already manifest in Uriel's account of the creation, in the crime of the Bacchantes, and in the threats of the Angel of the Pale Horse. In Act One we learn of another supernatural antagonist of the Deity who is more absolute in his enmity than those rebel angels whose disobedience has driven them to perdition: the mysterious "Worm that Dieth not," the force of total negation, the denial of life itself. The central event in the act is a symbolic battle between that creature and the Lion and the Eagle of the Throne, God's faithful guardians, from which the guardians retreat gravely wounded. The narration of their defeat is Moody's first explicit variation on the *Götterdammerung* theme implicit in Uriel's view of man as a finite extension of God's own being; for it represents the potential overthrow of the Deity himself by the Worm, now threatened as the necessary corollary to his projected destruction of his temporal counterpart.

But before that destruction takes place, Moody gives the Deity his due by allotting the second act to the Incarnation and Crucifixion—God's one great attempt to win man's voluntary submission through an act of empathy and love. Even the narration of these acts, however, is attended by strong suggestions of masochistic motives; and when the childlike Spirit of the Lamp refers in horror to "That Nothingness that sat upon the Throne" of Heaven during God's period of suffering and self-sacrifice on earth, she is not only revealing her naïve misunderstanding of the cause of his absence, but she is also intimating the futility of an act of love aimed only at inspiring man to sacrifice his own free nature out of mere gratitude.

The failure of the Incarnation and Crucifixion to accomplish God's purpose is apparent in Acts Three and Four, where the ranks of the condemned far exceed those of the redeemed in the Judgment-scene itself. Most of Act Four is devoted to a direct expression of what Moody had called "the point of view of the accusing human," as a group of unrepentant and unsubmissive sinners relate the various good reasons they "could not pay/The price exacted from us." Their defiant eleventh-hour self-justifications, in the name of human love, art, the joy of struggle, and the daily pleasures of the free sensual life, add up to a major variation on one of the central themes of the *Masque:* the inviolable sanctity of human personality, superior even in its evil manifestations to the kind of self-abnegation and acquiescence demanded of them in return for God's mercy. Finally, in Act Five we find that, with human life now annulled, all the might of Archangel Michael and his heavenly hosts is incapable of stopping the inexorable climb toward God's own throne of the "Worm that Dieth not," and the imminent downfall of Heaven itself—its angels, its redeemed humans, and its Ruler—before the force of absolute negation.

III   *The Positive Theme*

When the *Masque* was first published, some of Moody's friends took exception to his literal characterization of the Deity and the rather dreary and ignoble theology it seemed to embody. Typical of the poet's response is this passage from a letter to Mrs. C. H. Toy dated December 12, 1900:

> Your objection to the "theology" of the Masque would be well taken if there were any theology in it. There isn't an ounce, or at least if there is it is there against my will. Of course I didn't intend my "strangely unpleasant" God to be taken seriously. To me the whole meaning and value of the poem lies in the humanistic attitude and character of Raphael, the philosophic outlook of Uriel, and the plea for passion as a means of salvation everywhere latent. The rest of it is only mythological machinery for symbolizing the opposed doctrine—that of the denial of life. As Christianity (contrary of course to the wish and meaning of its founder) has historically linked itself with this doctrine, I included certain aspects of it in this mythological apparatus—always with a semi-satirical intention.[9]

The phrase "a semi-satirical intention" provides the indispensable gloss on Moody's characterization of the Deity and the general plot outlines of the *Masque*—though one which is easily lost sight of in the light of the high lyric manner that pervades most of the verse. As in the dramas of Moody's beloved Euripides, the lyricism of the *Masque* goes hand in hand with what is best described as a grim cosmic satire, leveled, as is much of Euripides' satire, at human conceptions of Godhead which seemed to the poet inadequate and pernicious. Clearly enough, the God depicted is not Moody's God, nor does he try anywhere in the work to characterize directly his alternative conception of the Supreme Being. For some idea of what that conception would have been like had the poet presumed to express it directly, we must turn to the utterances of those *personae* who plead the case for his personal humanism and his belief in "passion as a means of salvation." We have already noted one such plea in the speeches of the condemned sinners in Act Four. But "the point of view of the accusing human" is yet more fully represented by the chief onstage character in the *Masque,* Milton's "affable" Archangel Raphael, whose "speaking-out-in-meeting" on behalf of the humanity he loves takes up close to half of the total text. In the contrast between Raphael's humanistic affirmations and the suicidal negations of the Deity and his agents of destruction, we have not only the satirist's reduction-to-absurdity of orthodox eschatologies but also the lyric poet's intimations of his own theological position.

If Milton provided the chief source for the *dramatic personae* and much of the blank-verse style of the *Masque,* it was in Blake that Moody seems to have found the main inspiration for the substance of its positive doctrine. This is particularly true of Raphael's several long soliloquies, which might well have as their motto Blake's aphorism "Eternity is in love with the productions of time." The theme on which all of these soliloquies play their intricate variations is fully established in the opening speech of the Prelude, delivered while the archangel, on one of his frequent absences from Heaven, hovers alone over a sea-scape near a town on whose human life dawn is just rising:

> Another night like this would change my blood
> To human: the soft tumult of the sea
> Under the moon, the panting of the stars,
> The notes of querulous love from pool and clod,
> In earth and air the dreamy under-hum
> Of hived hearts swarming,—such another night
> Would quite unsphere me from my angelhood!
> Thrice have I touched my lute's least human strings
> And hushed their throbbing, hearing how they spake
> Sheer earthly, they that once so heavenly sang
> Above the pure unclouded psalmody.
> Sing as thou wilt, then, since thou needs must sing!
> For ever song grows dearer as I walk
> These evenings of large sunset, these dumb noons
> Vastly suspended, these enormous nights
> Through which earth heaves her bulk toward the dawn.
> With song I shelter me, who else were left
> Defenseless amid God's infinitudes,
> Bruised by the unshod trample of his hours.

This passage is followed by the first of many rhymed lyrics which alternate with the blank verse of the *Masque*—a gay song in celebration of the ever-recurring alternation of night, with its mystery and lunar passions, and day, with its clarity and solar ease. This is the keynote of all Raphael's subsequent speeches and songs: the beauty of process and variety, found only in the world of time and at its most intense in the sexual rhythms of the male-female relationship, which the archangel contemplates at the close of the first scene as he listens to an offstage girl's voice singing of erotic passion in the idiom of the Song of Songs. It is his worship of that beauty which makes Raphael praise the very restlessness and lack of stability whose manifestations incur Uriel's contempt for God's temporal creation in the same scene. It also underlies Raphael's lyrical effort, at the end of the long ode-like soliloquy that begins Act One, to suggest the sanctity of strife in the natural order and to excuse even the cruelty inherent in the survival-of-the-fittest principle as a necessary corollary to the violent energies of the erotic principle:

> *Drowsy with dawn, barely asail,*
> *Buzzes the blue-bottle over the shale,*
> *Scared from the pool by the leaping trout;*
> *And the brood of turtlings clamber out*
> *On the log by their oozy house.*
> *Round the roots of the cresses and stems of the ferns*
> *The muskrat goes by dodges and turns;*
> *Till she has seized her prey she heeds not the whine of*
> *   her mouse.*
> *Lovingly, spitefully, each*
> *Kind unto kind makes speech;*
> *Marriage and birth and war, passion and hunger and thirst,*
> *Song and plotting and dream, as it was meant from the first!*

The antithetical principle—that of completion, homogeneity, stasis—Raphael repeatedly associates with the mere denial of life. In his longest soliloquy, which occurs at the start of Act Three between the Crucifixion and the Last Judgment, he delivers an elaborate elegiac apostrophe to the suffering heart of man, with its good and evil inextricably compounded; and he condemns any separation of these forces as fatal to life itself. At this point, he still clings to a kind of desperate hope that the Deity he loves may not will that separation and thereby annul his most marvelous creation. Rumors that the failure of the Crucifixion to bring about a reconciliation between God and man have confirmed the Creator in his desire for a final cataclysmic judgment, arouse Raphael to an impassioned protestation of his disbelief that God could be "fool" enough to "dash in pieces" something He made out of his own intimate substance. Thereupon, in an attempt to find some hopeful interpretation of the Deity's recent actions, he wonders if perhaps the Crucifixion may have been the prologue to a new dispensation in which God, rather than judging man and destroying those who do not submit their wills to his, will at last "give the substance for the shade" and raise man to a higher plane of awareness and self-realization with his freedom intact. In this spirit Raphael implores the "doomed, rejected world" to awaken to the supreme gift of the Crucifixion and to accept, while it is still possible, the turn from vengeance to mercy which it may betoken.

But events soon prove him wrong; and, as the image of the Crucifixion is supplanted by that of the Last Judgment in the second scene of Act Three, Raphael becomes a type of the Romantic arch-rebel, rejecting the God who has betrayed his hopes for mankind and casting his lot with the many damned rather than with the few redeemed in the holocaust of Act Four. In his rebellion he is now joined by Uriel, who, having begun as a confirmed anti-humanist, has undergone a sudden and unexplained conversion to Raphael's point of view. Uriel's sober ratiocinations now become allied with the more emotional and intuitive attitudes of his fellow archangel; and they formulate together Moody's answer to the loyal archangel Michael's defense of the Last Judgment on the grounds that man's irreclaimable sinfulness left God no other recourse. That answer—centered largely in the dialogue of Act Three, Scene Two and Act Five, Scene Two—is the poet's own interpretative commentary on his behind-the-scenes plot and the ideological core of the *Masque*.

What it amounts to is a theodicy in which familiar nineteenth-century theories of progress are fused with the Transcendentalist idea of the identity of nature and the supernatural, man and the divine Over-Soul.[10] Apart from its satirical function as a criticism of Puritan views of Godhead, Uriel's account of the creation in the Prelude was also Moody's way of representing mythopoetically his conception of a dynamic rather than a static universal order. God and the cosmos are themselves imperfect, and the world of man and nature, which is their temporal replica, necessarily shares in that imperfection. Both, however, are engaged in a process of evolution through gradual self-purification, at the remote end of which lies that final fulfillment in which all evil and strife will vanish. Progress in the cosmic order is inseparable from progress in the temporal order; and, until the final goal is reached, evil and strife remain themselves the necessary conditions for such progress. As nature and man struggle toward the realization of their highest potential, God and the cosmos are aided in their own struggle toward perfection. Uriel asserts in Act Three, Scene Two:

> Not a heart
> O'ercometh evil and mounts up to good,
> But He o'ercometh and is lifted too.
> Each life of clay that flowered in fragrant deed,
> Each grass-blade that grew willingly, each bird
> That through the churlish weather hoarded song,
> Not only worked its own salvation out
> But helped Him in his old struggle with himself. . . .

The reason, then, why Raphael and Uriel must reject the God of the *Masque* is that, in seeking to eliminate the challenge of evil and man's freedom in the face of that challenge, He would eliminate struggle itself and thereby put an end to all progress in the cosmos. Instead of working with the aid of man to bring good slowly and painfully out of evil, the Deity has weakened at the peak of the challenge and submitted to a power beyond both good and evil—to his ultimate enemy the "Worm that Dieth not." By turning his wrath on a mankind whose moral being is inextricably bound up in his own, He has invited his own destruction by the force of absolute negation. At the end of the *Masque,* while the Worm is making its way toward the Throne of Heaven, Raphael reflects mournfully on what might have been; his reflections constitute a final summation of Moody's dialectics of struggle and a bird's-eye view of the Deity whom the poet might be inclined to place on the throne now to be vacated by the Deity he has renounced:

> Would He had dared
> To nerve each member of his mighty frame—
> Man, beast, and tree, and all the shapes of will
> That dream their darling ends in clod and star—
> To everlasting conflict, wringing peace
> From struggle, and from struggle peace again,

Higher and sweeter and more passionate
With every danger passed! Would He had spared
That dark Antagonist whose enmity
Gave Him rejoicing sinews, for of Him
His foe was flesh of flesh and bone of bone,
With suicidal hand He smote him down,
And now indeed His lethal pangs begin.[11]

There is in all this, of course, something of the Miltonic doctrine of the "fortunate fall." Though the *Masque* never alludes to any myth depicting some primal state of perfection from which man and nature were banished, but instead takes the state of the fall as the original condition, the moral implications are not much different from those in Book Twelve of *Paradise Lost*. In extending those implications from man to God himself, however, Moody suggests the essential opposition between his theodicy and the Calvinist one, even in the much modified version of Milton's epic. Moody's insistence on the inseparability of the human and the superhuman, and on their mutual imperfection, stands in open contrast to the Calvinist tendency to set as wide a breach as possible between human nature and the inscrutable perfection of the Deity and to emphasize the fall as a condition of absolute estrangement from the divine, except insofar as an arbitrary act of grace may close the breach for a chosen few.

Along with this goes Moody's rejection of the type of moral dualism implicit in the orthodox Christian view, particularly emphasized by the Calvinists, that the chief evidence of man's estrangement in the state of the fall resides in the innate sinfulness of the flesh. Moody was in no sense a facile primitivist, yet he did strongly oppose any reduction of moral issues to a neat antagonism of flesh and spirit. In his opposition he placed so heavy an emphasis on the beauty of natural passions that he sometimes gave the impression of advocating obedience to physical impulse as the one moral imperative. Actually, however, the point of the Bacchantes scene in the Prelude is that, when the senses and passions become an end in themselves, divorced from the higher purpose of man's evolution toward full self-realization, their life-sustaining forces are perverted into forces of destruction. God's mistake was in failing to make this distinction: seeing their perversion, He condemned the natural energies of man—whose power for good is latent in the shepherd boy's attractive description of the Bacchantes—as innately evil; and, in willing their annihilation, He destroyed potential good along with present evil. Uriel is explicit on this point in Act Three, Scene Two:

> Man's violence was earnest of his strength,
> His sin a heady overflow, dynamic
> Unto all lovely uses, to be curbed
> And sweetened, never broken with the rod!

Nowhere in the *Masque* does Moody deny the reality of evil or the validity of the human sense of guilt. As is apparent in poems like "Jetsam" and particularly in "The Daguerreotype," his own personal sense of guilt was sometimes very strong. Yet in these poems, as in the *Masque,* evil is associated chiefly with a failure to fulfill one's given potentialities, with stagnation or retrogression instead of progression toward higher states of being; and it is in such terms that Moody tries to reconcile the claims of flesh and spirit. In contrast to the rejected version of the problem of evil represented by the God he satirizes, he has Raphael, in Act Three, Scene Two, declare the essence of his own:

> Why did He quench their passion? I have walked
> The rings of planets where strange-colored moons
> Hung thick as dew, in ocean orchards feared
> The glaucous tremble of the living boughs
> Whose fruit hath eyes and purpose; but nowhere
> Found any law but this: Passion is power,
> And, kindly tempered, saves. All things declare
> Struggle hath deeper peace than sleep can bring:
> The restlessness that put creation forth
> Impure and violent, held holier calm
> Than that Nirvana whence it wakened Him.

IV *Evaluations*

From this analysis of the general structure and ideological meanings of the *Masque,* it can be inferred that Moody was working under a number of self-imposed technical handicaps. In substituting a theme-and-variations design for a more normal linear plot-line, he deprived the *Masque* of that strong forward momentum which is needed to sustain constant dramatic interest in a work of such length; and the design does make for a good deal of rather wearying repetition throughout the last three acts. In conceiving his *dramatis personae* largely as allegorical personifications, he generalized his background action almost to the point of total abstraction; and his treatment of the foreground *personae* sacrifices fullness and, in the case of Uriel, consistency of characterization to the need for mere voices to utter his ideas or the ideas he is satirizing. And his attempt to pitch all the blank-verse dialogue and most of the lyrics at the level of "sublime" rhetoric results in a frequent straining of language[12] and a stylistic monotony relieved only in such scenes as the brief one given to the shepherd's boy and his archaic colloquialisms. The best-written dialogue and soliloquies, on the whole, are those in the Prelude. Thereafter, we sometimes have a sense that Moody is forcing himself to draw out to a properly impressive length materials which have already absorbed his best eloquence. Raphael's soliloquies in particular grow increasingly diffuse after the first act; and all the blank-verse grows increasingly derivative. Even the most sympathetic reader may well become restive under the recurring mannerisms lifted from the style of *Paradise Lost*: the adjective-noun-adjective patterns, the resounding Latinate polysyllables in series; and the imitations of Latin syntax.[13]

Yet, though such derivations can simply be attributed to Moody's unconscious or semi-conscious reactions to his current labor on the edition of Milton, there is also good reason to see a significant conscious intention in several of the more heavily Miltonic passages. For, as was suggested in Chapter 1, Moody may well have conceived many of his literary "thefts" as comprising a kind of elaborate allusion; and in the present instance such allusion, if rightly understood, can function as an important ingredient of our experience of the whole work.

We have already seen how the *Masque* is, at least in part, an anti-Puritan document, an answer to Milton's attempt to "justify the ways" of the Puritan God to man. At the same time that he admired Milton enormously as a poet, then, Moody could also recognize in the Miltonic style itself an appropriate vehicle for pointing up, by direct association, his implicit criticism of the theological assumptions underlying *Paradise Lost*. We find this illustrated especially well in the passage from Uriel's account of the creation (quoted above), in which the very quality of the language emphasizes the evident, and perhaps the pointedly ironic, contrast between Moody's characterization of the orthodox Deity and that in Milton's epic. It is also illustrated in the general speech idiom of those characters ranged on God's side

—and therefore in a sense on Milton's—such as Michael and the Angel of the Pale Horse. There is, for instance, the latter's account, in Act One, Scene Three, of the defeat of the Lion and Eagle of the Throne by the "Worm that Dieth not," which has the familiar Miltonic ring appropriate to the speaker's role in the *Masque:*

> Deep in the purple umbrage droops the bird,
> His sick eye sealed beneath the weary lid
> Which scarce his right wing's torn and gaping gold
> Disfeathered hideth, since long hours ago
> He sidewise tucked his wounded head away,
> Shunning the light's offense; and through the boughs
> Let sink this mighty pinion sinister
> A vast and ruined length. . . .

But even conscious motives of literary allusion do not quite justify such transparent borrowings as these from Blake—chiefly from "The Tiger"—in Raphael's apostrophe to man during his Act Three soliloquy:

> Thou fiery essence in a vase of fire!
> What quarry gathered and packed down the clay
> To make this delicate vessel of desire?
> Who digged it? In what mortar did he bray? . . .

Or these, from the last scene of Marlowe's *Faustus,* in the rather bombastic and bathetic passage later in the same soliloquy where Raphael puts his hopeful interpretation on the Crucifixion:

> Lo! where God's body hangs upon the cross,
> Drooping from out yon skyey Golgotha
> Above the wills and passions of the world!
> O doomed, rejected world, awake! awake!
> See where He droopeth white and pitiful!
> Behold, his drooping brow is pitiful!
> Cry unto Him for pity. Climb, oh, haste,
> Climb swiftly up yon skyey Golgotha
> To where his feet are wounded!

Such unjustified borrowings are by no means so frequent as some of Moody's more severe critics would lead us to believe; yet they do stand out as evidence that by 1900 he was not yet wholly the master, and was sometimes still the victim, of his poetic influences.[14]

There are, on the other hand, passages in the *Masque* as impressively individual as anything in the shorter poems of the 1890's. When he subordinates abstract argumentation and rhetoric to lyrical description, Moody can also subordinate his influences to his own rich visual and auditory imagination. Uriel's account of the creation of Heaven during his expository narrative in the Prelude, for instance, may be cast in a recognizably Miltonic medium, but not to the extent of overriding our appreciation of a vivid imagery and supple rhythmic pacing for which no literary source can be held responsible:

> Heaven rose
> As if from sleep, and, lo, through all the void
> Clambered and curled creation like a vine,
> Hanging the dark with clusters of young bloom.
> Then from the viewless ever-folded heart
> Of the mystic Rose, stole breath and pulse of change,
> Delicious pantings such as seize the breast
> Of lovers when the love-tide nears its flood,
> Yet touched with endless potency of pain,
> As lips of mothers when their anguish ebbs
> And leaves the waifling life. Then first the Dove
> Began to mourn above the mercy-seat,
> And the dear sister spirits of the Lamps
> Bent all their shimmering wings one way to screen
> Their wicks from the wind-flaw. . . .[15]

The same may be said of Raphael's description, early in Act One, of the desolate mountain-and-valley landscape later to be the setting for the Last Judgment—a description based on Moody's visit to the Dolomite region of Italy and Austria during the summer of 1897:[16]

> The trees grow stunted in this keener air,
> And scarce the hardiest blossoms dare to take
> Assurance from the sun. . . .
>
> . . . .
>
> Such flowers as come, come not quite flower-like,
> But smitten from their gracious habitudes
> By some alarm, some vast and voiceless cry
> That just has ceased to echo ere I came.
> These white buds stand unnaturally white,
> Breathing no odors till their terror pass;
>
> . . . .
>
> . . . What giant plow

Harnessed to behemoth and mastodon
Set this slope furrow down the side of the world?
And to what harvest?

But the best passages in the *Masque* occur not during the
blank-verse speeches but in the rhymed lyrics, where Moody
achieves a compression and suggestiveness often lacking in the
more expansive and explicit pentameter dialogue. One of the
most praised of these is the chorus of offstage "Voices" in Act
One, Scene Two.[17] Here, along with a tastefully indirect reminiscence of Blake, we again see something of the quality of
good Symbolist poetry, as the literal function of the lyric—a
narration of the search for the "Worm that Dieth not" by the
Lion and Eagle of the Throne—takes second place to the larger
evocative overtones it throws off:

Through the vines of tangled light
In the jungles of the sun
Swept the Hunter in his might
And his lion-beagle dun
Gaped for prey to left and right.
O'er the passes of the moon
Strode the Hunter in his wrath:
The eagle sniffed the icy noon,
"Master, knowest thou the path?
Shall we meet thy foe-man soon?

"On what interstellar plain,
'Mid what comet's blinding haze,
Storm of star dust, meteor rain,
Shall we spy his crouching gaze,
Leap at him, and end thy pain?"
Peace is on the heavenly meres,
Sabbath lies on Paradise;
But the little Throne-Lamp fears,
For she sees the Master's eyes,
And she tastes the Master's tears.

Another effectively simple and tightly constructed lyric is that
of the Redeemed Spirits as they fly past on their way to Heaven
during the Last Judgment in Act Three, Scene Two—the one
passage in the *Masque* where Moody summons up a sympathetic eloquence for the point of view elsewhere rejected and
attacked:

In the wilds of life astray,
Held far from our delight,

Following the cloud by day
And the fire by night,
Came we a desert way.
O Lord, with apples feed us,
With flagons stay!
By Thy still waters lead us!

As bird torn from the breast
Of mother-cherishings,
Far from the swaying nest
Dies for the mother wings,
So did the birth-hour wrest
From Thy sweet will and word
Our souls distressed.
Open Thy breast, thou Bird!

If it is chiefly in such parts, rather than the whole, that the *Masque* may still be said to hold a secure value as a poetic and dramatic performance today, to some readers of Moody's own time the work in its totality represented a sustained embodiment of major literary genius. Though it received less critical attention than the 1901 *Poems* were to receive, and though in some reviews it came in for its share of condemnation, one critic in a prominent journal labeled the *Masque* quite simply "a great poem, great alike in conception and execution," and went on to declare, "as a work of constructive imagination, it ranks with the great masterpieces."[18] Even Robinson—from whom Moody expected little sympathy for its form and manner, and who did in fact express some initial qualms over Moody's plans—came in the end to develop a mounting enthusiasm for the completed work. After expressing tentative praise when the *Masque* was first published,[19] he finally went the limit in a letter of January 17, 1901, to the critic John Hays Gardiner:

> If you will read Moody's *Masque* I am sure that you will have a new opinion of the man. Barring six or eight scattered verses that are entirely damnable and unique in literature, the thing is an astonishing work of art and almost flawless in construction. The man has continued somehow to give unity, coherence, concreteness, and all the other things you people like to talk about, to the most difficult and unpromising material.[20]

But Robinson probably had come closer to the final truth in an earlier letter to Moody himself, written before he had read the *Masque*. In it he speculated that the ambitious work-in-progress that his friend had described to him would have "formative significance" as a "means of making your own poetical acquaintance" even if it did not stand the test of time as a total achievement in its own right.[21] That the *Masque* did have "formative significance" is beyond doubt. In committing his hitherto restrained ambitions to the challenge of the big poem, Moody had extended his poetic vision and exercised faculties whose development was essential to any endeavor at being the major poet he now clearly aimed to be. Moreover, the *Masque* had given fairly comprehensive definition to a philosophy in which the poet really believed and in which nearly everything he was to write from then on had its roots. With the *Masque* behind him, he could now go on to explore, with greater maturity and depth and more effective art, the themes and attitudes it had formulated.

CHAPTER 4

The Public Poet

THE FIRST YEAR of the new century found Moody on leave from the University of Chicago, living on and off in New York City and in various New England locales, and writing steadily. After winding up his labors on *The Masque of Judgment* late in January, he was occupied with two other large projects that year: completing the first version of the play *The Faith Healer;* and, from the early autumn, collaborating with Lovett on the *History of English Literature.* But the most important creative products of the year were several new poems, chiefly on contemporary political and social issues, which completed the contents of the 1901 volume and quickly became the most popular of all Moody's compositions in verse. Even before their appearance in the volume, some of these poems were already creating something of a national reputation for their author through their publication in the *Atlantic Monthly* and in *Scribner's Magazine*—a reputation to which the *Masque,* with its more obviously limited appeal, contributed in much smaller measure. Thanks to their repeated inclusion in anthologies, the same poems have remained Moody's best-known poetic works ever since; and it is largely on the basis of their contents that he has frequently been represented by anthologists and literary historians as first and foremost a poet of political and social protest.

The fact is, however, that, in subject matter and sometimes in manner, the 1900 poems constituted a fairly brief and temporary phase of Moody's career—though a phase whose significance, both in itself and for what it meant to his subsequent development, should not be underestimated. It would not be quite accurate to say that their direct concern with public problems of contemporary America marked a brand new departure in Moody's work; for we have already seen such a concern operating in the grim reflections on modern urban and industrial civilization that take up passages in "Jetsam," "Song-Flower and Poppy," and "Until the Troubling of the Waters." What is new in the 1900 poems is their general emphasis and the kind of poetic stance they often assume.

"Jetsam" and "Song-Flower and Poppy" were essentially introspective meditations, with the social scene providing the backdrop for a lyrical and discursive expression of the poet's personal religious, moral, and esthetic searchings. The real subject of "Until the Troubling of the Waters" was not the speaker's economic and social plight but her psychological struggles before an issue of religious faith. Now, however, society itself occupies the center of the poet's attention; and, with this shift of focus, his idiom undergoes certain alterations. In most of these poems we are aware of Moody self-consciously taking on the role of the public poet, speaking out or singing his views on current conditions in a voice meant to carry to large popular audiences. As though in relief at having finally put the abstractly mythical *Masque* out of his hands, he turns to the concrete facts of the world around him for his materials; and, while retaining much of the lyrical manner dominant in his earlier work, he tends now to turn that lyricism outward and to make it a vehicle for a critical scrutiny of an objective situation rather than for an examination of subjective states of mind.[1]

I *"An Ode in Time of Hesitation"*

Three political events which engaged the American public at the turn of the century—the Spanish-American War of 1898, the American annexation of the Philippines in the wake of that war, and the threatened partition of China by the major Western nations—provided subjects for Moody's poems "An Ode in Time of Hesitation," "On a Soldier Fallen in the Philippines," and "The Quarry." The first, published in the May, 1900, issue of the *Atlantic,* gained widespread attention from the outset and is still the most often anthologized and often discussed of all Moody's works.

Unlike certain of his more radical and perhaps more politically knowledgeable contemporaries, such as William Dean Howells and William Graham Sumner, Moody had been entirely in favor of the Spanish-American War. He regarded it, as did most of the nation, as a righteous struggle for Cuban independence and for the final elimination of oppressive Spanish rule in the Western Hemisphere. But when the peace treaty ending the war—which Congress had ratified in February, 1899—provided for the ceding of the Philippines to the United States, Moody could no longer assent to the foreign policies of the McKinley administration; and he soon became associated with a nationwide movement, comprising moderate liberals as well as radicals, formed to protest this clear instance of American imperialism.

Before long, the United States was fighting a small but brutal war against the very Filipinos who had aided in the struggle against Spain and who, having expected liberation and independence as a result of the victory, now resisted annexation by yet another foreign imperialist power. Reports of atrocities committed by the American fighting forces compounded the original evil of the war itself, which continued—despite large mass meetings conducted by the anti-imperialists and the outspoken opposition of prominent statesmen and writers—until the surrender of the last Filipino insurgents in April, 1902. While the war lasted, it received enthusiastic support from the more powerful political and commercial interests and the more influential journalistic organs throughout the country.[2] Moody's "Ode," coming at the crest of the minority opposition movement, had no more effect on national policy than did any of the other numerous writings of the anti-imperialists. It did, however, emerge as the one work to survive the immediate historical situation and to achieve a lasting place in American literature.

The "Ode" is simultaneously a poem of protest and of celebration. What it protests against is the corruption of America's national ideals; what it celebrates is those ideals themselves, as symbolized chiefly by the Civil War hero Robert Gould Shaw, the young and high-born New England colonel who had died while leading the first Negro regiment of the Union army in an attack on Fort Wagner in July, 1863, and had been buried in a common grave with the former slaves whom he commanded. In the summer of 1897, Moody, who was then in Europe, read a newspaper account of the unveiling on Boston Common of Augustus Saint Gaudens' monument to Shaw and his regiment, as well as a partial transcript of William James's oration dedicating the monument to Shaw's memory.[3] During the winter and early spring of 1900, Moody was living in Boston himself and saw Saint Gaudens' fine bronze sculpture with his own eyes. This experience, coupled with recollections of James's oration, provided the setting for the entire "Ode" and the principal source of contrast with the contemporary political evils against which the poem is directed.

Like "The Daguerreotype" and some of the longer lyric passages in the *Masque,* the "Ode" derives its elaborately irregular stanza forms and some of its rhetorical manner from the general tradition of the English Pindaric ode. More particularly, both its technique and its contents would have evoked associations for many of Moody's readers with the most famous earlier American effort in that tradition: James Russell Lowell's tribute to the fallen heroes of the Civil War, "Ode Recited at the Harvard Commemoration" (1865); and also perhaps with Lowell's shorter, less well-known ode to Shaw himself, "Memoriae Positum" (1863). Yet the associations with these poems involve contrasts which are probably more significant than the formal and stylistic similarities. Though Lowell's odes do contain passages that suggest anxiety over America's failure to live up to its original ideals, these remain subordinate to his celebration of the men who died in the cause of those ideals. In Moody's poem, on the other hand, the note of disillusion and protest is as strong as, and perhaps by the end stronger than, the note of affirmation. The very title testifies to this: America had entered a "time of hesitation," in which the kinds of heroism that had inspired Lowell's odes were being paralyzed by baser motives of self-aggrandizement, such as dominated American policy in the Philippines; and, while the country hesitated before its moral obligations, all Moody could "commemorate" was a kind of general hope that the better elements in the national character would soon reassert themselves and make real heroism again possible.

The actual subject of American imperialism in the Philippines does not enter the "Ode" until the fourth strophe. Prior to that, Moody devotes some sixty lines to an evocation of the affirmative spirit against which he will set the negative realities of the present. The mood of the first three strophes is one of expectancy and promise, and the central motif is that of rebirth. It is a "bright March morn": the poet, standing before Saint Gaudens' "solemn bronze," senses the imminence of spring in the air despite the present barrenness of nature; and he imagines the very ghosts of the figures in the statue stirring in apprehension of the coming renewal. Only in passing phrases like "The land they died to save from death and shame" and "her pangs," or the apparently casual remark that the people on the street pass the Shaw monument "Heedless," do we have any intimation of the later motif of national shame. The verse slips easily from direct, simply worded description of the present scene to a more grandiose and broadly cadenced idiom, as when the springlike atmosphere inspires the poet's imagination to expand outward toward unseen locales where spring is already a reality:

> The ice is runneled on the little pond;
> A telltale patter drips from off the trees;
> The air is touched with southland spiceries,
> As if but yesterday it tossed the frond
> Of pendant mosses where the live-oaks grow
> Beyond Virginia and the Carolines,
> Or had its will among the fruits and vines
> Of aromatic isles asleep beyond
> Florida and the Gulf of Mexico.

Then, in the long third strophe, Moody develops this sense of expansiveness to virtually Whitmanesque proportions as his vision moves gradually westward in a striking panorama of the entire American continent reawakening with the arrival of spring:

> Soon shall the Cape Ann children shout in glee,
> Spying the arbutus, spring's dear recluse;
> Hill lads at dawn shall hearken the wild goose
> Go honking northward over Tennessee;
> West from Oswego to Sault Sainte-Marie,
> And on to where the Pictured Rocks are hung,
> And yonder where, gigantic, willful, young,
> Chicago sitteth at the northwest gates,
> With restless violent hands and casual tongue
> Moulding her mighty fates,
> The Lakes shall robe them in ethereal sheen;
> And like a larger sea, the vital green
> Of springing wheat shall vastly be outflung
> Over Dakota and the prairie states. . . .

And so on, with mounting opulence of imagery and rhetoric, through the Rockies, the Arizona mesas, and the Sierras, as far as the thawing icebergs of the Alaskan sea; until the poet's vision comes to a halt where

> . . . Mariposa through the purple calms
> Gazes at far Hawaii crowned with palms

[74]

> Where East and West are met,—
> A rich seal on the ocean's bosom set
> To say that East and West are twain,
> With different loss and gain:
> The Lord hath sundered them; let them be sundered yet.

On this note, with its perhaps unfortunate reminder of the phrasing—if not the spirit—of Kipling's thrice-famous "Ballad of East and West," Moody finally arrives at his anti-theme. The tone and imagery suddenly darken as a "shade... of sorrow or of blame" enters from the direction of the distant Philippines where America is now engaged in a bloody attempt to destroy the natural barrier between East and West for her own selfish ends. From here to the end of the poem, this "shade" is cast over the promise of the spring scene and the inspiring image of the Shaw monument.

The fifth strophe seems to have been misunderstood by several of Moody's critics, particularly by Henry, who takes its rhetoric at face value as an earnest denial of the "besmearing rumors" concerning America's present shame.[4] A look at the strophe in its context will show how mistaken such a reading is:

> Lies! lies! It cannot be! The wars we wage
> Are noble, and our battles still are won
> By justice for us, ere we lift the gage.
> We have not sold our loftiest heritage.
> The proud republic hath not stooped to cheat
> And scramble in the market-place of war;
> Her forehead weareth yet its solemn star.
> Here is her witness: this, her perfect son,
> This delicate and proud New England soul
> Who leads despisèd men, with just-unshackled feet,
> Up the large ways where death and glory meet,
> To show all peoples that our shame is done,
> That once more we are clean and spirit-whole.

In view of what the poet has just said in the fourth strophe, and of all he will say in later strophes, this outcry is clearly ironic if not downright sardonic. The entire poem insists that, in fact, the "proud republic" *has* "stooped to cheat/And scramble in the market-place of war"; and, far from bearing witness to any *present* cleansing of America's political evil, Colonel Shaw and his regiment symbolize a *past* act of moral courage which stands as a constant reproach to the debased morality of the poet's own time. Moody's ironic contrast between past and present comes full force in the phrase "despisèd men, with just-unshackled feet," with its pointed double reference to the colored slaves whom Shaw gave freedom and dignity, and the colored Filipinos recently liberated from the tyranny of the white Spaniards but now subjected to that of the white Americans. The very banality and complacent righteousness of the language throughout the strophe point up the poet's aim of deriding those who would continue to believe piously in their nation's nobility while remaining "heedless" of its degeneration from the ideals for which Shaw and his men died.

In the sixth strophe all irony disappears from Moody's language as he turns back to his positive theme. His account of the battle of Fort Wagner, based in part on the details of James's dedicatory oration,[5] is fully in the spirit of the traditional ode—its tone solemn, fervent, high-serious. The image of Shaw before the battle takes on almost messianic qualities as the hero becomes also the agent of a spiritual transfiguration in his disciples:

> Crouched in the sea fog on the moaning sand
> All night he lay, speaking some simple word
> From hour to hour to the slow minds that heard,
> Holding each poor life gently in his hand
> And breathing on the base rejected clay
> Till each dark face shone mystical and grand
> Against the breaking day;
> And lo, the shard the potter cast away
> Was grown a fiery chalice crystal-fine
> Fulfilled of the divine
> Great wine of battle wrath by God's ring-finger stirred.

With this last extravagant conceit—which Robinson, despite his admiration for the poem as a whole, insisted was "with all respect to genius, really damnable"[6]—Moody makes his transition to the battle itself, the regiment's charge against deadly artillery fire from the fort, the death of Shaw and his men, and their burial together "By hasty and contemptuous hands." The imagery is sacramental: the limbs of the dead heroes, mingled "In nature's busy old democracy" (a Whitmanesque line which momentarily intrudes on the high, heroic idiom of the strophe), come literally and symbolically to fertilize the life that survives them in the mountain laurel and the rose. Fort Wagner itself becomes "no earthly hold/Of temporal quarrel" but a universal shrine commemorating the eternal struggle of good and evil. But Shaw's "bitter shade" appears in the role of accuser rather than redeemer in the seventh strophe. His eyes, much like those of Moody's dead mother in "The Daguerreotype," haunt the poet with silent reproach for his membership in a society that has repudiated its ideals. Again Moody, who assumes the role of America's champion, protests his refusal to believe that the older national spirit invoked by poets like Whitman and Whittier is now dead. Clearly enough, however, he protests too much; and the irony implicit in his denials becomes explicit when he sets against the memory of these poets his image of the uses to which language is now being put in America:

> Our fluent men of place and consequence
> Fumble and fill their mouths with hollow phrase,
> Or for the end-all of deep arguments
> Intone their dull commercial liturgies—

A specific reference may be intended in these lines to Senator Albert Beveridge of Indiana, one of the leaders of the pro-imperialist forces, whose much-applauded oratory in support of the Philippine annexation harped on America's role as a great commercial power whose chief motivation in international policy must be the acquisition of new foreign markets "and, if necessary, new lands" to guarantee the consumption of the surplus goods produced at home.[7] It is against such reductions of national purpose to mere commercial interests that Moody directs his sharpest and least ode-like invective, culminating in the often quoted reference to Milton's *Areopagitica* in the eighth strophe:

> Are we the eagle nation Milton saw
> Mewing its mighty youth,
> Soon to possess the mountain winds of truth,
> And be a swift familiar of the sun
> Where aye before God's face his trumpets run?
> Or have we but the talons and the maw,
> And for the abject likeness of our heart
> Shall some less lordly bird be set apart?—
> Some gross-billed wader where the swamps are fat?
> Some gorger in the sun? Some prowler with the bat?[8]

The outcry "Ah no!/We have not fallen so," which introduces the long concluding strophe, is not ironic in the way that the denials of America's shame were in the fifth and seventh strophes; nor does it mean that Moody is actually rejecting the accusations he himself has made. What he does reject is the idea that America's political corruption is universal and unredeemable. It is chiefly the country's leaders who are to blame for its imperialist actions; among the population itself, Moody reminds his audience, there are still men capable of the kind of heroism displayed "on the awful hill slope at San Juan" in behalf of the just cause of Cuba's liberation. But in putting those capabilities "to hire," as in the commercially motivated war against the Filipinos, the men in power are leaving no course open to the better elements in the population but that of revolt and retribution:

> With clamor, in the glare and gaze of noon,
> Or subtly, coming as a thief at night,
> But surely, very surely, slow or soon
> That insult deep we deeply will requite.

It is doubtful whether Moody meant to suggest literally that the American people would rise and overthrow their government. All he is trying to do from here to the end of the "Ode" is prevent the poem from seeming essentially a document of despair. The future tense in the verbs which describe what the people will do if their leaders continue in their present course —climaxed in the last line, "Blindness we may forgive, but baseness we will smite"—really suggests the imperative mood more than the declarative. Moody is exhorting, not prophesying; yet his very exhortation indicates that the optimistic spirit of the *Masque,* with its assumption of a fundamentally progressive movement in human and cosmic history, is still trying to operate. In the final analysis, the "Ode" lies somewhere between such firm patriotic affirmations as Lowell's two Civil War odes, and such latter-day poems as his descendent Robert Lowell's "Colonel Shaw and the Massachusetts 54th," which resets in the late 1950's the heroic subject of "Memoriae Positum" and Moody's "Ode" and offers virtually no hope for the resurrection of the spirit symbolized in Saint Gaudens' monument.[9]

Yet for all this, the last strophe of Moody's "Ode" comes as something of a letdown at the end of an otherwise moving performance. It is true enough that in the non-ironic passages throughout the "Ode," Moody's general rhetorical manner often seems to be laid on his emotions from the outside rather than to grow naturally out of the emotions themselves. But this is an inevitable quality of any modern poem composed with an eye to traditional modes of grand public utterance; and, if one allows for Moody's evident desire to place his poem in what had long been an artificial tradition—as one must, for instance, in the case of Milton's *Lycidas*—one can see honest and specific convictions, solidly grounded in concretions of imagery and situation, animating even the most artificially phrased passages in the earlier strophes. When he arrives at his conclusion, however, Moody seems to lose touch with such concretions and to resort to mere vague threats (like the one quoted above), or to easy biblical paraphrase like the following:

> The cup of trembling shall be drainèd quite,
> Eaten the sour bread of astonishment,
> With ashes of the hearth shall be made white
> Our hair, and wailing shall be in the tent.

The result is that, as the language grows increasingly general and abstract, so does the emotion; and we are finally left with a sense that, when it came to defining for himself and his audience the nature of the action which he would see substituted for the present hesitation of national ideals, Moody suddenly found himself with nothing to say. That he did have something to say is clear enough from the rest of the poem, but the language of the last strophe is not equal to its function in the total poetic statement of the "Ode."

II *"On a Soldier Fallen in the Philippines"*

The voice of the public poet is heard in less elevated tones throughout Moody's other anti-imperialist utterance, the short poem "On a Soldier Fallen in the Philippines," which Robinson once condemned as "the nearest to popular rot of anything you have done."[10] Though there is no evidence that Moody ever actually recited the poem to an audience,[11] its three ten-line stanzas—each containing two trimeter quatrains followed by a heptameter couplet, with a predominantly dactyllic bounce throughout—have all the qualities proper to an oral declamation. They comprise, in fact, a kind of mock funeral oration, probably occasioned, as one critic has pointed out, by the death in December, 1899, of the popular General Lawton while he was commanding an American unit in the Philippines.[12] Of course, Moody's sardonic elegy could apply to any soldier killed during the imperialist venture. Each stanza is built around a central ironic contrast: praise for the soldier's courage in performing to the death his assigned duties is set against bitter reflections on the nature of those duties. The irony of the poet's pretended message—that even in death the hero must remain deluded as to the cause for which he fought in order that his honor and peace not be disturbed—takes on its keenest edge in the deftly managed figure of speech, probably the best thing in the poem, with which the last stanza concludes:

> Let him never dream that his bullet's scream
> went wide of its island mark,
> Home to the heart of his darling land where she
> stumbled and sinned in the dark.

There is not even a hint here of the attempt at hopeful affirmation that characterizes the last strophe of the "Ode."

III *"The Quarry"*

In "The Quarry," on the other hand, Moody does venture such an affirmation as he turns his focus to a recent event which symbolized America's capacity for reassuming a noble role in international affairs. To Moody, the action of Secretary of State John Hay in the Chinese crisis of 1899 and 1900 went some way toward redeeming the evil of his country's policies elsewhere in the Far East. By means of his "Open Door Policy," Hay had effectively intervened to prevent the imperialistic governments of England, France, Russia, Germany, and Japan from dividing up and exploiting a weak and politically backward China; and he had guaranteed American support in maintaining independence and in instituting economic and political reforms in that nation.[13] Moody's tribute to this enlightened action takes the form of an allegorical animal fable in which an elephant, representing China, is about to be attacked by a group of murderous "brutes of prey," the imperialist nations; these are suddenly repulsed by an eagle, the United States. Around this simple plot, however, Moody weaves forty-eight lines of complex and sometimes highly enigmatic blank verse; and the special interest and excellence of the poem lie less in the basic allegory itself than in the ambiguities that pervade his elaborations on that allegory.

To begin with, the opening description of the elephant, which takes up nearly two-thirds of the poem, is out of all proportion to its function in the plot and contains an odd assortment of details that seem on first glance totally extraneous to the poet's purpose. Here are a few random excerpts:

> Upon his forehead sat a golden throne,
> The massy metal twisted into shapes
> Grotesque, antediluvian.
>
> . . . .
>
> A peacock spread his thousand dyes to screen
> The yellow sunlight from the head of one
> Who sat upon the throne, clad stiff with gems,
> Heirlooms of dynasties of buried kings,—
> Himself the likeness of a buried king,
> With frozen gesture and unfocused eyes;
>
> . . . .
>
> Between the carven tusks his trunk hung dead;
> Blind as the eyes of pearl in Buddha's brow
> His beaded eyes stared thwart upon the road. . . .

Clearly the description is more than was needed to suggest that the elephant is old and weak; and yet the entire passage functions as something more than mere decorative padding. Taken together, details like those in the quoted lines add up to what seems an indictment of the very civilization which America will later be praised for preserving: the elephant and its rider are obsolete, decadent, spiritually moribund. Such an indictment was undoubtedly part of Moody's aim. His imagery illustrates specifically the despotic feudal system which ruled over Chinese society at the time and, more generally, an entire historical mentality with which he had little sympathy.

Throughout the *Masque* and in some of the earlier poems, Moody had taken a philosophical position directly counter to the essence of Oriental thought, with its ideal of passivity, asceticism, and quest for escape from personality and the world of change into an impersonal Nirvana; and against that ideal he had set his own unequivocally Western vision of man and the universe. Yet at the same time, he still clung to the notion expressed in the "Ode" that East and West are naturally "twain" and that the Oriental nations must be left to work out their own destinies in ways indigenous to their own cultural history. For all his convinced philosophical Westernism, then, Moody could write not only lines suggestive of a distaste for Eastern religious thought and its social and political manifestations, but also lines suggestive of admiring wonder at the profound, if alien, beauties inherent in the ancient Oriental heritage:

> The trappings of the beast were over-scrawled
> With broideries—sea-shapes and flying things,
> Fan-trees and dwarfed nodosities of pine,
> Mixed with old alphabets, and faded lore
> Fallen from ecstatic mouths before the Flood,
> Or gathered by the daughters when they walked
> Eastward in Eden with the Sons of God
> Whom love and the deep moon made garrulous.

The ambivalences in his attitude toward China are resolved in the political policies which Moody upholds in the poem. The motive of the imperialist powers had been simply to violate China's integrity for the sake of economic exploitation; Hay's motive, Moody believed, was to help China reform its decadent political and social system, yet retain its essential character as a nation culturally different from those of the West. At the same time, China was to be permitted—through peaceful and equitable trade relations—to absorb some of the progressive mentality of the civilization to which Moody was personally committed. East and West would remain "sundered," but in a relation of mutual respect and mutually enriching interchange.

The second major ambiguity in "The Quarry" involves Moody's treatment of the eagle. When it first appears, the bird that symbolizes America seems to the poet simply another ravenous beast of prey come to claim its share in the spoils:

> Just as they gathered stomach for the leap,
> The sun was darkened, and wide-balanced wings
> Beat downward on the trade-wind from the sea.
> A wheel of shadow sped along the fields
> And o'er the dreaming cities. Suddenly
> My heart misgave me, and I cried aloud,
> "Alas! What dost thou here? What dost *thou* here?"

This impression is crystallized in the assuredly intentional pun on "trade-wind," with its intimation that America's role in the Chinese crisis may well be expected to follow the lead of its role in the Philippines, motivated solely by such commercial aims as Senator Beveridge had been identifying with ultimate national purpose. The poet is therefore surprised when, instead of joining the attack on the elephant, the eagle drives off the attackers themselves. His narration of this action is, however extremely brief; and it is followed by a further ambiguity as the eagle flies off after his successful intervention "Crying a word I could not understand."

Is Moody suggesting that the magnanimous motives which he would want to attribute to the eagle may not be the entire story; that, in view of the more characteristic features of current national thinking, there may be some hidden, and more selfish, policy behind the government's action in China? The question is never answered, but the very nature of his initial suspicions and the ambiguity in his subsequent phrasing seem designed at least to qualify the political affirmations embodied in the bare plot content of "The Quarry." As a poem of praise, it skillfully retains elements that resemble the poems of protest.

IV   "*Gloucester Moors*"

In all three of these political poems, the root of evil is located in what Moody considered the increasingly oligarchical character of modern industrialized America, and the betrayal of basic human rights to the avarice of the industrial ruling classes. Phrases like "dull commercial liturgies," "on the trade-wind from the sea," "grists of trade" and "grinding at the mill" (the latter two from "On a Soldier") dominate the didactic contents of the poems, and show how much Moody was affected by his contact with turn-of-the-century social critics like Henry George, Henry B. Fuller, and Hamlin Garland.[14] In the poem "Gloucester Moors," which became the title poem in reprints of the 1901 volume and achieved a popularity second only to that of the "Ode," Moody turns from specific political issues to a more generalized protest against the evils of contemporary industrial society. Its theme is adumbrated in a shorter poem which Moody also composed while living near Gloucester, Massachusetts, in the early summer of 1900—the somber lyric "A Grey Day." Though essentially a subjective expression of a private mood of dejection, the poem does open out in its last stanza to something suggestive of a larger social concern:

> I wonder how that merchant's crew
> Have ever found the will!

I wonder what the fishers do
To keep them toiling still!
I wonder how the heart of man
Has patience to live out its span,
Or wait until its dreams come true.

The plain diction and simple metric of this lyric, with its ballad-like combinations of tetrameters and trimeters, carries through to "Gloucester Moors." The poem begins as a pleasant, unpretentious little nature lyric, out of whose ostensibly random images Moody slowly forms the long sustained simile that becomes the vehicle for his theme of social protest. He locates himself on the open moor a mile inland from the port of Gloucester, and he devotes the first three stanzas to casual praise of the sunny afternoon and of the various flowers and birds that encounter his roving eye, in a manner sometimes reminiscent of Emily Dickinson at her simplest:

Over the shelf of the sandy cove
Beach-peas blossom late.
By copse and cliff the swallows rove
Each calling to his mate.
Seaward the sea-gulls go,
And the land-birds all are here;
That green-gold flash was a vireo,
And yonder flame where the marsh-flags grow
Was a scarlet tanager.

But we now become aware of a more disturbing element beneath the placid surface of the natural scene, as though the ocean, instead of stopping a mile away, actually continued underground and caused the apparently stable earth to "heave and dip." This good impressionistic observation becomes the basis for the more explicitly allegorical simile comparing human life to a "gallant, gallant ship" sailing the ocean of time; and, with the further reflection that the ship seems ignorant of its port and is commanded by greedy captains who sit "gorged at mess" while their oppressed crew labors to keep it afloat, Moody makes his transition to his didactic message. By the seventh stanza this message and the simile containing it have come full force:

By her battened hatch I leaned and caught
Sounds from the noisome hold,—
Cursing and sighing of souls distraught
And cries too sad to be told.

> Then I strove to go down and see:
> But they said, "Thou art not of us!"
> I turned to those on the deck with me
> And cried "Give help!" But they said, "Let be:
> Our ship sails faster thus."

The note of personal guilt suggested by his realization that he does not himself belong to the oppressed majority becomes stronger in the next stanza, in which Moody reflects ruefully on his own comparatively privileged state in a society based on exploitation of the masses. A lilting lyric refrain picked up from an earlier stanza is cut short by the poet's recollection of those who, condemned to sordid and ill-paid labor in the industrialized cities, are denied such easy relations with a bountiful nature as he has been enjoying:

> Jill-o'er-the-ground is purple blue,
> Blue is the quaker-maid,
> The alder-clump where the brook comes through
> Breeds cresses in its shade.
> To be out of the moiling street
> With its swelter and its sin!
> Who has given to me this sweet,
> And given my brother dust to eat?
> And when will his wage come in?

Finally, after a rather irrelevant digression to the literal ships with their literal crews that are presently putting in to Gloucester harbor, Moody returns to his simile in the last stanza and contemplates the ultimate destiny of his "ship of souls" in terms that suggest a waning of his optimistic theories of history before immediate sociological realities:

> What shapes, when thy arriving tolls,
> Shall crowd the banks to see?
> Shall all the happy shipmates then
> Stand singing brotherly?
> Or shall a haggard ruthless few
> Warp her over and bring her to,
> While the many broken souls of men
> Fester down in the slaver's pen,
> And nothing to say or do?

The question seems more rhetorical than real. Given the situation the poem has described, there is little reason to imagine a final happy homecoming for this particular *Pequod,* captained by men far worse than Melville's Ahab and with a crew far more helpless in its subjection than his. The poem ends as pure indictment, with little sense of possible remedies for the evils it exposes.

As a didactic poem, however, "Gloucester Moors" leaves something to be desired. One cannot help feeling that what Moody had to say might have been better said had he dispensed with the fanciful ship simile and spoken his mind directly. Indeed, the entire image seems a rather mechanical contrivance designed to connect the purely lyrical part of the poem with the didactic part; it does little, in the long run, to enhance the poignancy of the literal social facts which it metaphorically conveys. Those facts, to which Moody surely responded with honest and deep-seated feeling, suffice in themselves to make the poem moving, and, together with its rather uncharacteristic plainness of style, account for its popularity among his socially conscious readers.[15] But, as far as the poet's art is concerned, the passages of relaxed and pleasingly melodious nature description, only partly pertinent to the social theme, rather than the heavy allegorical apparatus used to dramatize that theme, emerge as the more memorable element. The personal lyricist tends to defeat the public moralist, and the poem thereby tends to defeat its own main purpose.

V *"The Brute"*

Just as "The Quarry" presented a qualified answer to the political pessimism of "On a Soldier," so "The Brute" presents a qualified answer to the social and economic pessimism of "Gloucester Moors." Several of Moody's critics are quite right in seeing "The Brute" as an anticipation of one of the major obsessions in twentieth-century literature and twentieth-century thought as a whole.[16] Its subject is the machine, symbolized vividly throughout the poem as a kind of Frankenstein's monster which has turned on its own creator and threatens to bring ruination on a world whose betterment it was designed to serve. Throughout the purposefully thumping trochaic tetrameters and heptameters of the first six stanzas, the spirit of "Gloucester Moors" prevails, though in somewhat louder tones. We see the allegorical monster betray all the nineteenth-century hopes that with increasing technological progress all men will have greater comfort and leisure and the human race will advance to higher planes of awareness where "We may rise and look about us and have knowledge ere the grave." Instead, the machine has come to strew its "cynic favors" only on "the strong and cunning few"—favors which even for them must ultimately amount to curses as they "stuff their maw with overplus until the spirit dies." For the rest of humanity technological progress has only meant the exploitation of cheap-labor markets and the sacrifice of bodies and souls to the Brute's insatiable need for manpower to keep him operating. In his senseless energy he has invaded and violated the sanctity of nature itself, and made the world a less congenial place even for the exploiters to live in:

> Quietude and loveliness,
> Holy sights that heal and bless,
> They are scattered and abolished where his iron hoof is set;
> When he splashes through the brae
> Silver streams are choked with clay,
> When he snorts the bright cliffs crumble and the woods go
> down like hay;
> He lairs in pleasant cities, and the haggard people fret
> Squalid 'mid their new-got riches, soot-begrimed and
> desolate.

But in the seventh stanza Moody's optimism begins tentatively to reassert itself as a "still small Voice" is heard speaking of envisioned times beyond the immediate present when the Brute will finally assume his intended role as the benefactor of all mankind and as the servant of ultimate cosmic purposes. From here to the end of the poem, this voice does all the talking. Like Raphael and Uriel in the *Masque,* it represents Moody's battered but still lively trust that present evil may prepare for future good, may even be necessary to maintain the condition of strife which alone can stimulate man to struggle toward higher self-realization. By the end of the last stanza, the very language and references hark back to the *Masque* as the voice describes the final redemption of the Brute in the service of the successful cosmic struggle:

> Then, perhaps, at the last day,
> They will whistle him away,
> Lay a hand upon his muzzle in the face of God, and say,
> "Honor, Lord, the Thing we tamed!

Let him not be scourged or blamed.
Even through his wrath and fierceness was thy fierce wroth
  world reclaimed!
Honor Thou thy servants' servant; let thy justice now be
  shown."
Then the Lord will heed their saying, and the Brute come to
  his own,
'Twixt the Lion and the Eagle, by the armpost of the Throne.

Yet the "perhaps" is significant, as is the fact that Moody
assigns these sentiments to a "still small Voice." The mood of
the poem is dominated by the larger voice of the present; and,
as in the conclusion of the "Ode," the future-tense verbs have
more the sense of desperate exhortation than of confident prediction. Like the English Victorian social critics, particularly
John Stuart Mill, Moody may have believed in material progress; but he could also see that, at present, such progress
was only material and therefore potentially more dangerous
than beneficial to the spiritual future of mankind. In his ener-
getic and often imagistically vivid expression of this view,
Moody goes further toward awakening the spirit of social concern and protest than in the more pervasively dissenting allegory of "Gloucester Moors."

VI *"The Menagerie"*

For all his theoretical belief in evolution, then, Moody tended
to feel its denial, or at least its retardation, more keenly than its
realization. Hence, in the whimsical dramatic monologue "The
Menagerie," he seems to have tried to exorcize some of his
doubts regarding his favorite theories by subjecting them to the
challenge of self-satire. "The Menagerie" is (with the exception of passages in the later poem "Old Pourquoi") Moody's
only extended excursion into poetic humor; and, in its ironic
questionings of basic humanist assumptions, it comes close to
being a mock-*Masque of Judgment.* Though not a public poem
in the same sense as the others considered in this chapter, its
reflections on general views of man's place in the universe are
closely related to the social and political disillusion that gave
rise to them. Moreover, in its experiment with colloquial speech
idiom, it forms part of Moody's overall attempt in the poems

of 1900 to bring his work closer to the contemporary scene and to address a broader audience than heretofore.

The speaker is a rather unprepossessing specimen of modern man who, after attending an animal circus in a state of mild intoxication, contemplates his place in the evolutionary process under the influence of his alcoholic haze and his disturbing encounter with his biological ancestors. The gist of his rambling meditation is a heightened sense of kinship with the creatures he has been observing, which so alarms him and offends his sense of dignity that he considers taking the pledge:

> I'll foot it home, to try and make believe
> I'm sober. After this I stick to beer,
> And drop the circus when the sane folks leave.
> A man's a fool to look at things too near:
> They look back, and begin to cut up queer.

All the way home, he continues to be haunted not only by the very human behavior of the circus animals but also by an uncomfortable feeling that they have been as much amused by him as he by them. This feeling prompts him to reconsider those inherited theories which would place him at the glorious apex of the natural hierarchy. The disconnectedly colloquial idiom of the early stanzas suddenly gives way to a sober and elevated mode of utterance as he reviews those orthodox evolutionary theories:

> Within my blood my ancient kindred spoke,—
> Grotesque and monstrous voices, heard afar
> Down ocean caves when behemoth awoke,
> Or through fern forests roared the plesiosaur
> Locked with the giant-bat in ghastly war.
>
> And suddenly, as in a flash of light,
> I saw great Nature working out her plan;
> Through all her shapes from mastodon to mite
> Forever groping, testing, passing on
> To find at last the shape and soul of Man.

He continues through four more stanzas in this manner, and in language pointedly similar to that of such standard expressions of cosmic optimism as Pope's *Essay on Man* and the later sections of Tennyson's *In Memoriam*. Then his grand flight is broken off abruptly by remembrance of the hysterical laughter

with which he had thought the lower animals had mocked
his own appearance as representative of nature's highest achievement:

> Helpless I stood among those awful cages;
> The beasts were walking loose, and I was bagged!
> I, I, last product of the toiling ages,
> Goal of heroic feet that never lagged,—
> A little man in trousers, slightly jagged.

The irony of this observation overlays his subsequent reflections,
again in the formal grand manner, on the omnipresence of
"soul" in all living beings and the mysterious quest that animates those beings, from the lowest on up, toward their ultimate fulfillment in the human soul. Again, both the style and
the sentiment of these reflections are undercut when the speaker
candidly reverts to the actualities of his personal situation:

> Man they desired, but mind you, Perfect Man,
> The radiant and the loving, yet to be!
> I hardly wonder, when they came to scan
> The upshot of their strenuosity,
> They gazed with mixed emotions upon *me*.

This leads him finally to the "moral" of the poem, a few
whimsical words of "advice" to his fellow humans cautioning
them against undue vanity and too close a consideration of the
facts of evolution. By the last stanza, all traces of the "sublime"
have vanished from his language:

> If you're a sweet thing in a flower-bed hat,
> Or her best fellow with your tie tucked in,
> Don't squander love's bright springtime girding at
> An old chimpanzee with an Irish chin:
> *There may be hidden meaning in his grin.*

The "hidden meaning" is, of course, that if evolution is not
simply a failure, it at least has a long way to go. As things
stand right now, the vision of man expressed by Raphael and
Uriel in the *Masque* is, at best, an optimist's dream.

Most critics who have given more than passing attention to
"The Menagerie," including those most delighted by its humor
and critical irony, have objected to what seems a basic inconsistency in the speaker's language and therefore in his characterization. Yet, as is perhaps evident from the summary

given above, his shifts back and forth from "low" to "high" idiom are quite deliberate and very much part of the point of the monologue. For one thing, it must be remembered that the speaker is only "slightly jagged," and the fact that the phrase itself is his own suggests a certain capacity for objective self-analysis even in his present condition. Secondly, for all the slanginess of his phrasing, he is obviously an educated man capable of dropping the vernacular and adopting a more learned and formal stance in the passages where he paraphrases ortho-dox evolutionary doctrines. Indeed, his shifts from "high" to "low" style correspond to shifts in the poem's content, from credulous celebration of the humanist view of man to skeptical questioning of that view from the standpoint of the plain-talking realist whose perspicacity is perhaps sharpened rather than dulled by the alcohol in his blood. In other words, the vernacular passages satirize the non-vernacular ones; and, though it may justly be argued that Moody sometimes gets rather carried away by his own eloquence in describing the evolutionary process, this is chiefly a fault in emphasis, and does not alter the fact that the poem as a whole is aimed at undercutting that very eloquence.

Nor is "The Menagerie," as quite a few readers felt at the time, "hopelessly out of place" among the other poems in the 1901 volume.[17] Though its manner is different from everything in the volume except the briefly colloquial opening of "Song-Flower and Poppy," its matter is very much of a piece with the other poems of 1900. It shows Moody facing up to the same doubts regarding optimistic views of man and the universe as in the poems of political and social protest. That such doubts never quite overcame his own optimism is evident in the more hopeful parts of "The Brute" and in most of his later writings; but, in confronting them as candidly as he had, he was pre-paring the way for a more mature and complex expression of the philosophical position he had enunciated in the *Masque*.

Moreover, in "The Menagerie," as well as in the other poems of 1900, we see Moody asserting his new independence of those literary influences that had made the *Masque* less than a thoroughly personal creation in several places. Where he is imitative now—as in the case of the general rhetorical manner of the "Ode" and its occasional Whitmanesque or Miltonic pas-sages, or in the case of the Popeian and Tennysonian reminis-cences in "The Menagerie"—his imitations are clearly conscious and always aimed at purposeful associations; mere derivativeness is rare. Without the 1900 group of poems, Moody's first volume would have been an interesting and promising young man's book, containing a few poems—"Jetsam," "The Daguerreotype," "Until the Troubling of the Waters"—which sometimes displayed a really individual poetic voice. With that group—of which "The Menagerie" is a prominent member—it was received as confirmation of a significantly new, original talent.

Moody did not remain long in the role of the public poet. The concern manifested in the poems of 1900 with things contemporary and specifically American would persist in some of the later poems and particularly in the prose dramas; but in these, as well as the verse dramas, the author's focus would again be on metaphysical themes and on problems of private belief and morality rather than on public social and political issues. As a man, Moody remained committed to all the causes upheld in his public poems, and his letters continue to show his absorption in those causes. But as a poet, he had had his say; and what he said was starting to make him famous.

CHAPTER 5

From Closet to Stage

I The Fire-Bringer: *Origins, Sources, Genre*

FROM THE AUTUMN of 1900 through the winter of 1901-2, Moody's productive energies were channeled into his labors with Lovett on A *History of English Literature;* those labors, coupled with heavy teaching duties at Chicago during the first half of 1901, made the period virtually a dead loss as far as his creative work was concerned. The early parts of the copious correspondence with Harriet Brainerd which began in May, 1901, contain several lamentations over what Moody considered the sheer hackwork involved in the scholarly enterprise and the frustration and even guilt he felt at being confined to such work at a time when his creative powers seemed on the verge of full fruition.[1] But the months of "drudgery" paid off: despite Moody's deprecatory attitudes, the book turned out to be a first-rate literary history; and its immediate success and promise of continued large sales made it possible for him to quit teaching in 1902 and turn full time to the principal business of his life, the writing of poetry and—more importantly from now on—of drama.[2]

The first thing Moody did after the *History* was completed was to take a trip to Europe which lasted from late April to late November of 1902. For some two months he traveled alone through much of Greece—on foot, by bicycle, and by donkey— and recorded his outward and inward experiences in long, often quite eloquent letters to Harriet. Then he settled for several weeks in Paris, where, together with his Harvard friend, the young poet and classical scholar Trumbull Stickney, he carried through a project initiated during his sojourn in Greece: the reading of the entire body of extant Greek tragedy in the original.

Out of these two intimate confrontations with Hellenic culture grew Moody's first dramatic masterpiece, the brilliant three-act verse play on the Prometheus myth entitled *The Fire-Bringer*. Begun in Greece and continued in Paris and during his subsequent trip to the Austrian and Italian Tyrol, the drama was largely completed by the summer following Moody's return to America and, after the addition of a few final lyric passages the following fall and early winter, was published early in 1904 by Houghton Mifflin.

Among the many observations he made to Harriet about the Greek authors he was reading, one recurrent note is Moody's insistence on the misunderstandings and distortions involved in the standard term "Classical." What seemed increasingly obvious as he read more and more deeply into the original texts was the highly "romantic" nature of their tragic conceptions and the strong Dionysian character of the substance contained within their tight and restrained dramatic forms.[3] This Nietzschean view of Greek drama, and of the Greek sensibility in general, lies behind Moody's adoption of a "Classical" mode in *The Fire-Bringer*.

He was, of course, conditioned in his attitude toward that mode not only by Nietzsche's theories but also by actual uses of the Prometheus myth in imaginative literature subsequent to the rise of Romanticism itself. Shelley's *Prometheus Unbound* was an inevitable influence; so was Bayard Taylor's elaborate four-act "lyrical drama" *Prince Deukalion* (1878), the second member of a trilogy of which the aforementioned *Masque of the Gods* was the first; and, most immediately, there was Stickney's own recently completed *Prometheus Pyrphoros*, a short closet drama which Moody later insisted on acknowledging as a direct source for elements in his own work when he co-edited his friend's posthumous collected poems in 1905.[4] Henry has quite adequately traced the parallels, as well as the more pervasive contrasts, between Moody's handling of his basic mythological materials and those of Shelley and Stickney; and other critics have done the same with regard to Taylor.[5] Despite these intermediary influences, however, Moody's real aim was to go back to the Greeks themselves and to recapture in his own terms some of the original and archetypally Romantic vision he saw animating their dramatic treatment of ancient myths. Aeschylus' *Prometheus Bound*—which, in its deceptively incomplete state as the one surviving member of a trilogy, disappointed Moody by what seemed to him a "dryness" of conception uncharacteristic of Greek tragedy[6]—provided

a source chiefly for general plot elements. In other of Aeschylus'
plays—like the *Agamemnon*—and also in such works as Sophocles'
Oedipus at Colonus and again Euripides' *The Bacchae*, Moody
found the kind of essential spirit he most wanted to emulate.[7]

Moreover, the Greek dramatists supplied Moody with something that Shelley, Taylor, and Stickney could not: real models
of theatrical structure and technique. Between the time he first
conceived and began writing *The Masque of Judgment* and the
time he conceived and began writing *The Fire-Bringer*, Moody
had developed a mounting interest in the theater and an increasing desire to write plays suited to stage production. As
early as April, 1898, during his first extended sojourn in New
York, he had met a number of practicing playwrights who,
though "not very big ones I suspect," had instilled in him
some of their "enthusiasm" and sense of "practical expedient."
"The great thing about them," he remarked, "is that they get
their things played, and that sort of thing, begad, begins to appeal
to me."[8] The following year he had—perhaps partly under their influence—abandoned his initial plan for writing *The Faith Healer*
in blank verse, and had begun a prose version designed for
stage performance. At the same time, however, his acquaintance
with the successfully produced verse dramas of the English
author Stephen Phillips and with the early plays of Yeats, which
were being staged in America as well as Ireland,[9] continued to
encourage Moody's interest in the notion of a new poetic idiom
for the American theater; and this interest—shared by friends
like Robinson and Josephine Preston Peabody—began to reassert itself soon after he had completed the prose version of
The Faith Healer in 1900. When Moody read Miss Peabody's
verse play *Marlowe* early in 1902, he wrote her excitedly, "By
all the Muses, we shall have an American drama yet"; and the
implication was clearly that he meant a producible American
verse drama.[10] Later in the same year, then, when he set about recasting the mythological materials already treated by Shelley,
Taylor, and Stickney, Moody also set about the task of bringing
those materials out of the "closet," to which his predecessors had
consigned them, and back into the theater, where they had originally found their natural home in the great age of Greek drama.

The theatrical appeal of *The Fire-Bringer* is, to be sure, directed chiefly at the kind of "élite" audience that Yeats sought
rather than at any sort of broad, popular one. For one thing, an
understanding of the play's action requires at least a generalized

knowledge of the myth on which it is based—a knowledge which the expository passages often refresh and clarify but do not supply from the ground up. Then too, many elements in the play share with *The Masque of Judgment* and with the nineteenth-century closet drama a recourse to frankly artificial literary techniques: its action and characterization are stylized and symbolic; its language is derived not from actual speech idioms but from traditional norms of elevated poetic diction; and at times the blank-verse dialogue, and especially the many rhymed lyrics interspersed with that dialogue, exhibit considerable compression of imagery and rhetoric.

Nevertheless, nothing in the play is unsuitable to representation on a normal stage, provided that stage is roomy enough to accommodate a rather large supporting cast and possesses the equipment needed for some of the special lighting and sound effects called for from time to time. Unlike the *Masque, The Fire-Bringer* includes no mere personified abstractions or disembodied allegorical voices in its cast; nor is anyone called upon to fly or to traverse vast tracts of space in a short time, as in the earlier work. With the exception of Prometheus and Pandora, all the *dramatis personae* are human beings, and even these two supernatural characters are almost wholly humanized. Long monologues, such as took up much of the *Masque,* occur less often; and, when they do, they are frequently kept from becoming static by palpable dramatic devices within the speeches themselves.

Above all, *The Fire-Bringer* has a real onstage plot with genuine suspense, a series of progressive climaxes, and the kind of graphic reversals and recognitions that Aristotle saw as essential elements in the best stage drama; and not only the blank-verse dialogue but also the lyrics themselves, both individual and choral, have important functions in forwarding the movement of the plot. In short, given an audience capable of comprehending verse whose concentration is surely no more demanding than Shakespeare's, and one possessing some minimal prior acquaintance with Greek myth, Moody's play can make for a very powerful theatrical experience. *The Fire-Bringer* was, in fact, scheduled for production in the winter of 1906-7 by the New Theater in Chicago;[11] and though that production never materialized, nor is there any record of later attempts to put the play on the stage, the New Theater's abortive project might still be successfully undertaken today.

II *The Play*

The general mythological context within which Moody locates the plot of *The Fire-Bringer* is summarized in a passage from Apollodorus that is quoted as an epigraph to the printed text. After the original Golden Age of the human race had declined through the Silver and into the Bronze Age, and after men had turned from their original virtue to an increasing pride and sinfulness, Zeus decided—much like the God of Moody's *Masque* —to abolish his own wayward creation in an enormous flood. But the Titan Prometheus had warned a few people of Zeus's intent; and, led by the shepherd-king Deukalion and his daughter-wife Pyrrha, they survived the flood by building a boat which carried them over the rising waters to the heights of Mount Parnassus:

> . . . *and there, when the rains had abated, he [Deukalion] landed and made sacrifice, praying for men to repeople the earth. Then Deukalion and Pyrrha took stones, and threw them over their heads; those which Deukalion threw became men, and those which Pyrrha threw became women. . . . Also Prometheus gave to them fire, bringing it secretly in a fennel stalk. When Zeus learned of this, he commanded Hephaestos to bind the body of Prometheus upon Mount Caucasus; and for the theft of fire Prometheus suffered this punishment.*

Both Aeschylus and Shelley had begun their dramas after the last event in this narration, focusing upon the subsequent moral struggle between an unrelenting Zeus and an unrepentant Prometheus. But Moody, following the lead of Taylor and Stickney, moved his focus up to events just after the flood. The central event is Prometheus' restoration of fire to a mankind rendered physically and spiritually impotent by its loss;[12] and the play ends at the point where the Titan begins to undergo his punishment for this second defiance of the Olympian gods. Like Taylor and Stickney, Moody makes Deukalion and Pyrrha the central representatives of the human race, but he surrounds them with a supporting cast of his own conceiving, comprised of their fellow survivors and the newly created "Stone Men and Earth Women." Prometheus becomes, of course, the full-fledged Romantic hero he had been for Shelley, as well as for Taylor and Stickney; and he is a dynamic counterpart to the largely passive Raphael of the *Masque*. But the humanitarian ideal symbolized in his actions and his final sufferings achieve still fuller expression in the character of Pandora—the original *femme fatale* of Greek myth, bringer of every affliction to mankind though also retainer of the delusive gift of hope—whom first Taylor and then Stickney had converted into a positive figure embodying the activating power of hope in her role as the lover and inspirer of Prometheus.[13]

In the case of each of these debts to his immediate predecessors, however, Moody expands considerably on rather simplified and sketchy materials. Prometheus, Deukalion, and Pyrrha grow from one-dimensional allegorical beings into rounded characters who invite real audience-identification; and Pandora's function develops from that of a minor and vaguely defined background voice to that of a major protagonist who participates fully in the onstage plot and whose personality—as expressed both in the dialogue and in her several fine lyrics—controls and directs most of the chief actions in the drama. Moreover, all the external materials borrowed from Taylor and Stickney, as well as Aeschylus and Shelley, are clearly re-adapted to Moody's own special philosophical purpose—a purpose integral to his most fundamental ideas and attitudes and, for all the apparent remoteness of his mythological sources, fully pertinent to his time and to our own.

III *Act One*

Act One opens on a situation that bears noteworthy resemblances to famous later expressions of twentieth-century despondency like Yeats's *The Second Coming* or Eliot's *The Waste Land* and *The Hollow Men*. The setting is a cliff on the slopes of Parnassus some time after the flood has abated. But, though Moody's Parnassus is equivalent to the Mount of Ararat where Noah, the Hebrew Deukalion, survived another flood to begin a new human race, it is an Ararat lacking a Covenant between God and man—a place of mere survival from which the fire of will and spiritual vitality is gone, and over which hangs the constant threat of final annihilation. Deukalion and Pyrrha, the latter having just awakened from sleep, sit before the unlighted wall of their cave, while their young son Aeolus—representing a human future deprived of the means of fruition—continues to sleep at their feet. Dimly seen in the dark background are the motionless crouching figures of the new Stone

Men and Earth Women, still retaining much of their original form as they await the inward power to come fully alive. The opening dialogue establishes economically and graphically the sense of man's present spiritual condition:

DEUKALION.

Thou hast slept long.

PYRRHA.

       I saw a burning lamp
That passed between the levret and the dove
On Zeus's altar, and a smoke went up.

DEUKALION.

Dreams: we are old. The green heart and the sear
He feeds with dreams; having some purpose in it,
Or else His idleness.

PYRRHA.

       No lamp was here?
No fire, no light?

DEUKALION.

       Some fire-sparks in the eyes
Of dull bewildered beasts that came to gaze,
And dully moved again into the mist.
They have forgot their natures, even as we,
And those who tremble yonder on the heights
For fear the ebbing deep should mount again,
Breathing this darkness have forgot ourselves,
Our natures, and the motions of our souls.

One need only compare this opening with the long and static soliloquy of Raphael at the start of the *Masque* to see how far Moody's dramatic powers have advanced. For all the stylized formality of the diction, this is real dialogue. Pyrrha's pathetic wish-fulfillment dream of the return of fire to earth, set against Deukalion's weary reflections on its futility, provides both exposition of the general situation and quick initial insights into their respective characters. Throughout the first part of the scene, even the internal rhythms of their lines, though contained within a uniform iambic pentameter metric, suggest differences in those characters. Pyrrha's attitude, influenced by her remembrance of Prometheus' past intervention on their behalf and by the lingering presence of Pandora, is hesitantly hopeful; and the cadences of her speeches have a certain animation and ex-

pansiveness when compared to Deukalion's stiffly laconic replies which convey his greater despair and fuller submission
to the waste-land situation. When she remarks with some excitement that she had sensed the presence of Prometheus during
her sleep, he cuts her off with the dry statement: "He came, in
darkness." When she eagerly asks "what word" the Titan had
brought, he responds in flat monosyllables: "I feigned to sleep.
I had no heart for speech." And when she wants to know how
Prometheus had behaved, he tells her in clipped, emotionally
neutral phrases that convey his apathy toward the possible
hope suggested in the Titan's visit and the singing of Pandora
which accompanied it:

> Stood awhile
> Watching thy slumber; touched the sleeping head
> Of Aeolus; gazed upward to the heights;
> Then vanished down the slope; and far below
> Pandora sang.

Though the style of both speakers becomes more animated in
the ensuing dialogue, the essential contrast between their states
of mind is sustained. The question-and-answer pattern of the
first few speeches continues; and Moody makes skillful use of
that pattern to weave necessary expository information into the
dialogue, as he has Pyrrha seek an explanation of her husband's vigorously positive past actions in the light of his present
despair and has him review those actions in order to expose the
delusions on which he now believes they were founded.[14]
We learn that, when Prometheus had warned him of the
coming flood, he had acted with prompt and firm authority in
leading himself and others to safety, and he had been motivated
less by concern for his own survival than by hopes for the
future development of the human race as embodied in his love
for his son Aeolus. These hopes had continued to impel him
later when he and Pyrrha, with the aid of Prometheus, had
created the new race of men and women out of stone. But in
the midst of that work the Titan had suddenly been forced to
flee, leaving the creation half-finished; time itself then seemed
to be suspended, perhaps "Caught in the rings of Python," the
dreaded monster who, like the "Worm that Dieth Not" in the
Masque, symbolizes absolute negation. Now the Stone Men and
Earth Women "appal" Deukalion with their helpless supplica-
tions for energy to become truly human, while the older sur-

vivors have become spiritually paralyzed by the absence of fire
and by the dread of greater punishments to come. Deukalion
himself, sharing that dread and drained of all capacity for
further striving, would now seek not to better their condition
but simply to maintain the *status quo* through total submission
to the gods "In fear and worship." Convinced that it was human
pride and willfulness which brought on both the flood and the
subsequent withdrawal of fire, he denounces the inspirers of
that pride and willfulness, Prometheus and Pandora, as deluders
whose continued attempts to benefit mankind can at best bring
on greater human suffering if not annihilation.

But his denunciation is suddenly interrupted by the distant
voice of Pandora, now heard for the first time in the play
singing an enigmatic but—at least to Pyrrha—inspiriting song
of hope which begins:

> *Along the earth and up the sky*
> *The Fowler spreads his net:*
> *O soul, what pinions wild and shy*
> *Are on thy shoulders set?*
> *What wings of longing undeterred*
> *Are native to thee, spirit bird?*

The Fowler is despair; the wings, hope. And on this note Prometheus makes his first entrance. For a moment it looks as
though he has come as the embodiment of Pandora's lyric intimations and as the fulfillment of Pyrrha's dream. The apparent
dramatic reversal turns back on itself, however, when we learn
that the Titan has just returned wounded and repulsed from his
first attempt to steal fire from Heaven in order to bestow it on
mankind. His anguished narration of the attempt and its failure
is one of the longest speeches in the play, and yet it sustains
dramatic interest through an imagery that grows increasingly
dynamic and a narrative pace that grows increasingly rapid,
as well as through the interjection of spontaneous outcries expressing the speaker's present emotional state. His plan had
been to surprise the gods during a period of suspended activity
which occurs by necessity at the close of "each great cycle of
Olympian years," when they all must withdraw to the "sacred
old Uranian field" and contemplate their limited existences
under the aspect of eternity. After describing that plan in fairly
slow-moving detail for twenty-six lines, he begins his acceler-
ating crescendo:

> Soft as light I passed
> The perilous gates that are acquainted forth,
> The walls of starry safety and alarm,
> The pillars and the awful roofs of song,
> The stairs and colonnades whose marble work
> Is spirit, and the joinings spirit also,—
> And from the well-brink of his central court
> Dipped vital fire of fire, flooding my vase,
> Glutting it arm-deep in the keen element.
> Then backward swifter than the osprey dips
> Down the green slide of the sea, till—Fool, O fool!
> 'T was in my hands! 'T was next my bosom! Fierce
> Sang the bright essence past my scorching cheek,
> Blown up and backward as I dropped and skimmed
> The glacier-drifts, cataracts, wild moraines,
> And walls of frightful plunge. Upon the shore
> Of this our night-bound wretched earth I paused,
> Lifted on high the triumph of my hands,
> And flung back words and laughter. As I dropped,
> The dogs of thunder chased me at the heels,
> A white tongue shook against me in the dark,
> And lo, my vase was rended in my hands,
> And all the precious substance that it held
> Spread, faded, and was gone,—was quenched, was gone![15]

Rashness has been his undoing, and Deukalion loses no time in telling him so. There follows a dialogue in which the now submissive king pleads with Prometheus—much as Oceanus had done in Aeschylus' play—to learn humility, repentance, and subjection of his will to Zeus's in order that both he and the humanity he loves may be spared the god's further vengeance. Prometheus' answers are outwardly defiant, but inwardly his failure has caused a total loss of self-confidence and hope; and later, after Aeolus has awakened and Deukalion and Pyrrha have gone off to seek roots and water for his meal, the Titan gives voice to a despair more complete than even Deukalion's as he yearns for his own annihilation:

> One deep, deep hour!
> To drop ten thousand fathoms softly down
> Below the lowest heaving of life's sea,
> Till memory, sentience, will, are all annulled. . . .

At this point the real reversal scene of Act One occurs. It is signaled not by anything in the action or dialogue, but by one

of Pandora's simplest and most memorable lyrics—sung as she
makes her first appearance onstage, amid the group of Stone
Men and Earth Women who have been crouching silently at
the rear:

> *Of wounds and sore defeat*
> *I made my battle stay;*
> *Wingèd sandals for my feet*
> *I wove of my delay;*
> *Of weariness and fear,*
> *I made my shouting spear;*
> *Of loss, and doubt, and dread,*
> *And swift oncoming doom*
> *I made a helmet for my head*
> *And a floating plume.*
> *From the shutting mist of death,*
> *From the failure of the breath,*
> *I made a battle-horn to blow*
> *Across the vales of overthrow.*
> *O hearken, love, the battle-horn!*
> *The triumph clear, the silver scorn!*
> *O hearken where the echoes bring,*
> *Down the grey disastrous morn,*
> *Laughter and rallying!*

What Pandora is singing about is, of course, that higher
courage and aspiration which lie on the far side of despair; and
toward these she would now direct Prometheus. On emerging
from among the crouched figures, she pretends—in another
effective dramatic touch—not to recognize her beloved in his
present defeated state. Yet she does proffer him a hollow fennel
stalk which can serve as a better carrier of fire than the fragile
vase he had used on his first attempt; and he, aroused by her
song and by the nostalgically erotic associations of the fennel
stalk, accepts it under the pretense of conveying it to the real
Prometheus. While Pandora continues to goad him out of his
hesitation, the Stone Men and Earth Women break out into
a short chorus praying for deliverance into full life by him who
helped give them birth. Then they disappear down the slope as
Pandora pointedly declares to the Titan, "They go to find Prometheus." With this the hero's hesitation ends: he follows them
down the slope on his way to a fresh attempt at stealing fire
from Heaven; and his final words contain significant echoes of
Pandora's own song:

Yea, I come,
I come; to find somewhere through the piled gloom
A mountain path to unimagined day,
Build all this anger into walls of war
Not dreamed of, dung and fatten with this death
New fields of pleasant life, and make them teem
Strange corn, miraculous wine!

Only now does Pandora acknowledge her recognition of her lover. Her curtain line, "Prometheus, lord!", is spoken as he vanishes on the quest for a rebirth of his own identity along with that of mankind.

IV Act Two

At the start of Act Two the action reverts again to a negative mood. Prometheus has been absent for a long time, and a group of the original survivors of the flood, having lost hope in his quest, gathers to offer an ultimate sacrifice aimed at forestalling a threatened return of the flood. For their principal victim they have chosen Aeolus himself; he, being "our best" and the one most likely to "fill the future," is the one whose death would most satisfy the gods. At this, Deukalion, provoked into a passionate entreaty on behalf of his son and the future he embodies, offers himself as a suitably noble substitute in the sacrificial rite. But they refuse him; and when, after his friend Lykophon has willingly placed his own daughter Alcyone on the altar, a terrible rush of thunder and lightning sweeps across the stage, Deukalion relents. He places Aeolus beside Alcyone with the words "The gods' dark will be done! I am content," and falls in a dead faint. Lykophon himself now assumes command in the king's place. Despite Pyrrha's desperate attempt to intercede and have the sacrifice delayed "till Prometheus comes or makes a sign," the new leader and his flock persist in carrying out the act which symbolizes their betrayal of man's future for the sake of present survival.

Once again, however, the distant sound of Pandora's singing voice signals a reversal just at the point where the mounting suspense is about to culminate in the sacrifice of the two children. A woman suddenly cries out:

Hush, hark, the pouring music! Never yet
The pools below the waterfalls, thy pools,
Thy dark pools, O my heart—!

Her disjointedly ecstatic outcry—another instance of Moody's inspired use of Symbolist technique—is followed by others of a similar nature, as Pandora's still wordless singing begins to awaken a mysterious sense of hope and a spiritual as well as erotic yearning in all of the crowd.[16] Deukalion himself is roused from his faint, though half-blinded now; and, while Pyrrha describes to him Pandora's approach at the head of the Stone Men and Earth Women, the two intended victims, Aeolus and Alcyone, rise dramatically from the sacrificial altar and point in rapt silence toward the sky on which the long-absent stars have suddenly reappeared. Gradually the stage, which has been covered with darkness since the start of the play, begins to light up. As it does, the words of Pandora's song suddenly become articulate—a stirring celebration of the revival of human desire and vital energy made possible by Prometheus' triumph over his own despair:

> *Because one creature of his breath*
> *Sang loud into the face of death,*
> *Because one child of his despair*
> *Could strangely hope and wildly dare,*
> *The Spirit comes to the Bride again,*
> *And breathes at her door the name of the child;*
> *"This is the son that ye bore me! When*
> *Shall we kiss, and be reconciled?"*
> *Furtive, dumb, in the tardy stone,*
> *With gropings sweet in the patient sod,*
> *In the roots of the pine, in the crumbled cone,*
> *With cries of haste in the willow-rod,—*
> *By pools where the hyla swells his throat*
> *And the partridge drums to his crouching mate,*
> *Where the moorland stag and the mountain goat*
> *Strictly seek to the ones that wait,—*
> *In seas aswing on the coral bar,*
> *In feasting depths of the evening star,*
> *In the dust where the mourner bows his head,*
> *In the blood of the living, the bones of the dead,—*
> *Wounded with love in breast and side,*
> *The Spirit goes in to the Bride!*

The scene is marvelously theatrical—so much so that it is able to sustain a heavy weight of lyrical utterance by which Moody suggests the sudden transformation of the earth and its inhabitants from their death-in-life state to one of fertility and joy. This utterance reaches its culmination in Pyrrha's vivid description—for which Moody provides dramatic credibility by having her present it for the benefit of the now blinded Deukalion—of nature's reawakening under the influence of the new light and its life-giving powers. At the very end of her speech, however, the rapturous mood abruptly turns into one of terror as the lesser light of the stars gives way to an unbearably bright sunlight. She cries, "O shelter me!/Bow down! Cover your eyes!"; and a group of "Confused Voices" is heard recoiling from "Terrible wings!—Light awfuller than darkness or the sea!" Now everyone except Deukalion is forced to shield his eyes from the searing brightness; then he, his vision suddenly restored but not to the extent of admitting the full blaze of the sun, takes over the role of describer and narrator. The whole stage becomes enveloped in a blinding haze of light symbolic of a spiritual illumination too intense for the recently benighted human race to sustain; and a "Man's Voice" is heard uttering sentiments similar to those of the chorus in Eliot's *Murder in the Cathedral* or to Eliot's own assertion in *Burnt Norton*, "Humankind/Cannot bear very much reality":

> My soul is among lions. God, my God,
> Thou see'st my quivering spirit what it is!
> O lay not life upon it! We not knew
> The thing we asked for. We had all forgot
> How cruel was thy splendor in the house
> Of sense, how awful in the house of thought,
> How far unbearable in the wild house
> That thou hast cast and builded for the heart!

Then, almost by way of dramatic confirmation of these sentiments, Deukalion himself, after recognizing Prometheus' own approach amid the blaze and at last acknowledging the Titan as his savior, dies under the strain of his new vision. The others, still unable to turn their eyes directly toward the sun, hear Pandora enter with the Stone Men and Earth Women to sing, *"invisible in the light,"* a short cryptic invocation to the new trinity of Dionysus, Eros, and Apollo which remains only cryptic until taken up again and elucidated in the final choral lyric of Act Three.

With the entrance of Prometheus himself, the dramatic tensions of Act Two reach a resolution; and the symbolism implicit in the prior action is crystallized. His first speech is a simple one-line statement to Pandora: "Thou gavest me the vessel; it is filled." She replies: "I am the vessel, and with thee 't is filled." Into this quite remarkable little interchange Moody manages to compress a summation, on three symbolic levels, of all that has gone before. The vessel is, literally, the fennel stalk, now filled with fire; it is also Pandora herself, as the vessel of hope now filled with realization; and finally, it is Pandora as the basic female principle, now mated with the fully manifest male principle in a fruitful union symbolic of the sexual vitality and fertility that have returned to man and nature with Prometheus' successful venture. This last meaning is emphasized when the Titan summons Aeolus and Alcyone to the altar on which they had almost been sacrificed and ceremoniously bestows on them, as future progenitors of the human race, the lighted fennel stalk:

> Unto this twain, man-child and woman-child,
> I give the passion of this element;
> This seed of longing, substance of this love;
> This power, this purity, this annihilation.
> Let their hands light the altar of the world.
> 'T is yours forever. I have brought it home!

Thereupon Prometheus exits; and, as he does, the blinding haze fades into the normal light of day at which humanity can again look directly.

The very last thing in the act, however, is a long lyric of Pandora's—probably the most diffuse and poetically uninspired of all her lyrics—which provides a bridge to Act Three by reminding us that all is not finished. Though vital energy and the capacity for growth have been restored, mankind is still a long way from final fulfillment and peace. After their own brief reunion, Pandora herself is again estranged from Prometheus; and her song is one of loneliness and longing for that distant time when all such estrangements will end in an ultimate consummation. Besides its general prophetic implications, the song also specifically foreshadows Prometheus' solitary suffering at the hands of the powers he has defied for the sake of humanity.

V *Act Three*

The action of Act Three centers on Deukalion's funeral—itself a symbolic event in that it introduces a motif of loss and mourning into the atmosphere of joy that had prevailed among the human characters at the end of Act Two. In rekindling the fire of life, Prometheus also necessarily reintroduced positive pain and sorrow as well as joy into human experience; and the principal theme throughout Act Three is the inseparability of these emotions in the universal human condition. Hence the opening chorus of Old Men, Girls, Young Women, and Young Men moves affectingly back and forth between lamentation over the old king's death, and praise of the pleasure-giving and life-giving powers of Eros and Dionysus. Later, while Pyrrha and Aeolus, accompanied by their handmaid Rhodope, are keeping watch over the tomb, an ominous cloud passes overhead; and Pyrrha says:

'T will rain; he brought us back the blessèd rain,
And storm, and natural darkness with the light. . . .
As also to our hearts the shutting-in
Of rain and natural darkness.

Even Pandora's voice, heard in the distance, is "sharp and agonized." When she enters, followed shortly by Prometheus, the rapture of their last encounter at the end of Act Two is replaced by a mood of sadness and foreboding which makes them seem even more like human beings than they do elsewhere in the play. Over the entire act hangs the threatening shadow of Zeus's mighty "bird of wrath," to which, in the end, Prometheus himself will succumb after a last desperate off-stage struggle witnessed by the human characters.

Before that, however, he delivers his parting message to those whom he has saved, combining assurances that the gift of fire is theirs to keep with admonitions to follow his own example in contending relentlessly against the "jealous gods" "With anger, and with laughter, and with love" which will assert their right to fuller and deeper realization of their human nature. For all the mournfulness of the scene and the sense of impending disaster to the Titan himself, his words are full of the kind of ultimate optimism that Moody had attempted to inspire in "The Brute" and in Raphael's speeches in the *Masque*. He even concludes by envisioning—in the one passage which exploits the idea of Prometheus' foreknowledge, integral to the original myth—a kind of final *Götterdammerung* like that depicted in the *Masque*:

> ... in the dim end of things,
> When the sun sickens, and the heaven of heavens
> Flames as a frosty leaf unto the fall,
> In swoon and anguish shall his [Zeus's] stormèd heart
> Cry unto us; his cry is ringing there
> In the sun's core! I heard it when I stood
> Where all things past and present and to come
> Ray out in fiery patterns, fading, changing,
> Forevermore unfaded and unchanged.

But once again it is to Pandora that Moody consigns his most eloquent expression of the optimistic spirit which underlies the action of *The Fire-Bringer*. After Prometheus has gone to endure his punishment and night has fallen on the last hopeful chorus of the now animated Stone Men and Earth Women, she sings her mystical vision of an ultimate reconciliation between man and the true God in a delicately wrought parable which conveys simple longing but also a kind of veiled prophecy:

> *I stood within the heart of God:*
> *It seemed a place that I had known:*
> *(I was blood-sister to the clod,*
> *Blood-brother to the stone.)*
>
> *I found my love and labor there,*
> *My house, my raiment, meat and wine,*
> *My ancient rage, my old despair,—*
> *Yea, all things that were mine.*
>
> . . . .
>
> *I saw the spring and summer pass,*
> *The trees grow bare, and winter come;*
> *All was the same as once it was*
> *Upon my hills at home.*
>
> *Then suddenly in my own heart*
> *I felt God walk and gaze about;*
> *He spoke; his words seemed held apart*
> *With gladness and with doubt.*
>
> *"Here is my meat and wine," He said,*
> *"My love, my toil, my ancient care;*
> *Here is my cloak, my book, my bed,*
> *And here my old despair.*
>
> *"Here are my seasons: winter, spring,*
> *Summer the same, and autumn spills*
> *The fruits I look for; everything*
> *As on my heavenly hills.["]*

The play ends with dawn rising over Deukalion's tomb, before which Pyrrha is silently kneeling, while a chorus of Young Men translates Pandora's vision into terms of its own awakened apprehension of infinite human possibility. Why some critics have found this last lyric "insolent," or felt that it seems purposefully to "drown" Pandora's voice, is hard to explain.[17] In actuality, the song elaborates and explicates Pandora's own invocation to the trinity of Dionysus, Eros, and Apollo in Act Two. It establishes this trinity—a synthesis of sensual and spiritual ideals— as the new humanistic vision which must supersede the fearful worship of Zeus. But the synthesis, though anti-dualistic, is still hierarchical; for, while celebrating the first two gods as bringers of sensual joy, the chorus names Apollo over and over as the supreme member of the trinity and supreme object of the new worship. Hence, far from "drowning" the sentiments of Pandora's last lyric, the young men are reiterating those sentiments as they express their own aspirations for union with a transcendent God of love:

> Eros, how sweet
> Is the cup of thy drunkenness!
> Dionysus, how our feet
> Hasten to the burning cup
> Thou liftest up!
> But O how sweetest and how most burning it is
> To drink of the wine of thy lightsome chalices,
> Apollo! Apollo! To-day
> We say we will follow thee and put all others away.
> For thou alone, O thou alone art he
> Who settest the prisoned spirit free,
> And sometimes leadest the rapt soul on
> Where never mortal thought has gone;
> Till by the ultimate stream
> Of vision and of dream
> She stands
> With startled eyes and outstretched hands,
> Looking where other suns rise over other lands,
> And rends the lonely skies with her prophetic scream.[18]

VI *Summation*

Nevertheless, these remain only aspirations; for Prometheus' gift has symbolized not their fulfillment but simply the conditions necessary for such fulfillment to be possible. By the end of the play nothing is finally resolved. Man is still alienated from the vengeful gods, commanded by Zeus, who presently reign on Olympus; and, as the Titan's own last admonition makes clear, these gods will fall and be replaced by greater ones only after man has waged a long and difficult rebellion against those elements in himself which create and foster them. This is probably the real meaning of that enigmatic line in Prometheus' speech in Act Three where he refers to man as "Himself the heavens, himself the scornful gods." There is, to be sure, some possibility that in this line and in the exhortation to perpetual rebellion which surrounds it, Moody may have been suggesting that the Titan has overreached himself by denying the existence of any supernatural powers outside of man's own personality, and he is therefore inviting retribution—in which case the passage would link up directly to the Bacchantes scene in the Prelude of the *Masque*. But it is more likely that the gist of the whole long speech is the by now familiar Moody idea that, as man struggles toward higher self-realization, his conceptions of godhead must undergo a corresponding evolution, and that both the human and cosmic orders require constant strife as a spur to such evolution.

The waste-land situation in the first half of the play is a projection of that inner waste-land in which such theological views as could identify the vengeful Zeus with the supreme deity have their origins. Man himself is the creator of that waste-land, and only by rising above his fear and moral torpor can he have insights into the true nature of the cosmos and can he convert his world into an image of that cosmos' own struggle toward perfection. Without denying the idea of a transcendent divinity, then, Moody is still laying his emphasis on the purely subjective problem of man's failure to nourish the divine fire within his own soul—a failure which was for him the supreme sin.

Perhaps the best key to this intention is found in Moody's comment on Shelley's *Prometheus Unbound* in A *History of the English Literature*. Though he considered the work Shelley's "highest achievement, . . . a fixed star in the firmament of poetry," Moody also felt that its philosophy was "immature" in intimating that "it is only some external tyranny—the might of priests and kings, the weight of 'custom,' the dark dreams of superstition—which keeps mankind from rising to his ideal stature."[19] For Moody—despite his poems of political and social protest—neither priests, kings, nor imperialist-minded presidents and senators could be blamed for man's alienation from the ideal. The true issues were neither social, political, nor even—in the objective sense—theological; but psychological and moral.

They were, moreover, psychological and moral in a very personal way. Passages like the following, in his July 13 and July 16, 1902, letters to Harriet, show how much the sense of profound estrangement and hopelessness depicted dramatically in Act One grew out of Moody's own struggles with his private demon of despair: "When I left Greece, ... I went down at once into such a valley and shadow of despair as I have never, I think, had to pass through before. Feeling round through my darkened kingdoms I could find no hopeful thing, no joy, no sovereignty. ... I felt spiritually deserted, God-forgotten, without power or hope or purpose." And: "... the trouble with me always has been that I was one of little faith. All along my life I see how a too quick despair has hurled me out of the path to which I had to struggle back with punishment and loss."[20]

In *The Fire-Bringer* as elsewhere, Moody's final optimism seems almost a desperate bulwark against a temperamental pessimism which often threatened to overwhelm his intellectual convictions, rather than the expression of a facile cheerfulness such as his harsher critics have charged against him.[21] Indeed, a major source of the power in all his best writings—and perhaps most especially in *The Fire-Bringer*—is the tension between his own natural propensity for despondency and negation, and his will toward joy and affirmation.

Though ideologically *The Fire-Bringer* is very much of a piece with *The Masque of Judgment,* Moody's dramatic and poetic means of restating the themes of the earlier work exhibit far more uniform maturity and skill. There are, to be sure, a few scenes—including ones from which excerpts have been quoted above—which still suffer from a certain diffuseness and a tendency toward bombast, and some judicious pruning of these scenes would certainly enhance a stage production of the play. Nor is the verse entirely free of literary influences: one is aware of a generally Keatsian or Shelleyan quality in several of the blank-verse speeches; Milton continues, understandably, to affect the tone and style of occasional narrative passages, chiefly in Prometheus' monologues, which deal with journeys and battles of the gods; and the conscious influence of Blake is often evident in Pandora's lyrics. Here and there, too, a line appears that is rather pointlessly Shakespearian—for example, Pyrrha's description of Deukalion at the time of the flood, "Why did'st thou bare thy white head to the storm . . .?", which comes right out of *King Lear*. And a particularly inappropriate Homeric echo occurs in the Chorus of Women in Act Two, where they express their fear that the long-absent Prometheus may have been defeated again by Zeus's agents: "Now thrice three times about the shining town/The thunder-wingèd chariot drags his corse."

All such instances of poor taste in drawing upon the work of predecessors add up, however, to relatively little in terms of the whole play; and compared with the *Masque*, the instances of diffuseness or bombast are few and far between. As far as Pandora's lyrics are concerned, those quoted above in their entirety show how well-assimilated and appropriate are Moody's indirect allusions to the Blakean lyric manner. Indeed, these lyrics, apart from their indispensable function in the dramatic design, emerge as some of the most successful poems *qua* poem that Moody ever wrote; they display a formal tightness and verbal restraint finer than anything in even the best blank-verse speeches, and a quality of ineffable suggestion that again aligns Moody with the authentic Symbolist tradition. Perhaps one of his early critics became a bit carried away when he re-remarked of them, "Lyric utterance in English has never achieved higher and purer strains than these," but it is possible to see some truth in his next remark: "We may say of them, as Symonds says of the lyrics in 'Prometheus Unbound,' that they 'may be reckoned the touch-stone of a man's capacity for understanding lyric poetry.'"[22] Even if one is not willing to go quite so far, one may still recognize in Pandora's songs, and in several of the vividly evocative images from the other passages quoted above, an uncommonly rich and, in the deeper sense, original lyric voice.

While he was writing *The Fire-Bringer*, Moody conceived the idea of making the play part of a trilogy on the "Promethean theme" he recognized as already present in the Hebraic-Christian materials of the *Masque*. He toyed for a while with the thought of adding a scene to the earlier work, "which will at once complete its own inherent idea and serve as a sufficient link of suggestion between the two."[23] But this plan was never realized, and, in the end, Moody simply allowed the connection between the first and second member to be, as he put it in an introductory note to *The Fire-Bringer*, "informal." Actually, the Bacchantes scene in the Prelude to the *Masque*, with its Greek setting and *personae* and Dionysian subject-matter, already provided something of a link; and inasmuch as the action of the *Masque* follows that of *The Fire-Bringer* in the trilogy, we may take that scene as symbolizing Dionysus' triumph over the Apollo whom the last chorus of the previous play had declared the supreme god, and hence a growing religious decadence which again threatens the human race with spiritual retrogression and eventually with annihilation.

Be that as it may, both plays are fundamentally about what Manly termed "the inseparableness, and, in a certain sense, the unity of God and man."[24] *The Fire-Bringer* shows man rebelling against the authority of the reigning deity Zeus, and the *Masque* shows the reigning deity of orthodox Hebraic-Christian theodicies rejecting man; but against these themes of separation Moody sets his belief in the ultimate oneness of the true Creator and His creation. He also sets forth in both plays his basic moral doctrine concerning the inseparableness of good and evil in the evolutionary process: *The Fire-Bringer* shows the birth of both qualities together in the restoration to man of will and passion; and the *Masque* shows how, by trying to separate them and retain the good while destroying the evil, the God of the Last Judgment would inevitably destroy them both together.

It now remained for Moody to depict a final reconciliation between the human creation and its Creator, such as Raphael and Pandora envisioned but neither of the first two members actually dramatized. In this reconciliation both man and God would be shown expressing the limits of their true natures, while the evil in life, rather than being destroyed, would be transfigured in the process of that reconciliation. This Moody would attempt later in *The Death of Eve*. Before he could apply himself to the completion of the trilogy, however, he became involved in another major dramatic effort. The theater continued to fascinate him and to attract his maturing talents; and, having written one mythological verse play aimed at a limitedly literary audience, he wrote another play, in a realistic medium and prose idiom, aimed at that larger public he had addressed in his social and political poems and would now address again from the commercial stage.

CHAPTER *6*

The Public Dramatist

I *The Origins of* The Great Divide

WITHIN A FEW WEEKS after he had written the last lyric of *The Fire-Bringer* and sent the completed manuscript to the printer, Moody was telling Harriet of a new play he had begun, this time on a subject drawn from contemporary life. It, too, was to be in verse, but a verse quite different from that used in *The Fire-Bringer*. His description of his intentions—which in many ways anticipates the theory of modern verse drama enunciated four-and-a-half decades later by T. S. Eliot and practiced in Eliot's own plays from *The Cocktail Party* on[1]—contains noteworthy indications of the direction Moody's dramatic thinking was beginning to take at the time:

> ...I have jumped into a big piece of work which makes my waking hours one debauch of stolid and silent excitement. Perhaps there is nothing in it, but I seem to myself to be on the point of solving the great problem of the application of blank verse to the realistic treatment of a modern theme in drama. ...I mean that in handling the subject I have now in hand— one of the modern subjects we have talked over and for which I am indebted to you, I seem to myself to have hit upon or to be about to hit upon a type of blank verse essentially new, which has much of the unconventionality and unguided movement of prose, in the passages where the emotional level is low, and which yet is capable of gathering itself up, when needed, into the passion and splendor which prose is incapable of. Co-operate with me in warding off from my head the punishment sent upon presumption, by letting this be as if it had not been said, until such time as I shall have pushed the experiment to consummation, and either proved or disproved its value.[2]

Moody never managed to push this particular experiment to consummation, nor does any manuscript or other record of the play itself seem to have survived. In fact, until the publication of the *Letters to Harriet* in 1935, none of his critics showed any knowledge of its existence; and the editor of those letters, Percy MacKaye, assumed that Moody simply abandoned the subject as well as the verse experiment when he turned to the composition of the prose play that was eventually to become *The Great Divide*.[3] We do know, however, that the prose play was based on a true contemporary story told him by Harriet;[4] and the fact that he had referred to the subject of the earlier verse play as one for which he was "indebted" to her would suggest that, rather than treating entirely new materials, *The Great Divide* may have represented a reworking in prose of the same materials which Moody had tried unsuccessfully to cope with in verse. Why he was unsuccessful is a matter for interesting conjecture; but, as will be seen later, his failure did not spell the end of his hopes for a new type of dramatic verse adaptable to contemporary subjects and speech idioms.

In any event, it was not until some time after his journey to the Arizona desert with Ferdinand Schevill in the spring of 1904 that Moody began work on the prose play which was to have one of the most successful runs to date in the American commercial theater. Actually, some of the inspiration for the play's Western setting and *dramatis personae* may be traced to a still earlier encounter with what was then the Wild West— a two-week camping trip in the Colorado Rockies which Moody had taken with Hamlin Garland in August, 1901, and which is memorialized in both the early letters to Harriet and Garland's volume of reminiscences *Companions on the Trail*.[5] During this trip—his first excursion farther west than the Chicago area—Moody had been particularly thrilled by his arrival at the highest point of the Continental Divide, where "the crazy little torrents" which separate there into Pacific-bound and Atlantic-bound "are all destined to great fates."[6] Later in the same trip, he had put up for one night at a deserted cowpunchers' hut with a group of tramp miners whom he found, despite a certain coarseness and uncleanliness, "good fellows" and whose image quite probably affected his portrayal of Stephen Ghent and some of the lesser characters in *The Great Divide*.[7]

But more immediate and far-reaching in its influence on the setting and spirit of the play was the 1904 trip to Arizona. Here Moody became acquainted, during a week's sojourn at Oraibi, with the Hopi Indians who figure in the background of the final version of *The Faith Healer;* he also became acquainted with the rugged beauties of the great Painted Desert which became the specific setting for Acts One and Two of *The Great Divide* and the focus for much of the play's symbolic imagery. His letters comment excitedly on the similarities he felt between "the color and form of the country, as well as the atmosphere," and those he had encountered on his journey through Greece two years before;[8] and his companion Schevill later recorded Moody's strong impression of the "inner relationship" between the dances and religious rites of the Hopis and "the spirit which gave birth to the Greek tragedy."[9]

Just as *The Fire-Bringer* owed its inception to the 1902 journey, then, so *The Great Divide*—even if its basic plot materials had already been established—owed much of its final substance to the 1904 journey; and the parallels Moody was impelled to draw between contemporary Arizona and primitive Greece correspond in many ways to parallels in the philosophical spirit of the two dramas.[10]

Though some letters near the end of 1904 contain brief references to his initial attempts at writing the play, the real business of putting it in shape was concentrated into a six-month period at the end of the next year, following Moody's slow convalescence from a serious leg operation which had taken place in April, 1905. The play was finished by January, 1906, and in February Moody began trying to peddle it to producers under its first title, *The Sabine Woman.* The rest of its history has been so fully described elsewhere that it may be very briefly summarized here.[11] In April *The Sabine Woman* had a short and moderately successful run in Chicago, where the noted actress Margaret Anglin produced it and played the female lead. Then the still more noted actor-producer Henry Miller took over the rights for a New York production, retained Miss Anglin in the same role, and cast himself in the male lead. During the summer, Moody revised the play and changed its title to *The Great Divide.* After a series of rather unpromising tryouts on the road, during which the play received damning reviews in most of the cities where it appeared, it finally opened in New York on October 3, 1906, and was an instantaneous success with critics and public alike. It ran uninterruptedly for some two years, followed by an equally triumphant American road trip and a successful run in London during the autumn season of 1909. It has been revived on the stage several times since, and was twice made into motion pictures—a silent version in 1917 and a "talking" version in 1924.

II *The Play*

The original true story as Moody received it from Harriet had all the trappings of a latterday sex-and-violence melodrama: "A girl of her acquaintance . . . had gone with her brother to a cabin in the West, had been left alone and had been attacked by three men. She had appealed to one to save her from the others and had agreed to marry him. The marriage did not turn out successfully, and resulted in divorce."[12] Yet, though George Pierce Baker was right when, in a commemorative essay about Moody published in 1910, he remarked that the very subject was one "from which our stage even a decade ago would have shrunk in timid trembling,"[13] the fact is that, from a mid-twentieth-century point of view, the play seems to treat sexual matters with fairly conventional indirectness and to play down rather than to exploit the sensationalism inherent in its raw materials. Melodramatic it certainly is in places, but, apart from the brief scene depicting the foiled rape, the melodrama is largely in the tradition of the standard nineteenth-century romance play: boy meets girl, boy loses girl, and—in a third act which alters the original story to supply a "happy ending"— boy saves girl's family from the poorhouse and finally regains girl.

Superimposed on this plot-pattern, as Henry has recognized, is the ancient one involving "a woman married by force or fraud who, bitterly resentful of her humiliation, is ultimately fascinated by her captor and learns to love him"—for which Henry cites a parallel in *The Taming of the Shrew*,[14] and which perhaps finds its closest serious parallels in Middleton's tragedy *The Changeling* and in the Roman legend of the Rape of the Sabines from which Moody drew the play's original title. Obviously enough, however, Moody took over such conventional plot devices with full consciousness of their conventionality in order to use them as a familiar, theatrically acceptable vehicle for his own favorite philosophical and psychological themes.

Those themes are centered almost entirely in the developing relationship between the two protagonists, the New Englander

Ruth Jordan and the Westerner Stephen Ghent; and, for the first two-and-a-half acts, their relationship follows the external facts of the original story quite closely. Act One is set in a cabin in the Arizona desert, where the nineteen-year-old Ruth has been living for some three months with her older brother Philip and his wife Polly, while attempting to restore the family's dwindled fortunes through the establishment of a new cactus-fiber industry. Also present is young Doctor Winthrop Newbury, a friend from back home who is Ruth's unsuccessful suitor. At length, Ruth is left alone when Philip and Winthrop take Polly off to the railroad station where she is to embark for a social jaunt in San Francisco designed to relieve her restiveness amid the loneliness and monotony of their new surroundings. Thereupon, three drunken men—Ghent, an American tramp miner, and a Mexican half-breed—enter with the intention of raping Ruth. After a frantic resistance, she suddenly offers herself in marriage to Ghent if he will rescue her from his companions, and he accepts. He buys off the Mexican with a handful of money and a crude gold chain and then wins a "stand-up" pistol duel with the other American. Then, having accomplished his side of the bargain, he holds Ruth to hers; and, after she has left an ambiguous explanatory note for her brother, the two ride off to be married.

Act Two takes place about a year later. Ghent is now—as he had confidently promised Ruth he would be at the end of Act One—a rich man, with a principal share in a thriving gold mine among the Cordilleras Mountains. He also is apparently a model husband, entirely devoted to Ruth and to his efforts at providing her with the "good life," as represented specifically by a luxurious new home he has commissioned an Eastern architect to design for their beautiful mountain retreat in the Cordilleras. Ruth, however, has been unable to forget the sordid origins of their marriage or to accept Ghent's present ways of making them up to her. While refusing to spend any of the money he has lavished on her except for basic necessities, she has secretly been selling her own fine weavings at the public market place in order to earn enough to repay Ghent the price he had originally paid for her and thereby to absolve herself of their bargain. With these earnings she finally manages to buy back from the Mexican of Act One the gold chain which has become for her a symbol of that bargain. Restoring this to Ghent, she leaves him and returns to Massachusetts in the company of Philip, Polly, and Winthrop, who have meanwhile tracked her down after a long search.

Act Three takes place six months later in the Jordan home, to which Ruth has withdrawn with her newborn child and where she is living as a virtual recluse, while undergoing a self-inflicted penance for her sinful marriage as well as for the ruination she brought on the family business enterprise by abandoning Philip. Only the aid of a mysterious "benevolent uncle" has saved the family from total destitution; and this uncle, we soon learn, is Ghent himself. Without Ruth's knowledge, he has followed her East and has been secretly supplying money to her mother and paying clandestine visits to his baby son. At length, Ghent puts in an appearance when Ruth is present and reveals his latest act of generosity in buying up and restoring to Philip the now thriving cactus-fiber business which his abduction of Ruth had caused her brother to lose. She, however, proceeds to destroy his glowing image by telling her family for the first time about the actual circumstances of her original disappearance and the nature of their marriage. There follows a violent scene in which the outraged Philip is prevented from avenging himself on Ghent only by the intervention of the now bitterly disillusioned Mrs. Jordan, who insists that Ruth and Ghent be left alone to work out their evil situation for themselves. Thus the scene is set for the climactic final dialogue, in which both protagonists undergo a transfiguring self-discovery and Moody converts his tragedy into a tragicomedy.

In order to understand the significance of this dénouement, as it applies both to the individual characters of Ruth and Ghent and to the larger issues which their relationship symbolizes, it is necessary to start from the beginning and consider the ways in which Moody develops the psychological and moral natures of his protagonists within this rudimentary plotshell, as well as the ways in which he makes his protagonists universalized symbols of his personal philosophical outlook.

By the time Ghent has entered the play near the end of Act One, Ruth's initial characterization is already fairly complete, and intimations of Moody's symbolic intentions are already fairly heavy. At the center of her character is a clearly defined though as yet only latent conflict between an inherited Puritan conscience and a personality whose natural expansiveness and capacity for uninhibited joy express themselves in a spontaneous attraction to all that is wild and mysteriously beautiful in the primitive Western landscape to which she has recently been transported. Though Philip and Polly are themselves rather stock type-characters, the contrast in their mentalities serves to emphasize the inner division within Ruth's more complex and individualized character: the stern and conventionally virtuous Philip represents an exaggerated version of her Puritan side; the fun-loving, somewhat frivolously anti-conventional Polly represents an exaggerated version of the impulse to rebel against her heritage in the name of the "Happiness" which Polly blandly declares is "its own justification." Likewise, the "good, . . . gentle and chivalrous" Winthrop stands for all that is best in traditional New England culture; and yet, as Ruth half-jokingly confesses to Polly, he also stands for all that is "finished," "rounded off, a completed product," unlike her own romantic dreams of a man resembling the primitive Arizona landscape, "the glorious unfulfilled."

Much of the offhand and light-heartedly humorous dialogue of the opening scene contains hints of Ruth's potential psychological and moral conflict, as well as foreshadowings—both subtle and broadly overt—of the actual events to come. At their most overt, they run like this:

POLLY.

Do you really mean to say that apart from your pride in helping your brother, making the project go, and saving the family fortunes, you really *enjoy* yourself here?

RUTH.

Since Phil and I came out, one day has been more radiantly exciting than the other. I don't know what's the matter with me. I think I shall be punished for being so happy.

POLLY.

Punished for being happy! There's your simon-pure New-Englander.

RUTH.

True! I was discovered at the age of seven in the garret, perusing "The Twelve Pillars and Four Cornerstones of a Godly Life."

POLLY.

Pointing at Ruth's heart, speaks with mock solemnity.
If Massachusetts and Arizona ever get in a mixup in there, woe be!

Rather more subtle than this dialogue in its establishment of symbolic metaphors for the play's literal contents is Ruth's sporadic monologue while she is later undressing for bed in the empty cabin. At one point, for example, having just sung a few snatches from a melancholy song including the lines, "Heart, wild heart,/... Flower and bird/Await but thy word," she addresses a bunch of actual wild flowers on the table: "Be still, you beauties! You'll drive me to distraction with your color and your odor. I'll take a hostage for your good behavior." She then places the "hostage" flower in her hair—an act which symbolizes her natural attraction to and her inbred suspicion of intense sensuous beauty; but it also ironically foreshadows the next scene in which she will be forced to give her own heart to Ghent as a kind of "hostage" for the good behavior of the men who have come to rape her.

If Ruth is characterized at the outset as a type of the New England sensibility reacting against itself under the influence of the Wild West, Ghent is characterized at the outset as a type of the lawless West who reacts against his own lawlessness under the influence of Ruth's authentic gentility. From the very start of the rape scene, Moody does all in his playwright's power to make Ghent's later nobility credible, but at the same time to depict him as a man whose present moral despair makes him capable of joining in the intended assault. After he has entered, he simply stands motionless by the table, *"gazing"* at at Ruth *"in a fascinated semi-stupor"* and taking no direct part in the other two men's efforts to subdue her. His very immobility and separateness from the violent action has the effect of attracting audience attention to him as an obvious source of appeal, even though it is clear that he is in on the rape; it also, of course, suggests something which he himself later makes explicit—that the sight of Ruth struggling with his companions brought on an immediate revulsion against the evil in his nature.

Fully aware of the depths of that evil, he is also aware of his power to redeem himself, given an external inspiration equal to the despair which had brought him to Ruth's cabin "blind-drunk and sun-crazy, and looking for damnation the nearest way." Such an inspiration he has intuitively recognized in Ruth; and, from the moment she makes her desperate offer, he becomes converted from a typical Western "bad man" to an embodiment of simple Western self-reliance and primitive

honor. His first gesture after disposing of his companions is
to lay his pistol within Ruth's reach and to turn his back on
her; and, though she explains away her failure to take advantage of this honorable gesture by invoking a familiar Puritan sentiment—"You must live—to pay for having spoiled your
life"—it is evident that part of the reason she cannot kill
Ghent, or take the other way out by killing herself, is that she
is already half-consciously identifying this strangely transformed man with her own dream of a lover made in the image
of the West's "glorious unfulfilled." In other words, though she
presumably goes off with him because her own code of honor
demands that she keep her side of the bargain, Moody also
takes pains—especially when he has her solicitously dress the
arm-wound Ghent has received in the duel—to suggest that
Ruth is already falling in love with her husband-to-be.[15]

When we next see them in Act Two, however, the "Great
Divide" between Ruth's Eastern and Ghent's Western sensibility has widened, as has the basic moral division within Ruth
herself. The original wound has failed to heal: her pride and
moral sense continue to be obsessed by the memory of the way
he had "bought" her for his wife; and, as she bitterly confesses
near the end of the act, she has not been able to rid her mind
of the image of that earlier Ghent who "stands behind you
now!—The human beast, that goes to its horrible pleasure as
not even a wild animal will go—*in pack, in pack!*"

Under the pressure of such obsessions, the Puritan in her has
reasserted itself with a vengeance. Her refusal to enjoy Ghent's
new wealth, and her self-abasing efforts to make money through
her own handiwork in order to buy back the gold chain,
are as much a form of self-castigation as a gesture of defiance
to Ghent or a means of earning her release from their marriage.
At the same time, some of the original attraction also remains:
her cruel reflections on the past alternate at times with out-
bursts like, "Oh, don't judge me! Don't listen to me! I am not
in my right mind"; and it is more than just self-defensive pride
which makes her assume the role of a happy and devoted wife
during her first encounters with Philip, Polly, and Winthrop.[16]
Indeed, Moody is quite skillful in suggesting something close to
the schizoid in Ruth's continual moral oscillations before her
Puritan conscience finally triumphs and she leaves her husband.

Yet it would be wrong to explain away all of Ruth's behavior
in Act Two as merely the reflection of a mental unbalance.

Much as our sympathies are now with Ghent, we are also made aware of some real justification for her bitterness, if not for the almost purely destructive forms it takes. After all, phrases like Ruth's *"in pack, in pack!"* do remind us of the enormity of the crime in which Ghent had nearly participated; and, if her wounded memory has perhaps had undue difficulty in healing, his has perhaps healed too easily. Despite his obvious reformation and success in fulfilling his earlier resolve to "Make this bad business over into something good for both of us," Ghent is still lacking in true moral maturity. Even before we learn anything of Ruth's attitude, we have already been given some sense, in his conversation with the architect and contractor, of Ghent's sincere but naïvely inadequate approach to the business of redeeming the past. He has much of the air of the prosperous entrepreneur, sure of his money-making gifts and dedicated to the proposition that bigger-and-better gold mines and larger and more sumptuous mansions are the key to the good life. Though his hearty manner is partly a pose, designed to hide from himself and others the actual present state of his marriage, it also reveals something significant about his way of thinking—as, for instance, in this brief interchange over the plans for the new house:

ARCHITECT.
This large room fronting the main arcade is the living-room.

GHENT.
I guess we'll have 'em all living-rooms. This place is to be lived in, from the word go.

ARCHITECT.
Humoring him.
To be sure, everything cheerful and open.

Later, Ruth herself reveals that Ghent has not always been this way, and that she had actually been on the verge of surrendering to his deeper attractions before their new prosperity again corrupted his image. When he poignantly reminds her of their first journey and reflects, "I thought—it seemed to me you had—begun to care for me," she replies:

That night, when we rode away from the justice's office at San Jacinto, and the sky began to brighten over the desert—the ice that had gathered here—(*she touches her heart*)—began to melt in spite of me. And when the next night and the next day passed, and the next, and still you spared me and treated me with beautiful rough chivalry, I said to myself, "He has heard my prayer to him. He knows what a girl's heart is." As you rode before me down the arroyos, and up over the mesas, through the dazzling sunlight and the majestic silence, it seemed as if you were leading me out of a world of little codes and customs into a great new world.—So it was for those first days.—And then—and then—I woke, and saw you standing in my tent-door in the starlight! I knew before you spoke that we were lost. You hadn't the strength to save us!

For her, the proof that he "hadn't the strength" lay in the very means he had chosen, and was still choosing, to save them—means which showed how much he himself was tied to the "little codes and customs" of that money-oriented society Moody had condemned in his earlier social poems: "While we were poor and struggling I thought I could do it—Then—(*she points toward the cañon*)—then that hole down there began belching its stream of gold. You began to load me with gifts—to force easy ways upon me—." The voice in the last phrase is, of course, that of Ruth's New England heritage; but what it says has a certain objective validity too.

In order, then, for Ghent's moral outlook to win a convincing, meaningful victory over Ruth's, as it does at the end of Act Three, Moody must first show it undergoing a critical trial from which it can emerge deepened and refined. This he does in the interval between the Act Two curtain and their final dialogue. During his six months in the East, Ghent has had his taste of real loneliness and deprivation; and his suffering has been compounded by his having to look on helplessly while Ruth's own suffering has brought her near to a physical and mental breakdown. He has come, among other things, to a palpable realization of the insufficiency of mere wealth as a means to happiness—a realization symbolized in the fact that he insists on keeping his financial aid to the Jordan family a secret from Ruth; for, "if she knew about it, she wouldn't stay here overnight." He has also come to see the true depths of the Puritan mentality, about which he has hitherto known very little; and the insights which Ruth's intense withdrawal and penitence have given him into that mentality reach their culmination when, in the end, even her mother, the person who has most benefited by his generosity and to whom he feels closest, reacts to Ruth's revelation of the truth about their marriage by exclaiming, "You ought to have—died—first!" Confronted with such insights, he now faces for the first time the idea that a reconciliation of the differences between his temperament and Ruth's may be impossible, may even be forbidden by some commanding law in the nature of things. By the time he is left alone with Ruth, he has therefore decided to abandon his attempts at winning her back and to return alone to the West.

In this frame of mind he enters the final scene. Typically enough, Ruth begins the scene by turning on herself in a spasm of remorse over having yielded to impulse and betrayed their secret to her family: "God forgive me! You never can." But this he chivalrously passes off as something to which he himself had driven her by coming to the house. The next few speeches summarize and crystallize the essential contrast in their moral characters and the reasons why there is apparently no hope of their coming back together. After confessing that "The way your mother took it showed me one thing.—I've never understood you, because—I don't understand your people," Ghent presents Ruth with the gold chain that has symbolized their relationship and now symbolizes its dissolution. Yet, when pressed by Ruth—who is again wavering—to tell her what he thinks is "the truth" about that relationship with regard to himself, he is moved to a last-ditch defense of its original potentialities:

> I drifted into one of your meeting-houses last Sunday, not knowing where else to go, and I heard a young fellow preaching about what he called "The Second Birth." A year and a half ago I should have thought it was all hocus-pocus, but you can believe me or not, the way he went on he might have been behind the door that night in that little justice den in San Jacinto, saying to the Recording Angel: "Do you see that rascal? Take notice! There ain't an ounce of bone or a drop of blood in him but what's new man!"

This statement Ruth counters with a résumé of her attitude toward his behavior in the wake of this "Second Birth": "If you had only heard me cry to you, to wait, to cleanse yourself and me—by suffering and sacrifice—before we dared begin to live! But you wouldn't see the need! Oh, if you could have felt for yourself what I felt for you! If you could have said, 'The wages of sin is death!' and suffered the anguish of death, and risen again purified! But instead of that, what you had done fell off from you like any daily trifle."

Then, with a gesture that probably owes something to the family-portrait scene in Ibsen's *Rosmersholm,* Ghent begins his reply by indicating the pictures of Ruth's Puritan ancestors on the wall and by blaming them for the destructive negativism of her moral views. Yet there is at least an undertone of desperate bravado in the argument he sets against those views: a rejection of "suffering and sacrifice" in favor of "joy, and selfishness" as the only moral imperatives that apply to such as they; and an almost arrogant attempt to justify the way he first won her by claiming that "most good women are taken that way, if they only knew." For a moment, it seems to be the old Ghent talking, and Ruth remains understandably cold to even his final appeal that she consider "the man you've made of me, the life and the meaning of life you've showed me the way to!"

The impasse seems complete: Ruth hides her face in her hands, and the stage direction calls for a long silence, at the end of which the somewhat hollow *"ring of exaltation"* which had been in Ghent's voice during the last speech *"is replaced by a sober intensity."* The words with which he breaks the silence amount to much more than a mere rhetorical ploy: "If you can't see it my way, give me another chance to live it out in yours." The entreaty is manifestly sincere, and, by way of proving his sincerity, Ghent now tells Ruth for the first time about the six lonely and miserable months he has spent in the East, "hanging about and bribing your servant for news"—during which he has come to recognize, even if he could not fully understand, the claims of self-denial as a means to redemption.

This recognition he embodies in a brand new proposal: "You ask me to suffer for my wrong. Since you left me I *have* suffered—God knows! You ask me to make some sacrifice. Well—how would the mine do? Since I've been away they've as good as stolen it from me. I could get it back easy enough by fighting; but supposing I don't fight. Then we'll start all over again, just as we stand in our shoes, and make another fortune—for our boy."

Whether because the last reference to "another fortune" strikes her badly, or because she has not yet fully taken in the meaning of Ghent's offer, Ruth simply *"utters a faint moan,"* allows her head to sink deeper into her arms, and makes no response to his imploring caress or to his concluding plea on behalf of their future and that of their child. At length he *"straightens up, with a gesture of stoic despair,"* and delivers a

farewell speech informed by a moral perception which recalls
the older Puritan atmosphere of works like Hawthorne's *The
Scarlet Letter* and which goes beyond even Ruth's in suggesting
the irrevocability of evil:

> I know what you're saying there to yourself, and I guess you're
> right. Wrong is wrong, from the moment it happens till the crack
> of doom, and all the angels in Heaven, working overtime, can't
> make it less or different by a hair. That seems to be the law.
> I've learned it hard, but I guess I've learned it. I've seen
> it written in mountain letters across the continent of this life.
> —Done is done, and lost is lost, and smashed to hell is smashed
> to hell. We fuss and potter and patch up. You might as well
> try to batter down the Rocky Mountains with a rabbit's heart-
> beat! *He goes to the door, where he turns.*
> You've fought hard for me, God bless you for it.—But it's been
> a losing game with you from the first!—You belong here, and I
> belong out yonder—beyond the Rockies, beyond—the Great
> Divide!

Only now is Moody ready to dramatize the final reversal
which gives the play its happy ending. As Ghent is about to
leave for good, Ruth suddenly rises, *"with streaming eyes,"* and
cries "Wait!" From here to the end, she does most of the talking; and we are made aware that a tremendous psychological
pressure has at last been lifted from her. She herself now reviews her own past behavior in rapid, almost breathless phrases,
reminding him that she had acted in the only way her upbringing and deeper nature made possible, but that, "when I tore
down with bleeding fingers the life you were trying to build for
us, I did it only—because—I loved you!" Yet now she has suddenly become capable of expressing that love in another way
than "by wretchedness, by self-torture, by trying blindly to pierce
your careless heart with pain." For what Ghent has just said has
all at once released the other side of her nature, long repressed
under the weight of her Puritan conscience, but whose struggle
for liberation has been manifest in all her agonized oscillations
through the last two acts:

> O, as I lay there and listened to you, I realized it for the first
> time—you had risen, in one hour, to a wholly new existence,
> which flooded the present and the future with brightness, yes,
> and reached back into our past, and made of it—made of all of
> it—something to cherish! . . . You have taken the good of our

life and grown strong. I have taken the evil and grown weak,
weak unto death. Teach me to live as you do!

With this plea, sne places the gold chain around Ghent's neck
as a symbol of the original sin of their relationship, now transformed—like Hester Prynne's "A" in the brighter scenes of *The
Scarlet Letter*—into a symbol of the good which can grow out
of such evil. The play ends with Ruth and Ghent fully reconciled
and looking ahead in joyful hope to a new future for themselves
and their child.

III *The Double Reversal*

None of Moody's critics seems to have recognized the real
significance of this double reversal, whereby Ruth submits to
Ghent's views only after he has first submitted to hers. Yet,
besides being a very effective dramatic device for delaying the
final climax and providing an extra element of suspense just
before the last curtain, the double reversal is also at the core of
the play's meaning, and reflects back on all that has gone before.

It is true that throughout the play Ruth's negative morality is
associated with that denial of life which Moody had elsewhere
depicted as the deepest of all evils; this association is perhaps
made most explicit in the way she is shown raising her child in
Act Three—"with the most watchful, the minutest care," as her
mother observes, "but ... exactly as if it were a piece of machin-
ery." Nevertheless, there is also something profound in the
tough Puritan vision which underlies her heroic austerity, just
as there was something rather too facile and even shallow in
Ghent's earlier approach to their moral problem. We must remember that Moody nowhere denies that Ghent's part in the
rape attempt of Act One was a serious sin, requiring a serious
expiation. It is only after Ghent has come to see this for himself,
then, and has learned to appreciate the validity in the Puritan approach to expiation, that Ruth can appreciate the greater validity of his own final approach. By the last scene he not only is
a man who has suffered but also is a man whose whole way of
thinking and living has been challenged by an intense encounter
with its opposite. And out of that encounter his moral vision has
risen to a higher plane where it can at last assert a stronger
claim on Ruth's conscience than her own negative vision. In
giving up the gold mine and the "easy ways" it represents, in
experiencing for himself the power of suffering as a means of

purification, and in at least admitting—as he does near the end —that some sins may not be redeemable except by surrendering the fruits of those sins, he actually incorporates the better elements of Ruth's morality into his own. Hence Ruth's line "Teach me to live as you do" does not mean "Teach me to live as you *have* lived," but "Teach me to live as you *now can*." It takes a purified version of Ghent's basic moral outlook to convert Ruth from a denier to an affirmer of life.[17]

The central symbolic meaning of *The Great Divide* is therefore nothing so simple as the triumph of the West over the East—of nature over civilization, freedom over law, the present over the past. These dichotomies are certainly present in the relationship between Ghent and Ruth, who symbolically represent the two sides of the American experience as well as of the universal human condition. Yet Moody is concerned not with widening the "Great Divide" between East and West but with closing it; and, though his personal sympathies clearly lay more with the West than with the East, he was still enough of a New Englander himself to see that the Ghents require the Ruths as well as vice versa. Ghent symbolizes the West not as self-sufficient nature but as promise—a promise whose realization depends in large part on contact with tradition, represented at its best in that side of Ruth to which Moody constantly draws our admiration.[18] By the Act Three curtain, both protagonists have undergone a kind of conversion as a result of such contact; and both thereby transcend their earlier selves to become fully defined embodiments of Moody's positive morality and the hopeful vision of the future he had expressed in poems like "The Brute" and in the characters of Raphael, Prometheus, and Pandora.

Like Aeolus and Alcyone in *The Fire-Bringer*, Ruth's and Ghent's child contains within him the seeds of a higher civilization to come; with his parents' achievement of a reconciliation based on love and positive striving to bring good out of evil, it becomes possible for him to cultivate those seeds in healthy freedom. Hence their reassertion of their own capacity for growth prefigures a progressive future for America in the same way that Prometheus' restoration of fire had for Greece. As in *The Fire-Bringer*, however, Moody makes his optimistic vision "earn" its triumph by confronting it with an antithetical vision powerful enough to elicit real struggle before such a triumph can be won.

IV *Style and Dramaturgy*

Because of the play's essentially realistic technique, the prose style of *The Great Divide* naturally lacks the dense texture of the dialogue in the verse dramas; and, for the most part, Moody's use of language tends to be limited to the requirements of simple theatrical expediency. At the high moments in the action, on the other hand, there is often a corresponding heightening of the idiom, in which the poet in Moody briefly declares himself. We see such a heightening, for example, in Ruth's speech about the marriage journey near the end of Act Two and in Ghent's Act Three farewell speech. In these an intensification of imagery and figurative language, as well as a strong rhythmic quality which almost turns into meter at times, might even be vestiges of the earlier blank-verse version.

Then, too, there runs throughout the play an unobtrusive but important image pattern drawn from geography, which, by the end, takes on symbolic dimensions of its own and reinforces the symbolism inherent in the action and characters themselves. At the center of this pattern is of course, the basic image of the American East, the American West, and the geographical "Great Divide" which separates them; and this image reaches its metaphorical and symbolic apex at the conclusion of Ghent's farewell speech. In the same speech, another recurrent image reaches its apex in the line "I've seen it written in mountain letters across the continent of this life," which takes its most immediate symbolic associations from a speech by Polly just a few pages earlier, where, in one of her more perspicacious moments, she had answered Mrs. Jordan's remark that Ghent "seems to me a good man" by declaring: "Oh, he's *good!* So is a volcano between eruptions. And commonplace, too, until you happen to get a glimpse down one of the old volcanic rifts in his surface, and see—far below—underneath the cold lava-beds—fire, fire, the molten heart of a continent."

Such metaphorical devices do more than contribute to the individual characterization of the play's protagonists; they have the effect of identifying those protagonists with the entire land they inhabit, and their struggles toward self-realization with a corresponding struggle in the cosmic process itself.

Considering his total lack of practical theater training, Moody's handling of the more commonplace theatrical amenities is remarkably professional throughout—almost to the point of "slickness" in places. Though only Ruth and Ghent are fully rounded *personae*, the various type-characters who make up the supporting cast are skillfully employed in the standard functions of helping forward the plot line and of setting off elements in the central relationship via parallelism and contrast. Thus Philip and Winthrop, as simplified specimens of the New England male, contrast directly with Ghent's frontier masculinity. The compatible but colorless and ultimately unsatisfactory marriage relation of Philip and Polly contrasts with the stormy but intense and ultimately magnificent relation of Ghent and Ruth— a contrast which becomes poignantly explicit in some of Polly's own speeches in Act Three. And, among the lesser characters, there is a clear contrast between the blunt Western humor of the old miner Lon in Act Two and the genteel New England humor of old Doctor Newbury, Winthrop's father, in Act Three, which further establishes the difference between the Arizona and the Massachusetts spirit.

Most of the orthodox devices for "comic relief" are, however, concentrated into the role of Polly, a rather ambiguously conceived character who at moments seems to take on a kind of choral function as the playwright's own interpreter; but who is elsewhere obviously limited in her perception and given to superciliously "romantic" ideas of glamor which blind her to the real complexities of things, especially with regard to Ghent. In the first role, her humor is that of conscious wit; but in the second, one feels that she may herself be an object of Moody's satire.[19] Either way, she comes the closest of anyone in the play to resembling a typical character out of the drawing-room comedy of the time; and, as such, she does much toward retaining contact between the play's more unusual and demanding aims and the conventional expectations which Moody's audiences would have brought into the commercial theater of 1906.

Yet the enormous popularity which *The Great Divide* achieved, though it might not have been possible without appeals to such expectations, was really due to a deeper appeal which Moody's philosophical and psychological themes made to that American public for whom, and about whom, the play was written. Far from being a mere "pot-boiler," as one later critic has charged,[20] *The Great Divide* was a major event in the history of American drama largely because of the way it adapted commercial-theater commonplaces to the service of uncommon and serious ideas. During at least a decade after its first production, the play stood out in the estimate of critics as the brightest source of hope for a revolution against the dull mediocrity which had long dominated the American stage.[21] Given the conditions which prevailed on that stage at the time it was written, and allowing for occasional antiquated techniques that identify it with its age, *The Great Divide* still holds up unusually well as a dramatic experience today. A theater historian writing in 1930 was well justified when he remarked that "With a play like this the modern drama in America was coming of age."[22]

CHAPTER 7

Later Poems

FOLLOWING the publication of the 1901 volume, Moody's output of non-dramatic verse gradually decreased as his creative attentions became concentrated on the drama. Of the twelve surviving pieces which Manly included in the posthumous *Poems and Plays* under the heading "Second Coming, and Later Poems," only six were published in journals during Moody's lifetime;[1] and it is possible that the others—mostly personal love poems to Harriet—were written with no thought of publication. The majority of the poems belong to the years 1903 and 1904; after that, Moody's dramatic labors seem to have left him less and less time or material for other kinds of creative effort.[2]

That this falling off reflected a basic change in his literary affections is borne out by an interview, recounted in a current journal, in which Moody commented about present prospects for American literature with the observation: "Our poetry, I admit, is suffering a backset, but do you know why that is? The whole modern tendency is toward the drama as the most important literary form. It's the highest form of art—no doubt about it! Even the popularity of the novel is on the decrease. The drama, like our present life, is highly vitalized; it is pithy, difficult, concise."[3]

Nevertheless, the small corpus of Moody's late non-dramatic verse, though uneven, contains some of the best and most individual writing he did outside the dramatic mode.

I *General Characteristics of the Later Poems*

There is scarcely a trace in these poems of the social and political themes which figured so prominently in the latest poems written for the 1901 volume. Apart from some generalized reflections on the present decadence of American religious insti-

tutions in "Second Coming" and on the emancipation of woman
in "I Am the Woman," the only piece which directly recalls the
earlier protest poems is the slender nonsense song "The Counting Man," where pure children's doggerel alternates with satirical jibes at the American commercial mentality:

> Eeny, meeny, miney, mo, —
> All the children in a row.
> Cracka feeny, who is he,
> Counting out so solemnly?

At the same time, little is left of that earlier Moody manner—
the remotely literary Pre-Raphaelitism or *fin-de-siècle* estheti-
cism dominant in many of his early lyrics during the 1890's. He
may, in fact, have intended to express an outright repudiation
of that manner in the strange little tirade "Musa Meretrix"
("Prostitute Muse")— a poem which he said "was written about
nobody in particular, though I had in mind I forget which one
of the many who have made shipwreck on the 'Art for Art's
sake' fallacy."[4] The object of his sometimes bombastic indigna-
tion is the ungrateful Muse who betrayed this anonymous representative of *fin-de-siècle* poetics into writing a kind of poetry
which, though Moody once emulated it himself, now seems to
him "flaunting rubbish." Toward the poet himself, Moody's
attitude is a combination of admiration and half-contemptuous
pity—admiration for the absolute artistic dedication by which
he "ate not, drank not, save for thee [the Muse]"; and pity for
the futility of that dedication, misdirected as it was to a
"Flat brothel-jestress, thing of sale." In the partly earnest and
partly ironic tribute of the second stanza, in which the virulent
tone is momentarily softened, "Musa Meretrix" seems to foreshadow Ezra Pound's similarly ambivalent appraisals of the
poets of the 1890's in *Mauberley*. Moody writes:

> I see again his dream-worn hand
> Shaken by my poor praise, his brow
> Flushed by the words I scarce knew how
> To speak at all, so shadowy grand
> He stalked there in Song's lonely land,
> Under the vow.

This does not mean, of course, that Romantic lyricism as such
has disappeared from Moody's verse, or that his surface manner
is, for the most part, any less artificial than in the earlier poems.

What chiefly distinguishes his later lyricism from that of his youthful work is that in content it is far less literary, less imitative, and more closely bound up with real personal experience which gives it a greater sense of emotional immediacy. In the poems "The Moon-Moth," "My Love is Gone into the East," "The Three Angels," "A Prairie Ride," and "I Am the Woman," the informing experience is quite simply Moody's ardent love for Harriet. In "Old Pourquoi" and "Second Coming" it is actual events which occurred during his travels in Europe; and even the three poems—"The Death of Eve," "The Fountain," and "Thammuz"—whose subject matter is derived from literary sources, translate their raw materials into terms clearly and uniquely identifiable with Moody's personal way of seeing and thinking. A Romantic he remained to the end, but more in the sense of trying to revive that original Romanticism he discerned in "Classical" Greek literature than of emulating the latter-day distillations of the Pre-Raphaelites and the *fin-de-siècle* esthetes.[5]

II *"The Moon-Moth"*

In the longest, most elaborate of the poems about his love for Harriet, the ode-like lyrical meditation "The Moon-Moth," Moody's general style and handling of narrative elements bear resemblances to the earlier lyrical meditation "Jetsam." Like "Jetsam," the later poem makes some use of techniques comparable to those of the most difficult French Symbolist poetry, and Charleton Lewis attributed his own admitted trouble in making sense of its contents to those techniques and to Moody's attempt to "make the ultra-violet rays visible."[6] Yet the obscurities of "The Moon-Moth" can be, and have been, overestimated. Compared with "Jetsam," for example, the poem follows a quite consecutive narrative sequence, despite its deliberate blurring of transitions and logical connectives; and it is fairly explicit in defining at least the basic sense of its symbols. Though Moody obviously wanted those symbols to suggest more than can be stated about them, his meanings do lend themselves to paraphrase, at least up to the point where they become pure evocation.

The setting is the summit of Acrocorinth, a high hill overlooking the ruins of ancient Corinth, which Moody had visited during his 1902 trip to Greece. The two main symbols are the ruins

of an ancient temple to Aphrodite, associated throughout with
the eternal force that inspires human love; and a "rainbow-
colored" lunar moth—one of the many bright "creepers and
flyers" that are now the only inhabitants of the site—associated
with another such creature which had once visited him and
Harriet at an ecstatic moment when their own love was coming into being. Surrounding these two symbols are various
images representative of time and space—the vast sense of historical time evoked by the Greek landscape spread out below
the poet and the ancient myths whose spirit still seems to pervade it; and the vast sense of present space evoked by Moody's
reflections on the distance that now separates him from Harriet.
As the poem proceeds, however, both time and space come to
lose reality for the poet, who is falling under the influence of
the supernatural love-principle embodied in the temple ruins.
At length, by means of one of his freshest and most richly evocative conceits, Moody effects a subtle transition from his normal waking state, conditioned by temporal and spatial cognition, to a half-sleep in which such cognition is briefly suspended
and only the eternal aspects of things have substance:

> Mountains and seas, cities and isles and capes,
> All frail as dream and painted like a dream,
> All swimming with the fairy light that drapes
> A bubble, when the colors curl and stream
> And meet and flee asunder. I could deem
> This earth, this air, my dizzy soul, the sky,
> Time, knowledge, and the gods
> Were lapsing, curling, streaming lazily
> Down a great bubble's rondure, dye on dye,
> To swell the perilous clinging drop that nods,
> Gathers, and nods, and clings, through all eternity.

In this state he has a dream somewhat comparable to a medieval love vision; in it he imagines himself an apostate votary
of Aphrodite supplicating the goddess for readmittance to her
favor and for the long-overdue fulfillment of his amorous needs.
On waking, he finds the atmosphere of his surroundings and
his inward mood miraculously altered. Though the moonlit
night scene in which the dream was set has given way to the
twilight of finite reality, presences from the dream still linger;
and these now become incarnated in the sudden appearance of
the moon-moth, which he imagines has crossed the sea as an

emissary from Harriet and at the same time, because of associations between its colors and the birth of Aphrodite, has
crossed from eternity into time as an emissary of the goddess:

> O missionary
> Winds of the far and dear!
> O elfin ship, why flap your gallants there?
> My heart has many a brimming estuary
> Where you can ease you from the endless air,
> The ocean light you sailed to bring me news of her!
> . . . .
> . . . flame of pearl, vapor of pearl,
> Breath and decantment of sea-buried gems
> That with the foam-born Woman did upswirl
> To wreathe their brightness round her breast and limbs
> And give their color to the cup that dims
> Earth's piercing cry to music, . . .

For a while, then, the lesser reality of the poet's solitude is
supplanted by a higher reality in which time and space seem
annulled and he has a sense of Harriet's actual presence before
him, "More palpable" than in any previous meeting because
wholly of the spirit. Thereupon the moon-moth itself flies off;
and, as it does, this presence also disappears, throwing the poet
back on normal reality and leaving him intensely homesick and
ridden with longing for the physical Harriet. In the end, however, these feelings give way to one of calm joy, as his remembrance of this brief conquest over time and space settles in as
a kind of permanent testimony to the eternal quality of their
love:

> For us the future was, the past will be,
> And all the holy human years are new,
> And all are tasted of eternally,
> And still the eaten fruit shines on the tree. . . .

Perhaps because of its ostensible obscurities, perhaps because
it is probably the most extreme example of Moody's "sublime"
rhetorical manner, "The Moon-Moth" has been one of the most
neglected poems in all his work. It may well take a new revolution in poetic taste, a major reaction against the tight-lipped,
anti-rhetorical, anti-meditative bias of Imagism, Objectivism,
and their aftermaths, to bring a poem like this into its own.
Yet it is a poem whose entire spirit and technique resemble

those of a later poet who has somehow continued, despite his vehement non-adherence to the prevailing literary fashions of his time, to evoke admiration—the Hart Crane of "Voyages," "The Broken Tower," and the "Atlantis" section of *The Bridge*. Like Crane, the Moody of lyrical meditations such as "Jetsam" and "The Moon-Moth" seems almost purposefully to overwrite, as though intending to overwhelm us by the sheer internal pressure of his thought and emotion, irrespective of any rational sense of congruity between that thought and emotion and the external situation against which they weigh. And like Crane, Moody can, at his best, generate enough force from within to create, rather than simply reflect, intensities in the reality without. In this he was, as was Crane, a Romantic in one of the more fundamental and important senses of that complicated term.

III *Other Love Poems for Harriet*

A much lighter and even whimsical treatment of the same general subject as that in "The Moon-Moth" occurs in the short song "My Love is Gone into the East." Written from Harriet's point of view while Moody was in Europe, the song seems to retain much of the style and atmosphere of the earliest lyrics; but it does so in a way that is largely ironic, and Moody may well have meant to provoke a smile from Harriet at the reminiscence of his own youthful poetic manner in the opening stanza:

> My love is gone into the East
> Across the wide dawn-kindled sea;
> My love remembreth naught of me
> Nor of my lips nor of my breast,
> For he has gone where morning dwells
> Into the land of dreams and spells.

The poem's real subject, after all, is not the exotic romance of this "land of dreams and spells," but the lover's fidelity to the lady he has left behind, as embodied in the wistful little "cricket" voice of the last stanza, which sings to her at night of his inevitable return west.

"The Three Angels," written in commemoration of the evening when Moody and Harriet first silently acknowledged their love (perhaps the event at which the "moon-moth" had been present), gives way in its weaker moments to stale conventionalities of phrasing ("Like flame afar her life did rise," etc.)

which threaten to reduce its emotions to bathos. Those emotions do, however, manage to survive in the poem's central metaphor, introduced by the dawn scene impressionistically described at the start:

> Before my feet the curving strand
> Unblurs its outline from the sea,
> And light feels upward like a hand
> To find if yet creation be. . . .
>
> And sure at length that all is good,
> Upon the pavement of the deep
> Dawn walks with wings that burn abroad
> And lifted hands that seem to keep
> Attention till a word be said;
> And now day lifts above its head
> A harp that soon these hands will sweep.

The implicit parallel between this image and the subjective experience of awakening to love is hinted at rather subtly in the light imagery of the next five stanzas, until it becomes fully explicit in the metaphorical identification of the concluding stanza:

> O angel day, O seraph bright!
> As thou upon the mortal deep
> We o'er these coasts of deathless light,
> With lifted wings strong silence keep.
> Between the plumed and whispering fires
> We raise on high the golden lyres
> Which soon our burning hands shall smite!

In "A Prairie Ride," written in commemoration of a later experience of rapturous communion during a horseback ride with Harriet through the Midwestern countryside, conventional rhetoric is more fully subordinated to concrete imagery drawn from Moody's immediate environment, and the effect of emotional directness is consequently greater. Though Robinson probably had a point when he complained that the poem seems "an unfinished experience,"[7] there is still a clear overall coherence in its apparently improvised details. The following lines, for example, are typical not only of the almost onomatopoeical rhythms and of the animated visual imagery which characterize Moody's affectionate description of Harriet's horsemanship, but also of a metaphorical pattern which runs through the whole poem as Moody seeks to evoke a sense of identity between Harriet and nature itself:

> . . . within the rings our laughter made,
> Bending like a water-arum
> Where impetuous waters meet,
> Rhythmic to the strong alarum
> Of her horse's rushing feet,
> Before me and beside me and on before me swayed
> Her body like a water-arum blade,
> Like a slanted gull for motion,
> And the blown corn like an ocean
> For its billows and their rumor, and the tassels snapping free
> As whittled foam and brine-scud of the sea.

The significance of this pattern then comes full force in the poem's final image—a kind of Wordsworthian recollection-in-tranquillity whereby Harriet takes on virtually mythic qualities as a being somehow directly communicant with basic life forces:

> . . . often here, above the weary feet
> That pour along this fierce and jaded street,
> As from a taintless source
> Of power and grace,
> Anxious and shrill and sweet
> I hear her strong unblemished horse
> Neigh to the pastured mothers of the race.

Indeed, if we compare the image of Harriet which Moody presents in poems like "The Moon-Moth" and "A Prairie Ride" and in many of his letters, with more conventional images of the Romantic heroine—as, for instance, in his own earliest verse —we have a vivid illustration of Henry Adams' distinction between woman as "force" and woman as "sentiment."[8] There was certainly a strong element of "sentiment" in Moody's view of his future wife, but more prominent and significant was the element of "force"—the tendency to exalt her into a symbol of the essential procreative energy in nature and of the eternal female principle as such. We must remember that Harriet was some eleven years older than he, and evidently a woman of considerable strength, vitality, and independence; it is not surprising, then, that she came to be associated with that maternal ideal which Moody had previously associated with his dead mother's image in "Good Friday Night," "Jetsam," and "The

Daguerreotype." At the same time, it was obviously an ideal-ization of Harriet's actual role as his beloved and his spiritual mentor which underlay the role of Pandora in *The Fire-Bringer*. And Moody's heroic treatment of the title character in the nar-rative poem "The Death of Eve" and in the later play on the same subject, as well as his attempt to depict the quality of universal womanhood in the poem "I Am the Woman," are both inspired by this idealization.

IV *"I Am the Woman"*

Since the poem "The Death of Eve" treats the same general materials as those dramatized in the one completed act of the play, a consideration of its contents will be postponed until the next chapter. Suffice it to say now that, as narrative verse, the poem is a rather static and discontinuous performance; apart from a few good lyrical and descriptive passages scattered through the narrative, it is not nearly so fine a creation as the play which was, in a sense, to supersede it. Some of the poem's spirit and implied ideology can, however, be inferred from the contents of "I Am the Woman."

This semi-dramatic monologue has perhaps come in for more damnation from latter-day critics than any other single poem of Moody's: Gregory and Zaturenska, for example, cite it as a no-table illustration of the unwittingly "mock-heroic" quality they find in Moody's more ambitious verse;[9] and a more recent com-mentator passes it off as simply "one of Moody's worst poems."[10] But, though the language of the incessant dactyls does not al-ways produce the high epic effect which Moody clearly wanted to create through association with the classical dactylic hex-ameter, the poem does have real incantatory power and does contain some substantial ideas equal to its magniloquent rhetoric.

In one sense, the speaker seems a propagandist for turn-of-the-century feminist ideas, an eloquent rebel against age-old male domination and that traditionally sanctioned misogyny which lays on the head of woman all the trouble in the world. In another and more important sense, she is the female principle incarnate, embodying in her dual nature Moody's familiar rejec-tion of the flesh-spirit dichotomy and his equally familiar views regarding the inseparability of good and evil in the evolving human condition. The opening lines set forth these central themes with a rhythmic and verbal vigor whose effect is surely more "heroic" than "mock-heroic":

> I am the Woman, ark of the law and its breaker,
> Who chastened her step and taught her knees to be meek,
> Bridled and bitted her heart and humbled her cheek,
> Parceled her will, and cried, "Take more!" to the taker,
> Shunned what they told her to shun, sought what they bade
>   her seek,
> Locked up her mouth from scornful speaking: now it is
>   open to speak.
>
> I am she that is terribly fashioned, the creature
> Wrought in God's perilous mood, in His unsafe hour. . . .

Much of the poem is constructed around a series of paradoxes which elaborate the one in the first line: the speaker refers to herself as "the rapture . . . the shame, and the power"; as "harlot and heavenly wife"; or as the mother of the world's Cains and of the world's Abels, who can without discrimination "comfort and feed the slayer, feed and comfort the slain." Such paradoxes rise to their climax in the lines in which she identifies herself simultaneously with Eve and the Virgin Mary:

> I say to you I am the Mother; and under the sword
> Which flamed each way to harry us forth from the Lord,
> I saw Him young at the portal, weeping and staying the rod,
> And I, even I was His mother, and I yearned as the mother of God.

Being both the daughter of God and His mother, she is not only the bringer of mercy as well as suffering, good as well as evil, but is also the link which joins the Creator to His creation—and, therefore, a symbol of Moody's favorite theological premise: the interdependence of the natural and supernatural orders in their quest for self-realization. After an extended development of this theme, it is summarized in the closing lines, where the defiant tone which has characterized the speaker's language in the earlier stanzas suddenly gives way to one of almost weary supplication. The paradoxes are all recapitulated in four lines of effective antithesis, but now they introduce a rather lamely managed prayer for their final resolution:

> I am the Woman, ark of the Law and sacred arm to upbear it,
> Heathen trumpet to overthrow and idolatrous sword to shear it:
> Yea, she whose arm was round the neck of the morning star
>   at song,

Is she who kneeleth now in the dust and cries at the secret door,
"Open to me, O sleeping mother! The gate is heavy and strong.
Open to me, I am come at last; be wroth with thy child no more.
Let me lie down with thee there in the dark, and be slothful with
     thee as before!"

Robinson was right, as usual, when he called the word
"slothful" a "false note."[11] In fact, one can only regret the
preciousness and bathos of the entire last line (as well as what
seems an odd metrical lapse in the first half, which even an un-
naturally heavy stress on "with" does not quite repair). What
Moody evidently intended was to have the speaker envision
herself as the appropriate agent of that ultimate reconciliation
between man and his natural and divine origins which will end
all struggle and bring peace to the universe. But his phrasing
here does lapse into what might justly be called the "mock-
heroic," and its effect is subversive to the otherwise consistent
and convincing tone of the poem as a whole.

V "Old Pourquoi"

The motif of cosmic rebellion which figures so largely in
Moody's trilogy, and is clearly touched on by the speaker of
"I Am the Woman," recurs under a guise of comic narrative in
"Old Pourquoi"—a poem for whose subject matter he went all
the way back to the walking trip through Normandy which he
had taken with Mason during the summer of 1895. The incident
around which the narrative is built is summarized in Mason's
own diary under the date August 26, 1895: "Met on the open
road an old man dressed very meagrely, with slippers open at
the toes, ragged shirt, and bare head, who lifted his hands elo-
quently, and chanted to the empty landscape." Mason then re-
produces the tune of the chant as he took it down at the time,
and the single word which comprised its text: "Pourquoi?"[12]
For all we know, the chant might have been nothing more than
a snatch of a popular love song. But, as recollected some nine
years later, the aged solitary wanderer and his haunting voice
appealed to Moody's inveterate fondness for myth-making; and
"Old Pourquoi" became another of his *dramatis personae* who
symbolize the eternal questioning and questing spirit of man.

Moody had the good sense, however, to treat his materials in
a predominantly light manner—though, underneath that manner,

of course, elements remain of the grimmer cosmic satire drama-tized in *The Masque of Judgment*. Much of his humor consists in a partly nostalgic, partly disdainful reflection on his own past image as a young man. At the beginning, for example, after he has unpretentiously sketched the scene on the flat Norman plain near the sea just at nightfall, he pokes some good fun at the far more pretentious youth he had been nine years ago, and at the free-and-easy confidence with which he and the young Mason had been given to dispose of the eternal mysteries:

> All afternoon our minds had reveled
> In steep, skylarking enterprise;
> Our hearts had climbed a dozen skies,
> And fifty frowning strongholds leveled
> Of Life's old enemies.
>
> A trifle, here and there, was spared
> Till morning found us more adept;
> But, broadly speaking, we had swept
> Earth of her wrongs; light had been flared
> Where the last Error slept!

The last two lines ironically prepare the way for a sudden darkening of the atmosphere with the old man's appearance on the road, flinging his one word of challenge at all such com-placencies of thought and conscience, "As if some great dis-honoured dust/Came crying its ancestral wrong,/And found no listener just." Yet his weird chant seems to rebuke not only these complacencies, but also those universal forces which conspire to keep mankind itself ignorant and helpless; and the self-depre-cating whimsy of the previous stanzas now gives way to a fiercer kind of grotesque humor as the absurd figure of the aged Frenchman is associated with some "immortal jest" in which "satire was the cosmic mood." When the earlier kind of humor reappears, it has lost some of its light naturalness and has be-come strained and heavy-handed—particularly where Moody recollects his fury at what seemed mere musicologist's pedantry in Mason's insistence on copying out the old man's tune: " . . . your pencil flew/In quirk and quiddet vile"; ". . . in disgust I seized your hand,/And thundered, 'Scratching music, clod?' "[13]

But the real substance of the poem's concluding sections is not so much the image of Moody laughing at his earlier self, as that of him identifying his present self with "Old Pourquoi's" magnificent tragi-comic gesture of defiance. His chant becomes the poet's own vehicle for challenging current theologies and for restating his persistent theme of man's estrangement from the divine:

> Pourquoi? Pourquoi? Yes, that was all!
> Only the darkest cry that haunts
> The corridors of tragic chance,
> Couched in the sweet, satirical,
> Impudent tongue of France.
>
> Only the bitterest wail flung out
> From worlds that traffic to their mart
> Without a pilot or a chart;
> With "What?" the body of their doubt,
> And "Why?" the quaking heart.

And the poem concludes with another of Moody's recollections-in-tranquillity, in which both the surface absurdity and the deeper seriousness of the remembered event assume permanent significance for his imagination as a reminder of his own initiation into the rebellious spirit which animates his major writings:

> Old bard and brother to the Sphinx!
> I wonder what abysmal luck
> Had left your face so planet-struck,
> And driven you on such horrid brinks
> To play the run-amuck.
>
> I wonder down what road to-night
> You shuffle; from what plunging star
> Your gnarled old hands uplifted are,
> Between moth-light and cockshut-light,
> Calling young hearts to war!

VI   "Second Coming"

Probably the best-known of Moody's later poems is the one Manly chose as the title poem for the entire group—"Second Coming." Based on an incident from the 1902 trip through Greece, the poem is a longer and more complex companion-piece to the earlier "Good Friday Night." Its form—the spare quatrain made up of three tetrameters followed by a trimeter, which Moody had also used to good effect in Pandora's last song and, with the addition of an extra tetrameter, in "Old Pourquoi" —represents a variant on the form he had first hit upon as an appropriately simple vehicle for narrating his experience during the 1897 Easter procession at Sorrento. "Second Coming" begins, in fact, by recollecting that earlier experience; then it proceeds to describe a similar vision or hallucination which the now more mature and less impressionable poet had while visiting the island of Crete. Significantly enough, this second encounter occurs in a place rich with associations from ancient Greek myth, as well as with an almost intoxicating amalgam of present-day Eastern and Western, Moslem and Christian cultures. The first seven quatrains slowly build up these contrasting qualities in the atmosphere; and the sense of mysterious incongruity in the descriptive details prepares us for the lack of surprise and even for the feeling of inevitability with which the poet greets the appearance of a figure he takes to be Christ:

> . . . Seraglio windows, doors that reek
> Sick perfume of the mass;
>
> The muezzin cry from Allah's tower,
> French sailors singing in the street;
> . . . .
> Yonder on snowy Ida, Zeus
> Was cradled; through those mountain haunts
> The new moon hurried, letting loose
> The raving Corybants,
>
> Who after thrid the Cyclades
> To Thebes of Cadmos, with the slim
> Wild god for whom Euripides
> Fashioned the deathless hymn. . . .
>
> —'T is strange! No wonder and no dread
> Was on me; hardly even surprise.
> I knew before he raised his head
> Or fixed me with his eyes
>
> That it was he; . . .

The encounter lasts for only an instant, after which the poet, in "sweat and shuddering of the mind," stumbles away and finally comes to rest at a picturesque spot on the shore, where he attempts to take stock of himself. After an hour in which "all my being.../Has sat in stupor without thought,/Empty of memory, love, or power," his personality reasserts itself; and, as it does, the sense of paralyzed awe is immediately replaced by a characteristic "ghostly protest":

> "Yea, it is I, 't is I indeed!
> But who art thou, and plannest what?
> Beyond all use, beyond all need!
> Importunate, unbesought,
>
> Unwelcome, unendurable! . . ."

A comparable rejection of Christ had also been Moody's initial attitude in "Good Friday Night"; but there, it will be remembered, this quickly gave way to feelings of remorse when he recognized the stranger for what he seemed to be. Now, however, Moody recalls those feelings only to deny their pertinence to his present situation:

> "To the vague boy I was before—
> O unto him thou camest well;
> But now, a boy no more,
>
> Firm-seated in my proper good,
> Clear-operant in my functions due,
> Potent and plenteous of my mood,—
> What hast thou here to do?"

His protest then takes a form already familiar to the reader of the *Masque* or of *The Fire-Bringer*: against the historical image of the humble and ascetic Christ, Moody sets an antithetical image, drawn from the earlier stanzas, of the sensual and life-giving Dionysus (the god for whom "Euripides/Fashioned the dealthless hymn" in *The Bacchae*); and he insists that Dionysus' claim to his personal allegiance and general relevance to the situation of modern man is as great as, if not greater than, that of the Christian ethos which once triumphed over him:

> "Yeς, I have loved thee—love thee, yes;
> But also—hear'st thou?—also him
> Who out of Ida's wilderness
> Over the bright sea-rim,
>
> With shaken cones and mystic dance,
> To Dirce and her seven waters
> Led on the raving Corybants, . . ."

Thereupon, as the poet's immediate view of the Mediterranean becomes imaginatively extended out through the Straits of Gibraltar and across the Atlantic to America itself, he invokes the decadent Christianity of his own native land as evidence of the spiritual bankruptcy which the original Christian vision has suffered: today's descendants of the once mightily devout Puritans may "spend for thee nor count the cost;/But follow thee? Ah, no!" Finally, Moody summarizes the grounds of his protest with a flat declaration which reminds one of Henry Adams' contemporary lament over what he termed "the stupendous failure of Christianity":[14]

> "Thine image gently fades from earth!
> Thy churches are as empty shells,
> Dim-plaining of thy words and worth,
> And of thy funerals! . . ."

Moody's address to the figure he has identified with Christ concludes, however, on a rather different note. Though the sudden and quite effective turn in the last stanza stops well short of the spiritual reversal in "Good Friday Night," it does give to "Second Coming" some of the same open-endedness and sense that there may be more to the situation described than has been or can be stated. If the preceding stanza recalls Adams, this stanza recalls Yeats's Magi, who, "Being by Calvary's turbulence unsatisfied," still look ahead with a certain hopefulness, however tentative and ambiguous, to the possibility of a new vision, a new dispensation, which may yet arise out of the demise of the original Christian one:[15]

> "But oh, upon what errand, then,
> Leanest thou at the sailor's ear?
> Hast thou yet more to say, that men
> Have heard not, and must hear?"

The poem's title, then, may be interpreted as a triple pun: it refers, first, to the "second coming" of the vision or hallucination which Moody himself had experienced five years earlier at Sorrento; second, to the intimation of an actual "second coming" in Christ's apparent presence on the shores of Crete in 1902; and third, to the concluding hint of some future revelation whereby the present Christian one, as well as that embodied in the Dionysian mysteries, may be transcended.

Just what form this revelation might have taken in Moody's imagination can only be inferred from his general religious position in the *Masque* and *The Fire-Bringer*—where, it will be remembered, neither historical Christianity nor the exclusive worship of the Dionysian principle had represented a satisfactory resource; though, as in "Second Coming," the latter had turned out rather better than the former. In "Second Coming" the dominant note is still the rejection of what Moody considered the essentially negative and spiritually enfeebled Christianity in which he had been raised, and to which not even the thought of its founder's return to earth can draw his present allegiance. As for the prophetic intimation at the end, it, too, is purposefully couched—like that which concludes Yeats's famous later poem of the same name—in the form of a question rather than an assertion.

Yet our final sense of the poem's meaning is, as in the case of "Good Friday Night," largely dependent on the question of just how literally Moody took and wanted us to take his identification of the "leaning figure by the boat" with Christ. Lovett, who categorically accepts the vision described in both poems as literal, remarks: "No one who knew Moody can doubt that these were real experiences."[16] On the other hand, when Moody himself was later asked to supply additional descriptive materials for a proposed illustration to "Second Coming," his account seemed to suggest something less than absolute credence in the literal identification:"... the person ... was curiously spiritual in feature, slightly bearded, bare-headed, dressed in the long flowing gown of the Greek priesthood, rusty black in tone. He looked like an Armenian."[17] Moreover, it might well be argued that, had he undergone a real confrontation with a resurrected Christ, Moody's subsequent reflections would seem at best supercilious. Of course, we must allow for the fact that the poem itself was written more than two years after the event it describes; and, whatever may have been the nature of his original response, it is clear that Moody's reflections on the experience emerged from his normal personality and his normal philosophical attitudes as they became re-established with the passing of time. Nevertheless, one cannot help feeling that the poem is substantially weakened by Moody's equivocal handling of the experience itself, and by the lack of congruity between the poem's experiential and ideological contents.

VII *"The Fountain"*

In the dramatic monologue "The Fountain," Moody takes up the Spanish legend of the quest for the Fountain of Eternal Youth and makes it over into an ambiguous but often imaginatively vivid allegory of modern man's quest for spiritual rebirth.

Like the earlier poem "Until the Troubling of the Waters," this one is written in a fairly spare and straightforward blank verse, though its verbal texture gains density in the climactic moments and in the four rhymed lyrics which Moody weaves into the monologue-proper. The speaker is an aged member of a once large and joyfully confident exploring party which, after years of fruitless search and heartbreaking pursuit of false leads, has become a mere "handful, heroes of a dwindling hope." His words are ostensibly addressed to his despairing companions in an attempt to urge them forward on their quest for the miraculous fountain even though the goal of the quest has come to seem more and more of an illusion. Actually, however, the poem has—like "Until the Troubling of the Waters"—less the quality of a true dramatic monologue than of an internal meditation set in an outward dramatic situation. Most of what the speaker says amounts to little more than a retrospective account of events with which his listeners are well acquainted; and, except in his final peroration, he seems to be talking much more to himself than to those listeners. Moody's real concern, obviously enough, is with the allegorical applications of the speaker's thoughts; for the most part, he seems indifferent to problems of literal credibility or of surface dramatic effectiveness.[18]

The desert setting clearly symbolizes the modern spiritual waste-land depicted in *The Fire-Bringer*—beset with mirages, with perfidious or well-meaning but misleading guides, yet also with elusive intimations of some eventual rebirth. These intimations are centered in the four enigmatic lyrics which the speaker has heard sung by persons who appeared to have found the miraculous fountain and to have gained eternal youth from its waters. Though in the case of all but the last, the places where the singers claimed to have undergone their rejuvenation turned out to have lost their miraculous powers, the words of their songs still haunt the speaker as a source of hope. But the purely tentative and generalized nature of that hope is suggested both by the fact that all previous guidance has proved unavailing and by the pointed admonition of the last singer—the only one who had refused to try leading the speaker and his companions to the waters from which he himself had drunk:

> "Not with searching, not with strife,
> Not by traveler's true reporting,
> Nor by signs of old importing,

Win ye to the Fount of Life.

. . . .

For ere with striving you are come
The fountain's singing heart is dumb,
Faded its spell; . . .

At the end of the poem, then, it is the sentiment and phrasing of this fourth lyric which becomes the text for the speaker's concluding exhortation to his fellow wanderers:

> Though order and the comeliness of truth
> No more reign constant in the spirit's house,
> Though far and near shift places, and our sleep
> Tangles itself with what we are awake,
> Yet, O worn brothers, much-enduring men,
> Without search, without striving, go we on,
> For I am told at heart that we shall find! . . .
> Perhaps within the pictured water-jars
> They [the natives] fill and place for us along our path;
> Perhaps in stooping where the wild and tame
> Fight for the thread of moisture in the rocks;
> Perhaps as ghosts beside the ghostly lakes
> Which noonday paints upon the distant sand;
> Perhaps far sunken by a canyon pool,
> Under the soft rein of a cataract
> Which leaps and scatters down the walls of Death.

Both passages appear to strike a rather un-Moodyan note of quietism, suggesting as they do an appeal to passive faith, rather than his more usual appeal to the spirit of struggle and rebellion, as the means toward spiritual illumination and rebirth. This note is also sounded in the reflections with which the speaker introduces his exhortation, where he marvels at the inexplicable friendliness of the desert natives who have lately been supplying the wanderers with food and other less tangible moral assistance—symbolic, evidently, of the gratuitous benefits bestowed on those who merely persist in faith and hope, without specific striving for a specific goal. The same sentiment had, in fact, been expressed indirectly but with a special eloquence as early as the third lyric—a "bright, disturbing song" sung by a rejuvenated woman, and very like one of Pandora's lyrics in form and style, though its content seems to move from something reminiscent of Pandora to something purposefully antithetical to the spirit she represented:

> "*I saw a thousand gates unclose,*
> *A risen woman in each gate;*
> *Each woman cried, 'For thee I rose:*
> *Waitest thou? I can wait!'*
>
> "*I scared the stars above the sun,*
> *I shook the old roots of the sea,*
> *The anchored continents did shun*
> *My importunity.*
>
> "*I cried, 'I will not suffer death,*
> *Nor shameful age, the death in life!*
> *What from our love God hidden hath*
> *Be wrung from Him with strife!'*
>
> "*In faintness once again I lay,*
> *And saw those gates unclose about me,*
> *I heard the thousand women say*
> *'How long, then wilt thou doubt me?*
>
> " '*For thee, I rose, for thee I wait*
> *Who am thyself, long, long uprisen;*
> *Come to the Fountain; it is late;*
> *And darker grows thy prison!'*
>
> "*All mutinous thoughts away I flung,*
> *And I, a risen woman, trod*
> *Those liberties where gushed and sung*
> *The living wells of God.*"

It is difficult to know what to make of such an apparent rejection of those "mutinous thoughts" which figure so largely in Moody's moral outlook elsewhere—nor can we explain it away by citing the fact that the singer of this lyric had been the mate of one of those who proved a false guide; for her "message" is substantially the same as that contained in the fourth singer's song. In the final analysis, however, the note of quietism, strange though it is, is really secondary to another and much more characteristic theme which seems to be the central point of the poem as a whole.

The key to this theme may be found in the fourth singer's lines "*Not by traveler's true reporting,/Nor by signs of old importing,/Win ye to the Fount of Life.*" "Traveler's true reporting" and "signs of old importing" might best be translated as convention, creed, dogma—any doctrine imposed from the outside rather than growing out of the individual's unique relation to himself and to the universe. If so, the main allegorical meaning of all the failures which the speaker and his companions have previously endured is manifest: though the fountains to which they had been guided may have proved true sources of rejuvenation for their guides, those same fountains had had no miraculous powers for them simply because what brings spiritual rebirth to some may not bring it to others. Hence the fourth speaker's refusal to specify the fountain from which he had drunk symbolizes his wisdom in seeing that the way to salvation cannot be prescribed and that the most he could do was to inspire the wanderers with his song into finding their own way, through faith and hope, toward their own proper fountain. This, then, may be the real gist of the speaker's final peroration—that "search" and "striving" after a goal defined by others and limited to the significance it has had for others can never bring one to his own self-realization. If the poem's other moral implications seem hazy and oddly inconsistent with Moody's normal views, this implication is quite clear and fully in keeping with that pronounced individualism and rejection of doctrinaire theology which he had inherited in part from the American Transcendentalist tradition.

VIII *"Thammuz"*

Moody's purely lyrical treatment of the same theme of rebirth in the short poem "Thammuz"—whose subject and manner bear close affinities to central passages in *The Masque of Judgment* and *The Fire-Bringer*—is one of his most memorable creations outside the drama. It is worth quoting in its entirety:

> Daughters, daughters, do ye grieve?
> Crimson dark the freshes flow!
> Were ye violent at eve?
> Crimson stains where the rushes grow!
> What is this that I must know?
>
> Mourners by the dark red waters,
> Met ye Thammuz at his play?
> Was your mood upon you, daughters?
> Had ye drunken? O how grey
> Looks your hair in the rising day!
>
> Mourners, mourn not overmuch
> That ye slew your lovely one.

Such ye are; and be ye such!
Lift your heads; the waters run
Ruby bright in the climbing sun.

Raven hair and hair of gold,
Look who bendeth over you!
This is not the shepherd old;
This is Thammuz, whom ye slew,
Radiant Thammuz, risen anew!

As one early critic recognized, Moody is actually dealing here
with a composite myth of his own making.[19] He merges the
Phoenician fertility god Thammuz (or Adonis), who was killed
by a wild boar and came back to life every spring, with the
Greek Orpheus and Pentheus, both of whom were torn to pieces
by a group of frenzied Bacchantes, the first for shunning their
revels and the second for refusing to acknowledge the godhead
of Dionysus. The merger is, of course, purposeful; for Moody
knew enough mythology and anthropology to recognize in all
three myth-complexes—those involving Thammuz, Orpheus, and
Dionysus—mutually reinforcing elements of the death-and-resur-
rection theme he set out to treat in this lyric.

Much of the poem's effectiveness derives from its supple
sound pattern and delicate nuances of tone, as well as from
economy created by the omission of superfluous connectives.
It is, in fact, structurally and verbally one of the tightest pieces
of verse in Moody's work. Even his handling of the meter enhances the perfectly symmetrical balance between the first and
second stanzas and the third and fourth. For example, the line
"Crimson stains where the rushes grow" introduces an anapestic
lilt into the regular trochaic pattern as it describes the pollution
of the River Adonis by the dead god's blood; and this is exactly
paralleled in the later line which describes the transformation of
the blood into a sacramental image: "Ruby bright in the climbing sun." Just as quietly skillful is the way Moody turns the
Bacchantes' hair from "grey" to "raven" and "gold" at the moment their remorse is lifted and they become reborn with their
recognition of the risen god; or the way he withholds all indication of the speaker's identity until it can coincide with that
recognition. Then we ourselves share the shock of the Bacchantes'
abrupt realization that it is the god himself who has been speaking so tenderly to his own slayers and forgiving them for obeying
their own natures: "Such ye are; and be ye such."

Above all, unlike most of Moody's poetry, "Thammuz" achieves its effects totally without discursive commentary; all the work is accomplished by simple juxtaposition of images, rhythms, and tones. In managing this technique, Moody may be said to have shown himself ready to participate in the Imagist revolution which began soon after his death. Yet his own characteristic strengths, as we have seen, lay elsewhere—not in the impersonal precision of sensory detail which vivifies external realities for their own sake; but in that intellectual and emotional pressure from within which works to transmute those realities into symbol. Even "Thammuz," for all its seeming objectivity, is essentially a metaphorical statement of an unstated but palpable philosophical idea; and it was perhaps such a refusal to accept the phenomenal world as self-sufficing, more than his technical conservatism, which later prompted the most militant of the Imagists, Amy Lowell, to remark, "I wonder if he [Moody] could have kept us back."[20] His readiness to comprehend the aims of the Imagists, and his capacity for using some of their chief techniques, would probably never have meant a willingness to constrict his own talent and vision within the limitations of those aims and techniques.

CHAPTER 8

Cosmic Reconciliation, in Prose and Verse

I *Competing Allegiances*

DURING THE LAST two-and-a-half years of Moody's active career—from the autumn of 1906 to the spring of 1909 —his creative allegiances were caught in a conflict between the attractions of the commercial theater and a desire to continue his work in the verse drama and specifically to bring his trilogy to completion. Even while *The Great Divide* was enjoying its triumphant New York run, he continued to assert his belief that "Poetry is the salvation of the stage"[1] and to cast about for materials suitable to a new dramatic endeavor which would exemplify that belief. In fact, the idea for such a drama, based on the same general subject he had treated in the narrative poem "The Death of Eve," had already begun taking shape in his mind during the summer of 1906, while he was still hard at work revising *The Great Divide* for its New York production.[2] He seems to have made some start toward writing the play that autumn;[3] but the idea did not really crystallize until the following spring, when he suddenly recognized in it the potentiality for a full-scale resolution of the themes explored in the *Masque* and *The Fire-Bringer*. A letter to Harriet dated May 1, 1907—written from Florence during a trip which Moody was taking through Italy with Ridgely Torrence—reveals some of the understandable excitement he must have felt at having thus hit upon a way of finishing off his trilogy:

> . . . as I was walking along the street thinking of nothing but the good feel of the sun and the good taste of the air, suddenly something clicked inside my head, a kaleidoscopic down-rush and up-thrust and over-tumble of broken pictures and half-thoughts passed before my mind, whirled a minute, settled into place, and behold! there was the third part of my

trilogy. . . . It is the *Eve* play, combined with a continuation
and culmination of the 'Judgment' theme as it is left at the
end of the *Masque*. This element of the poem must lock the
whole—I mean all three parts—together, but it will be brief, for
I feel that the subject is one which won't stand extended
handling. Also, your conviction that the theme of the third part
must lie in the words of the Apocalypse, 'The old earth has
passed away, and a new earth, etc.' finds a place in my present
conception; . . .[4]

From June to September of that year, Moody was settled in
Chicago and on Mackinac Island; and, though the absence of
any letters from those months leaves his activities uncertain,
it is probable that, by the time he went to New York in mid-
September, he had written most if not all of the one act of *The
Death of Eve* which has come down to us. In the meantime,
however, he had begun early the same year to try recasting the
old prose play about the faith-healer Schlatter, which he had
completed in 1900, into a new form capable of being produced
on the commercial stage. Once he was back in New York—
where the success of *The Great Divide* had given him a considerable reputation in the commercial theater and had created
a demand for more plays by the same author—he set aside
the verse drama in order to try finishing the new version of *The
Faith Healer* in time for a projected production the following
autumn.

At the time, Moody hopefully remarked that "with this long-
delayed task out of the way I can go at the *Eve* with a more
single mind";[5] but the fact that none of his many letters from
September, 1907, on makes any mention of his working at *The
Death of Eve* would indicate that his hopes for eventually turning his full attention back to that play were frustrated by his
labors on *The Faith Healer*. Those uncommonly arduous labors
occupied Moody right up to March, 1909, when this second
version, in four acts, was given a one-week tryout run in St.
Louis. The St. Louis production, however, did not satisfy the
audience, the majority of the reviewers, nor the author.[6] Once
again—though his health was already seriously weakened by
previous overwork, an attack of typhoid fever he had suffered
the year before, and the first manifestations of the brain tumor
which was to prove fatal a year-and-a-half later—Moody applied himself to rewriting the play, finishing the third version
"after six or seven weeks of very strenuous labor."[7] This three-

act version is the one which Henry Miller produced on Broadway in January, 1910, and which became the standard text of *The Faith Healer* when it was published by Macmillan later that year.[8]

II The Faith Healer

That Moody's commitments to the commercial theater, then his protracted illness, and finally his death prevented him from the completion of the trilogy, the ambition closest to his heart, is a matter for genuine regret—all the more so because the play which did occupy so much of his time and diminishing energy during his last years was a theatrical, and in some ways a literary, failure. The New York production of *The Faith Healer* fared no better, and perhaps a bit worse, than the St. Louis one;[9] and, though a few subsequent commentators have praised the play rather generously and even rated it above *The Great Divide* as a work of art, most of Moody's later critics have justly agreed with the judgments of his first reviewers.[10]

It is true enough that in secondary elements, *The Faith Healer* shows a decided advance over the earlier play. Moody's realistic portrayal of his social milieu, a turn-of-the-century Midwestern farm community stirred to an intense religious revival by the coming of a messiah-like faith-healer, is surely the finest thing about the play. And among the supporting cast are several characters—particularly semi-humorous "local color" types like Matthew Beeler (in whose home all the action is set) and the old Negro Abe—who emerge as more richly conceived and memorable creations than any of the subsidiary characters in *The Great Divide*. But, when it came to handling his central protagonists and the central thematic design of the play, Moody succumbed before a challenge which very few dramatists can be imagined as meeting successfully in the medium of prose realism.

Unlike the plot of *The Great Divide,* that of *The Faith Healer* has no direct source in fact, since those reports about Schlatter himself which Moody had read in newspapers in 1895 figure only in the remote background of the events actually dramatized on the stage. The closest thing to a literary source was probably Bayard Taylor's *The Prophet* (1875)—an undistinguished five-act, blank-verse closet drama based on the career of the Mormon leader Joseph Smith, which was noted in Chapter Two as a possible source for at least one line in "Until the Troubling of the Waters," and may well have exerted a strong influence on Moody's first effort at writing the play in blank-verse.[11] But by the time he wrote the final version of *The Faith Healer*, this influence had faded to the point where all the two dramas really have in common is the fact that both deal with an American prophet-messiah figure, that both concern themselves in some measure with the phenomenon of faith-healing (though in *The Prophet* this is a very minor motif), and that Moody's heroine Rhoda has the same name as the protagonist's wife in Taylor's work.

On the other hand, both the next-to-last and the last versions of Moody's play do owe something of importance to a book which, though it can hardly be called a source for the dramatic structure and events as such, did affect his view of basic psychological and theological questions as they bore on his handling of the central character. On January 8, 1907, just as he was taking up the play again for the first time in over six years, Moody wrote to Harriet:

> I am re-reading Wm. James's wonderful book, *Varieties of Religious Experience*, with a view to better understanding my man Schlatka.[12] Do you know the book? The main text might not interest you, but you would be carried away by the 'documents' cited in illustration. These are numerous and amazing; and they range over all history. Already I feel a sounder grip on my theme from studying them. James's treatment is masterly. He gives the cynics and the skeptics all they ask, and then proceeds quietly to spread out the documents—chiefly autobiographical, until the mind gradually loses its resistance, and is overwhelmed and confounded by the heaped-up evidence. Not that James has a thesis to prove; he merely investigates and compares, but the conviction which emerges, that there is a living divine spirit at work in the world, by excluding which we are lessened and by receiving increased, seems at last inescapable.[13]

The "theme" on which Moody felt he was gaining a "sounder grip" as he read William James's book was presumably one that had also been central to his earlier conception—the triumph of religious faith over modern scientific naturalism and skepticism. But we may speculate that his conception of the faith-healer himself, as an embodiment of that theme, underwent some further development in the light of James's persuasive documents. In fact, the account which Ulrich Michaelis gives the

heroine of his earlier life, the mystical vision in which his special "calling" was revealed, and his subsequent experiences of
growing power to perform miraculous cures and to bring spiritual enlightenment to others, might be considered Moody's
imaginative contribution to the autobiographical "case histories"
by which James had sought to establish the validity of supernatural psychic experience.[14] The specific phenomenon of the
Christian Science movement was, of course, wholly incidental
to Moody's interest.[15] What he was out to defend was not any
particular theological or ecclesiastical system but simply that
"conviction of a living divine spirit at work in the world" for
which he found a close-to-home dramatic symbol in the contemporary American faith-healer.

At the same time, Moody also tried, like James, to "give the
cynics and the skeptics all they ask" by creating a number of
secondary characters—especially Beeler and the young doctor
George Littlefield—who are quite eloquent in challenging
Michaelis' vision of himself and his mission and who represent,
at various levels of learning and sophistication, the modern
scientific spirit. Until near the very end, Moody makes all due
concessions to the view, most fully expressed by Littlefield, that
there is a purely naturalistic explanation for all Michaelis' healing activities; and, even at the end, he does not try so much to
deny those explanations as to show how nature itself may become spiritualized through active faith and a superior type of
human love.

For, along with the faith-versus-skepticism theme, the play
also has a love theme; indeed, the central plot-element is a
conflict, ultimately resolved, between Michaelis' consecration to
an exalted religious mission, and the claims of the flesh and of
normal humanity represented by his love for the play's heroine
Rhoda Williams. Such a conflict had evidently been part of
Moody's design from the time he first conceived the idea for
The Faith Healer. Henry reports Harriet as recalling that, in
Moody's original plan, the hero was to end up by renouncing his
love in order to remove all impediments to the pursuit of his calling; and that later—perhaps in the first completed version—Moody
reversed this and had the hero renounce his calling in order to
marry the heroine.[16] But by 1907 Moody had come to see his
materials in a new light; he had recognized in them a choice
opportunity for expressing one of his favorite ideas—that rejection of metaphysical and moral dualism which had been so

central to the ideology of his trilogy and had perhaps been most succinctly expressed in the concluding stanza of "Song-Flower and Poppy":

> How long, old builder Time, wilt bide
> Till at thy thrilling word
> Life's crimson pride shall have to bride
> The spirit's white accord, . . .

Hence, with his habitual fondness for reconciling contraries by way of symbolizing the ultimate unity of all being, Moody decided to recast his materials so that the hero could win the heroine and also retain his miraculous powers and sense of religious consecration; in fact, he decided to make one dependent on the other. In Act One—which takes place the morning of the day before Easter—though Michaelis has already demonstrated his continuing powers by curing Beeler's long-invalided wife Mary, he is suffering from deep feelings of guilt over his growing desire for their twenty-year-old niece Rhoda; and he fears that this betrayal of his ascetic role has incapacitated him for further pursuit of his mission. By the end of Act Two— which takes place that afternoon—he appears to have lost his healing powers altogether: Mary Beeler has suffered a relapse; a sick child brought to Michaelis by a desperate young woman from town—clearly the same woman who had been the speaker in "Until the Troubling of the Waters"—has failed to respond to his ministrations; and the hero's guilt has intensified into a total despair and conviction that he has been rejected as God's servant on earth. He has therefore resolved to give up his religious mission and surrender to his passion and common human needs by running off with Rhoda. But in the climactic scene of Act Three—which, pointedly enough, takes place early Easter morning—Moody has Michaelis recover his powers and rise out of his despair into a higher faith than he has heretofore known. He does so because Rhoda has at last revealed the truth about her own sinful and unhappy past; and, in seeing how her love for him has since purified her moral being, Michaelis realizes that his own love, rather than negating his mission, derives from the same divine origin as that mission itself.

But, as every hostile critic of *The Faith Healer* has recognized, Moody's dramatization of his reconciliation motif is neither dramatically nor psychologically convincing. To at least one

critic, Hermann Hagedorn, the play was doomed from the start
by the very thesis Moody set out to demonstrate:

> Michaelis serves two masters, passion and the healing Christ.
> He comes to grief, and no statement on the part of the dramatist
> that Michaelis's healing power is restored because the woman he
> loves is herself in dire spiritual need can persuade us that it is so.
> No man can pursue a human passion and at the same time
> successfully cleanse the multitude with the pure fire of his faith.
> The play is psychologically wrong.[17]

There is probably some truth to this argument; yet, even if
there were not—even if we are ready to accept the abstract
validity of Moody's thesis—the fact is that as a dramatist he
fails to make that thesis concretely persuasive. Neither Michaelis nor Rhoda emerges as a plausible psychological creation:
throughout the play their mutual passion is something we are
told about rather than made to feel with immediacy; and, when
it is suddenly converted from a source of guilt to a source of
miraculous regeneration, we are left with a sense that Moody
has imposed an abstract idea on a realistic situation to which it
simply does not apply. In the same way, Rhoda's revelation
about the evil in her past life seems almost an afterthought designed to combine the theme of the unity of flesh and spirit
with that other familiar Moodyan theme: the necessity for evil
as a spur to full realization of the good. Her past sin remains
about as abstract as Michaelis' present passion; and Moody does
not help matters by trying to concretize that sin in the person
of Doctor Littlefield—who by a convenient coincidence turns
out to be not only the dogmatic young Positivist called in to
minister to the sick after Michaelis has temporarily lost his
powers, but also Rhoda's original seducer during her earlier
life in St. Louis.

Probably the weakest scene in the play is the climactic one
midway through Act Three in which Littlefield is depicted as a
kind of mustache-twirling villain of a nineteenth-century popular melodrama, from whose evil overtures the hero saves the
heroine by the force of his own now exalted love. In fact,
through the whole of Act Three, the religious and psychological
issues—which have been explored with honest complexity during passages in the preceding acts—become increasingly sche-
matized and sentimentalized. The saintly man of feeling, em-

bodying absolute good, triumphs over the coldly intellectual and sexually perverted man of science, embodying absolute evil; and the play concludes with a large offstage choir singing *"a great hymn, of martial and joyous rhythm"* in celebration of that triumph and of the implied cosmic reconciliation in Michaelis' recovery of his miraculous gift through a love which has made the flesh itself divine.

III   *The Failure of Language*

Perhaps, in all fairness, we should not blame Moody for thus using a device which has since become the stock-in-trade of the Hollywood "religious epic." But there is significance in the fact that he does fall back, at the high moment of the drama, on a purely mechanical sound-effect aimed at eliciting an easy emotional response from his audience. Considering the materials with which he was dealing, it is understandable that he would have sought some means of transcending his realistic medium in order to arouse feelings of exaltation equal to his supernatural, and supra-rational, theme. Indeed, however successfully he may have used the realistic medium in *The Great Divide* and in his handling of the subordinate characters throughout *The Faith Healer* (especially the excellent dialect of Beeler and Uncle Abe), it is evident that Moody suffered under its limitations when it came to dramatizing those special states of soul which were his real concern in the case of Michaelis and Rhoda. His hero and heroine lack credibility chiefly because we are obliged to see them from the outside, through what they do and what they say in the language of normal human speech—what one person might literally say to another in an actual life-situation. Committed to that language as the norm for his dialogue, Moody was thus deprived of those verbal resources which Harley Granville-Barker has ably described as necessary for the exploration of character at levels deeper than those available to the prose realist:

We need a language . . . capable of expressing thought and emotion combined, and, at times, emotion almost divorced from thought. It is plain that a merely rational vocabulary and syntax will not suffice. But the poet knows how to work on his hearers by subtler ways; openly by the melody and rhythm of words, more powerfully by suggestion, association, by stimulating our imagination. He appeals, past reason, past consciousness often, to our entire sentient being. His are the means, then, by which we can best be persuaded, for the time, that these characters in a play are, soul and body, living creatures like ourselves.[18]

Whether or not this idea is universally applicable, it certainly applies to *The Faith Healer*. To bring characters like Michaelis and Rhoda really alive, Moody needed a form of expression in which spiritual states incommunicable at the level of realistic prose discourse could have been evoked. He needed melody, measured rhythm, metaphor, verbal suggestion and association, as constant rather than merely sporadic elements in the texture of the dialogue; in short, he needed poetry. But he settled instead for devices like the grand offstage choir and the occasional "purple" passages—chiefly in Michaelis' speeches—which have neither the virtues of good realistic prose nor those of true verse. For example, here are excerpts from two speeches in the Second Act, where Michaelis is trying to overcome his mounting despair by giving in to his guilty desire, and is beseeching Rhoda to do the same:

> Out there, at this moment, in city and country, souls, thousands upon thousands of souls, are dashing in pieces the cup that holds the wine of heaven, the wine of God's shed blood, and lifting the cups of passion and of love, that crown the feasting table of the children of this earth! Look! The very sky is blood-red with the lifted cups. And we two are in the midst of them. Listen what I sing there, on the hills of light in the sunset: "Oh, how beautiful upon the mountains are the feet of my beloved!" . . .

> All my life long I have known you, and fled from you. I have heard you singing on the hills of sleep and have fled from you into the waking day. I have seen you in the spring forest, dancing and throwing your webs of sunlight to snare me; on moonlit mountains, laughing and calling; in the streets of crowded cities, beckoning and disappearing in the crowd—. . . .

Failing as they do to cohere in some overall structural and rhythmic pattern, speeches like these simply stand out as incongruous exceptions to the prevailing idiom of the dialogue. And this incongruity will almost certainly—unless Michaelis is played by an extraordinarily gifted actor—prove embarrassing in any stage production of the drama.

In the final analysis, then, the most basic failure of *The Faith Healer* is one of language. Conversely, the language of the verse drama which Moody never got to finish because of his labors on his prose drama is its strongest asset. Despite its comparative brevity, the one surviving act of *The Death of Eve* stands as an open-ended but esthetically rounded creation; and, in many ways, the act is Moody's finest achievement. Published under the subtitle "A Fragment" in the 1912 *Poems and Plays*, it was scheduled for stage production by the New York Poetry Society in 1924; but, as in the case of the projected Chicago production of *The Fire-Bringer*, this never came off.[19] Since then, there have apparently been no attempts to put *The Death of Eve* on the stage. Yet, even more than *The Fire-Bringer*, it is an eminently stageworthy play; and in 1941 Alfred Kreymborg, while somewhat indiscriminately lumping together the first two members of Moody's trilogy as works "inconceivable" in the theater, did choose the third member for his far-ranging *Anthology of Plays in Verse from the Ancient Greek to the Modern American* as "a complete drama in itself" and as one meriting inclusion among an international selection of plays tried and tested in the practical theater.[20]

IV The Death of Eve

At the ideological heart of Moody's design for *The Death of Eve* was the same moral thesis which he tried to work into the Rhoda-Michaelis relation, and which had been central to the ideology of the *Masque, The Fire-Bringer, The Great Divide*, and poems like "The Brute," "I Am the Woman," and the narrative poem on which the play was based—that evil, as a manifestation of an imperfect but evolving universe, springs from the same essential creative source as good; and it provides the condition of strife necessary for the good to transcend its present limited state in the general cosmic progress toward perfection.

This thesis receives perhaps its most concentrated expression in Moody's work through the character of Eve, the original bringer of evil into the world, who now becomes, in her old age, the embodiment of that higher good which evolves out of man's struggle with evil. Like Raphael and Prometheus before her, Eve is depicted as a type of the Romantic rebel; and, as with those earlier Moody heroes, what she is rebelling against is that imperfect God whose image is associated with negative prohibitions which reflect his alienation from humanity. At the same time, she is depicted as having undergone a long period of purgative suffering which has prepared her to envision another God beyond that image—one who has himself evolved to a higher state of perfection in the course of her own suffering. Under the influence of such a vision, she has determined to disobey the earlier God's edict against re-entering the Garden of Eden, from which she and Adam had long ago been expelled, in order to effect a final reconciliation between herself, as representative of the human race, and this greater God whose moral development has paralleled hers. In that reconciliation would be established a true convenant between God and man, and all life would be transformed according to the prophecy in the *Apocalypse* which Moody and Harriet agreed should form the theme of the concluding member of the trilogy.[21]

Though Moody did not live to realize all of this design, the play's one completed act contains the whole of it in germinal form. The plot of the act represents an elaborate expansion, with some important changes, of a brief passage in the earlier narrative poem. There, Moody had rather sketchily described how the aged Eve, having dreamed of being reconciled with God before her death, makes her way back into Eden where she sings an exultant song expressing both her defiance cf the original prohibition and her longing for reconciliation; and where she finally dies a peaceful death in which Moody faintly suggests some sort of transfiguration. On her journey to Eden she is accompanied by her eldest son Cain, whom she visited after many years of estrangement following his exile for killing Abel, and whose crime she took on herself with the symbolic act of kissing the sign which God had set in his forehead as a permanent memento of that crime.[22] All action prior to the scene in Eden is narrated in short flashbacks, one of which describes Eve's solitary arrival at and subsequent sojourn in the city of Nod, where Cain has lived out his long exile as king of a savage desert people. This flashback is the passage on which the first act of the play is based:

> She gave her message darkly in the gates,
> And waited trembling. At day-fall he came.
> She knew him not beneath his whitened hair;
> But when at length she knew him, and was known,
> The whitened hair, the bent and listening frame,

The savage misery of the sidelong eyes,
Fell on her heart with strangling. So it was
That now for many days she held her peace,
Abiding with him till he seemed again
The babe she bare first in the wilderness, . . .
Then, leading him apart, Eve told her wish,
Not faltering now nor uttering it far off,
But as a sovereign mother to her son
Speaks simple destiny. He looked at her
Dimly, as if he saw her not; then stooped,
Sharpening his brows upon her. With a cry
She laid fierce, shaken hands about his breast,
Drew down his neck, and harshly from his brow
Pushing the head-band and the matted locks,
Baring the livid flesh with violence,
She kissed him on the Sign. Cain bowed his head
Upon her shoulder, saying, "I will go!"

The changes which Moody made in transferring these materials to the play were aimed not only at giving them greater
theatrical effectiveness but at extending and enriching their
symbolic meanings. For one thing, instead of having Eve come
to Nod alone, he now has her come with her young grandson
Jubal, who in the poem had simply been referred to as "songs-
man of the tribe" and the last one to see Eve before her mysterious departure. Instead of having her merely give her message at the gate and then wait for Cain to come at dawn, he
now has Eve and Jubal disguise themselves as suppliants from
an outlying district of Cain's realm, humbly awaiting the king's
visit to the Seat of Supplication outside the gate where he is
accustomed to hear his subjects' grievances.

In creating the role of Jubal and in altering the opening
scene, Moody was, of course, providing Eve with a necessary
confidant and establishing a plausible context for an initial
dialogue in which basic expository information could be con-
veyed; and this exposition he manages quite skillfully. Jubal's
ignorance of the purpose behind Eve's decision to visit Cain
after so many years of bitter estrangement, and his youthful
wonder at the general alteration in his grandmother's behavior,
give credibility to the questions and snatches of retrospect narrative by which he seeks to have Eve explain the reason for
their journey. Through these and Eve's guardedly reticent replies, Moody establishes both immediate exposition—Eve's and

Jubal's long and exhausting journey across the desert and their present situation as incognito suppliants to the mighty and terrible Cain; and the general background of that situation—the sudden change which came over Eve and impelled her to set out on her quest, her futile attempts to win approval for the quest from Adam and her various sons, including even the ghost of Abel, and finally her choice of her adoring grandson as the only one fitted to accompany her. At the same time, Eve withholds just enough information—especially about the nature of the vision which brought on her change—to arouse suspense and to impel our attention forward to the approaching encounter with Cain; and our own suspense is objectified in Jubal himself.

Yet Jubal is much more than merely a device for accomplishing exposition and objectifying audience suspense. He is a fully characterized *persona* who plays a functional role in the main action; and his youthfulness and innocence present a constant contrast to the aged and world-weary Cain, as well as to Eve herself. The same is true of the young orphan maid Abdera, who had not appeared at all in the narrative poem but who becomes the fourth of the play's major *personae* when she emerges from Cain's city, where she has spent most of her life as a lonely outcast, to join Eve and Jubal at the Seat of Supplication and to offer herself as a voluntary sharer in their fate. She, too, plays an important expository role in helping characterize Cain before his own appearance onstage; for it is from her that we first learn how "old" the king has grown, how his own subjects mutter that "as he grows more weak he grows more cruel," and how at times, when remembrance of his ancient crime comes over him, he suffers violent fits of madness. But she, too, has important dramatic and symbolic functions of her own. Inevitably, of course, Abdera and Jubal fall in love; and, as the play proceeds, their love assumes a significance comparable to but much more fully delineated than that of Aeolus and Alcyone in *The Fire-Bringer*. By the end, it is clear that they are to be seen as the future progenitors of that higher human race for which Eve is seeking a new dispensation.

Besides Jubal and Abdera, Moody also adds to the cast of the narrative poem a women's chorus whose brief appearance midway in the act both characterizes the population of the city over which Cain rules and symbolizes the general mentality of a human race alienated from its God and desperately in need of that new dispensation. The women, with Abdera in their midst, pass the Seat of Supplication on their way to the city well where they have come to fill their water jars; and they take the opportunity to throw malicious taunts at Eve and Jubal, as well as at Abdera when she tries to defend the silent strangers. There is a note of sheer sadism in the chorus' taunts, and it is appropriately balanced by a note of masochism in the song they sing—one which reflects the unhealthy psychological and moral atmosphere of Nod and, in a broader sense, seems to represent a kind of perverted Calvinism whereby Moody depicts the God against whom Eve has been inspired to rebel:

Even though, even though!
Be it ours to flee and double, be it His to bring us low.
Blessed she who tastes his arrow and lies broken in the wood.
She has fled, she has fallen: it is good.

Finally, in the confrontation scene between Eve and Cain which forms the dramatic and symbolic climax of the act, Moody introduces one major change into the events sketched in the poem: he omits the period during which Eve "held her peace" and simply dwelt with Cain awaiting the opportune moment to declare her intention of returning to Eden with him as her guide. Up to a point, such a waiting period seemed to be part of Moody's design, and he does have Eve and Cain start up the stairs to the city where they will abide together "till such a time/As these our wounds are healed." But right then he effects a new and significant plot reversal which precipitates Eve's final revelation of purpose, her decisive gesture of kissing the sign on Cain's brow, and his conversion to that purpose. Just as they are about to enter the city, the Death Angel Azrael suddenly manifests himself to Eve. With this recognition that her death is imminent, she proceeds to tell Cain everything then and there and, having kissed the sign, to set tomorrow dawn as the time for their departure.

Such a change was, of course, partly necessitated by simple requirements of theatrical economy; but it also gave Moody a chance to work one last and very effective climax into a scene constructed in a series of mounting dramatic and emotional reversals, as well as to concentrate into that one scene all the main symbolic meanings of the whole projected drama. For now Eve's defiance of the moral edict which had estranged her from Cain becomes fused with their joint resolve to defy the moral edict which had exiled them both from their birthplaces; and their own reconciliation becomes fused with their joint resolve to force a final reconciliation between themselves and God.

V *Dramaturgy and Poetry*

Moody's well-matured theatrical instincts are apparent not only in his adroit handling of plot elements—suspense, recognitions and reversals, and the continual rises and falls of tension which occur within the overall dramatic crescendo climaxed at the very end—but also in his decision to limit his cast to a small, tightly integrated number of human characters. Except for Azrael—who appears for only a moment far in the background and has no lines—there are no supernatural or purely allegorical figures in the act; and the four major *personae,* as well as the chorus, have very much the quality of realistically conceived human beings, while at the same time retaining their functions as symbolic archetypes.

Eve in particular emerges as a memorable example of Moody's capacity for combining high heroic grandeur with psychological realism. One early critic not normally given to superlatives called her "the most tremendous creation in modern English drama," and by "tremendous" he probably did not mean to convey a value judgment so much as a sense of the larger-than-life passion and dignity which Moody infuses into the role.[23] Yet the primal mother and supreme rebel is also a particularized specimen of normal humanity; she has her own psychological quirks and her own quite simple maternal affection for Jubal, Abdera, and above all Cain. Throughout the act she is a figure whose emotions readily invite audience identification.

Cain, too, has considerable tragic stature in his role as the tortured exile and reluctant king of a people with whom he has little in common and whom his bitterness and guilt-ridden memory drive him to govern with cruel austerity. He is also, however, simply the rejected son craving a motherly love of which he has been deprived and forgiveness for a misdeed he has long outgrown. The psychology of this mother-son relationship, quite as much as the universal moral issues symbolized by Eve's visit to Cain, gives the confrontation scene its power; and, despite the stylized formality of the dialogue, the action by which Eve finally brings psychological peace to her anguished son and finally liberates her long-repressed maternal

needs can, if skillfully and honestly performed, have as much
direct pathos as a comparable action in a good modern domestic drama.

On the other hand, it is the poetry in *The Death of Eve* which
makes the play more than just a good modern domestic drama
transferred to a biblical context and thereby given larger symbolic dimensions. Most of the dialogue shows greater original-
ity and technical mastery in the handling of dramatic verse
than Moody had shown anywhere except in the very best passages of *The Fire-Bringer*. The Miltonic elements which had
been so prominent in the *Masque* and were still present in parts
of *The Fire-Bringer* have now been virtually eliminated, as have
transparent derivations from other poets except, in two small
but unfortunate instances, from Shakespeare. The first of these
occurs when Eve at last drops her veil to reveal her identity,
and Cain, seated in the Judgment Seat opposite the Seat of
Supplication and surrounded by his priests and officers, rises
in horror at what he takes to be her ghost, since up to now he
has believed vague reports of her death. His outcry is a taste-
less echo of Macbeth's lines on seeing the ghost of Banquo:

> Thou hag of hell,
> Glare not upon me with those caverned eyes!
> *To his officers.*
> Whoever has done this, his life shall pay.
> Do ye spread out your nets among the dead,
> And toll them here out of the earth and air
> To daunt me, and to shake me from myself?

The second occurs later in the same scene, while Eve and Cain
are alone and she, having seen the Death Angel, is trying to
overcome Cain's resistance to her plan for re-entering Eden.
As yet she has not performed the ultimate symbolic act of kissing the sign on his brow, and is still using lesser means of
winning over his will. In this particular speech she seems to
be half-ironically adopting a courtly tone appropriate to her
assumed role as a petitioner to the all-powerful king of Nod;
yet ironic or not, the pseudo-Shakespearian stance and tone introduce a false note into an otherwise highly charged dramatic
interchange:

> Touching this same journey,
> I humbly do beseech thee, look thereon,
> And be well pleased to lend thy royal favor,

Thereto the needed beasts and muniments
Proportioned to the distance and the time; . . .
And that our starting be by dawn to-morrow.—
Unless, by favor, thy decreeing lips
Should breathe "To-night" and do it. Might it be?
'T is but an hour to moonrise, and the moon
Is at her full, or nearly. Say'st "To-night?"
Aye, aye, thy silence cries I have a son!
—To-night! That is right royal.

But considering the standing practice among nineteenth-century
verse dramatists, particularly Shelley and Byron, of simply para-
phrasing whole passages from Shakespeare at moments when the
Shakespearian manner seemed appropriate, we might forgive
Moody for indulging in that practice only twice. Better still,
we might allow ourselves the charity of agreeing with Charleton Lewis—who also condemned the *Macbeth* echo in the first
passage—that such a lapse of taste "would never have passed
Moody's final revision" had he lived to complete and revise the
play.[24]

Elsewhere, the verse is much truer to Moody's personal idiom,
much better adapted to the speakers and specific dramatic
situations, and answers much better to Granville-Barker's description of a "patterned language" whose "more than rational
power" can stimulate an audience's imagination to a heightened
apprehension of theme and character.[25] For the most part, the
diction and syntax are simpler than in the *Masque* and in *The
Fire-Bringer*, and all the dialogue is theatrically functional.
There are no long set-speeches, in fact very few long speeches
of any kind; and, though the texture of the imagery is quite rich
throughout, Moody tends to let that imagery speak for itself,
without the heavy ballast of rhetoric and allusion which sometimes weighted the style of his earlier verse dramas. Here, for
example, is one of Cain's more moving speeches during a moment of relative calm in which he and Eve are reminiscing
nostalgically over the early days before his crime:

There was a day when winter held the hills
And all the lower places looking sunward
Knew that the spring was near. Until that day
I had but walked in a boy's dream and dazzle,
And in soft darkness folded on herself
My soul had spun her blind and silken house.
It was my birthday, for at earliest dawn

You had crept to me in the outer tent,
Kissed me with tears and laughter, whispering low
That I was born, and that the world was there,
A gift you had imagined and made for me.
Now, as I climbed the morning hills, behold,
Those words were true: the world at last was there;
At last 't was mine, and I was born at last.
I walked, and on my shoulders and my reins
Strength rang like armor; I sat, and in my belly
Strength gnawed like a new vinegar; I ran
And strength was on me like superfluous wings. . . .

If we compare a speech like this with any of Michaelis' more
heightened utterances, we see the difference between a strained
and unnatural prose out of harmony with all that surrounds it,
and a dramatic verse well suited to its context and integrated
with the dialogue as a whole by its use of metrical and stylistic
techniques which are sustained from the beginning to the end
of the act. Visually, the speech is quite vivid; but much of its
effectiveness, like that of all the best verse in the act, is also
due to its stimulation of less conscious levels of audience
awareness through direct appeal to the auditory imagination.
The very stylization of the meter, besides enhancing our readiness to accept the stylization in the language itself, operates
throughout the dialogue as a norm of expectancy against which
are counterpointed the actual speech rhythms, with their constant variety resulting from devices like alternation of longer
and shorter cadences, end-stopped and run-on lines, or con-
formity to and violation of the basic iambic pattern. And this
counterpointing, like that in music, can work on an audience's
emotions in a way more subtle and more telling than anything
which even the most rhythmic and "melodious" prose—lacking
as it does the stability of a continuing metrical norm—can perhaps ever achieve.

Moreover, in addition to its overall metrical unity, *The Death
of Eve* is also given dramatic coherence by a number of recurrent image patterns which Moody handles with far greater
subtlety than those in his prose plays. These cannot be adequately illustrated short of quoting nearly the entire act, but
we may see the way the general technique works by considering what are probably the two most important patterns. The
first begins in the very opening lines:

EVE.

Yea, Jubal?

JUBAL.

Nothing, mother.

EVE.

Thy lips moved;
The hand upon thy knee rose as in question,
And fell as in reply.

JUBAL.

I slept; I dreamed.

EVE.

Sleep yet; the heat is strong.

The interchange bears evident similarities to the beginning of *The Fire-Bringer*, and Moody may well have intended to establish a parallel between the bare desert scene which forms the backdrop and the desert setting in the first member of his trilogy. But more important than this retrospective analogy is the new thematic element introduced by the reference to Jubal's hand rising and falling in sleep; for there are many similar references throughout the play to the characters' hands which serve almost as stage directions tying one episode to another by immediate visual as well as verbal analogy. For example, later in the same scene, Jubal—speaking as he often does in a respectful third person—is groping for an image to convey his sense that there is more to Eve's purpose than the simple one she has asserted: "To look upon my first-born's face again,/And know him what he grows to." At length his eyes move to her hands, and perhaps through association, conscious or unconscious, with his own earlier dream, he hits on something very close to the truth:

JUBAL.

. . . Eve sits here, . . .
Within her hands—Alas, I speak too near!

EVE.

Speak on.

JUBAL.

And in her hands—I know not how
To say my meaning.

EVE

Say, though.

JUBAL.

On her hands,
That lie so quiet and so empty here,
A look as if they seized the hands of God,
And dragged Him with her through his holy mountain
Unwillingly to do her glorious will.

Two scenes later, Abdera—at the end of a speech in which she
attempts to account for her immediate and overwhelming attraction to Eve and Jubal—introduces the second of the play's
two chief image patterns while at the same time adding her
bit to the now well-established pattern of hand imagery:

ABDERA.

I was brought young to Cain's fierce citadel.
And since, day after day, season by season,
Now stark alone and now in bands of trouble,
The hurt and hungry people gather in,
To crouch upon this stone. Some I have feared,
Yea, hated for the wickedness in them,
Being myself made wicked by that hate;

. . . .

To-day I came, and lo, nothing to wonder,
Nothing to question of! Two trees of life
Planted from always unto everlasting
By the still waters; and my quiet soul,
With outspread hands and upturned countenance
In the bright shadow, saying, "Glory, glory!"

JUBAL.

Low.
One tree.

ABDERA.

Low to Jubal.
Thy parable?

JUBAL.

Indicating Eve, who sits in reverie.
She is the tree;
And I with thee stand singing in her shadow.

Through the rest of the scene between Eve, Jubal, and Abdera,
the same tree image recurs several times, and always with

[176]

strong symbolic implications. Though by her reference to "two trees" Abdera has simply meant to indicate Eve and Jubal, Moody also seems to be intending further associations with the two original trees in the Garden of Eden, that of Life and that of forbidden Knowledge. And, though Jubal's reply is in one sense simply a grand compliment to Eve, in another its phrasing intimates that her nature contains the fruits of both those trees and that they become one in her. Hence the image may be said to point ahead cryptically to the new dispensation Eve seeks from God, in which Life and Knowledge may become one for a reborn humanity, represented by Jubal and Abdera singing in the shadow of Eve's reconciling spirit.

Both these image patterns are invoked at moments of high emotional intensity during the final scene between Eve and Cain. The tree image appears—again associated with that spiritual unity enjoyed before the sin which estranged man from God—in Eve's passionately nostalgic recollection of Cain as an innocent youth: "O green tree! O the young man in the house!/ A gold frontlet of pride, and a green cedar!" The hand image appears at the most intense moment of all, when Eve uncovers the sign on Cain's brow and takes on herself the guilt of Abel's murder, thus bringing peace to Cain and assuring his participation in her quest.

> 'T is not thy head
> Weareth this Sign. 'T is my most cruel head,
> Whose cruel hand, whose swift and bloody hand
> Smote in its rage my own fair man-child down.
> Not thy hand, Cain, not thine; but my dark hand;
> And my dark forehead wears the sign thereof,
> As now I take it on me.
> *She kisses him on the Sign.*

Only now is that same hand ready to fulfill the implied prophecy in Jubal's earlier speech—to "seize the hands" of God himself and to unite "her glorious will" with the divine will.

In the effectively quiet close of the act, Eve's accomplishment of this final objective is so clearly foreshadowed that we almost do not need a second and third act to complete the symbolic design. Eve and Cain mount up through the city gate from which they will re-emerge at dawn, followed shortly by Jubal and Abdera, who will accompany them to Eden and in whose innocent love the sense of man's estrangement from God is already virtually overcome:

JUBAL.

O Abdera, the strangeness of the world.

ABDERA.

Not strange.—Strange, strange before; no longer so.

JUBAL.

Look where the star leans flaming from his throne
And viewless worlds are suppliant in his porches.
They pass through the gate and disappear, climbing upward.[26]

VI *Sources and Influences*

Though the plot and characterization of *The Death of Eve* are largely Moody's own creation, the play does owe debts of varying degrees to certain works of his predecessors. In the remote background hover early nineteenth-century closet dramas like Blake's little parable *The Ghost of Abel,* from which Moody seems to have derived a hint for the retrospective narration of Eve's encounter with her dead son's apparition; and Byron's "mystery" play *Cain,* from which Moody probably derived little more than the notion of expressing the spirit of Romantic rebellion through a symbolic reworking of materials from Genesis. Closer still, at least in time, was the strangely interesting blank-verse drama *Cain* which Moody's friend George Cabot Lodge had written in 1904, and in which Eve is also depicted forgiving Cain for the murder of Abel and becoming identified with him as a rebel against the negative morality represented by the Old Testament Jehovah.[27]

Critics have also pointed out the influence of a narrative poem called *La Vision d'Eve,* by the late nineteenth-century French Parnassian poet Léon Dierx, on several details in Moody's play: the use of the Death Angel Azrael; the portrayal of Cain's lonely suffering during his exile in Nod; and the general idea, though not the style, of a brief and moving speech in which Cain recollects the first incident that had given Eve forebodings of his later crime and the suffering to follow:[28]

> The first that I remember of my life
> Was such a place, such a still afternoon,
> I sitting thus, thy bright head in my knees,
> And such a bird above us as him yonder
> Who dips and hushes, lifts and takes his note.

> I know not what child's trespass I had done,
> Nor why it drove the girl out of thy face,
> Clutched at thy heart with panic, and in thine eyes
> Set shuddering love.

Finally, the work which probably had the strongest influence on both the spirit and the general dramatic design of *The Death of Eve* was, characteristically enough, not a product of latter-day Romanticism or post-Romanticism but of Classic Greek drama. No critic appears to have recognized the similarities between Moody's one act, plus the subsequent action as sketched in the narrative poem, and Sophocles' *Oedipus at Colonus.* Yet in several significant ways Moody seems to have conceived the last member of his trilogy as a counterpart to the last-written member of that trio of plays on the Oedipus myth which, though not in the strict sense a trilogy, did amount to such by the time Sophocles had added the *Oedipus at Colonus* to the *Oedipus Rex* and *Antigone.* It was not so much that Moody was imitating Sophocles—for his style and the details of his dramaturgy are quite different—as that he seemed to be deliberately setting up suggestive analogies between his treatment of the Hebraic myth and Sophocles' treatment of the Hellenic one which Moody considered an archetypal expression of the religious vision he aimed to express in his own trilogy.

Like Sophocles' aged Oedipus, Moody's aged Eve is a character who has suffered at great length for an original sin and who is now ready to offer that suffering as sufficient claim to a reconciliation with the divine power she has offended—a power which, like the Greek Eumenides, has itself progressed in the meantime to a higher state of being. Just as Oedipus began as a wandering suppliant to the Athenian king Theseus, so Eve begins as a wandering suppliant to Cain; and just as Oedipus was accompanied by his young and innocent daughter Antigone, so Eve is accompanied by Jubal. Both Oedipus and Eve are characterized by an odd combination of humility and pride —humility in their roles as exiled criminals and helpless petitioners to a powerful king; pride in their roles as bearers of a vision whereby they will become the agents of a new covenant between humanity and the supernatural. At the end of the *Oedipus at Colonus,* this covenant comes into being with the hero's death and transfiguration in the sacred Grove of the Eumenides; and had Moody finished his play he would cer-

tainly have expanded on the brief passage in the narrative poem
which also suggests Eve's death and transfiguration in an Eden
now freed from the stigma of human sin.

VII *The Uncompleted Design*

In fact, between the evidence contained in the narrative
poem and that in the Sophocles play, we can derive a fairly
good idea of the general directions Acts Two and Three would
have taken. For more particular details, we can turn to firsthand recollections of Moody's conversations about *The Death
of Eve* as recorded first by Manly and then by Harriet:

> The other acts . . . two in number, were to be diversified by
> many illuminating incidents, among them the instinctive wander-
> ing of the age-stricken Adam back to the Garden, ostensibly
> following Eve, but really yearning forward to participate in the
> new and glorious solution of life. In the third act there was to
> be a song by Eve, the burden of which would be the inseparable-
> ness of God and man, during which, as she rises to a clearer
> and clearer view of the spiritual life, she gently passes from the
> vision of her beholders; while, delicately symbolizing the
> permanence and beauty of the earth, Jubal and Abdera draw
> together with broken words of tenderness.[29]

> . . . at the conclusion of the drama, if he had finished it, he
> intended to put a lyric murmur of pure human joy, based upon
> their consciousness of mutual life, into a duet between Abdera
> and Jubal, which was to give the feeling of renewal of the world
> after Eve's song of reconciliation. This lyric, as he explained
> it to me, would have given an unsurpassed assurance of happiness,
> truth, and beauty, as forever established on earth.[30]

We might be tempted to speculate that the successful achievement of these plans would have been beyond Moody's powers.
The long song of reconciliation which Eve does sing in the
narrative poem is not one of his most inspired lyric creations,
and it would have been quite inadequate to the ambitions he
had for this last scene in the drama. On the other hand, Moody's
conception of his materials had become considerably richer and
more mature between the time he wrote the poem and the first
act of the play; there is a good reason to believe, therefore, that
he would have improved upon that lyric, and upon everything
else in the poem's conclusion, had he been able to see the play

through to its own conclusion. As it stands, the one completed act of *The Death of Eve* is an impressive achievement, and one which Moody might conceivably have ruined by trying to dramatize the symbolic implications already inherent in its contents. If, however, he had lived to revise those occasional passages in which his inspiration clearly failed him, and had then gone on to write two more acts as good as the first, he might have contributed something really momentous to the modern drama.

VIII *Conclusions*

In October, 1906, when Moody was first starting work on *The Death of Eve*, a certain Mrs. Le Moine had suggested that he might try transferring its story "to modern life," and he had reported himself as answering "that's just where it was already, and I didn't intend to expose it to cobwebs and museum shelves by putting Adam in creased trousers and Eve into glove-fitting etcetera."[31] All he meant, of course, was that despite the apparent remoteness of the play's characters and setting, its thematic contents were universal and it was therefore, in a fundamental sense, modern. Nevertheless, Moody never ceased to believe in the validity of a remark he made to Percy MacKaye in August, 1904, while he was still perhaps hopeful of realizing his initial project for writing *The Great Divide* in verse: "... I am heart and soul dedicated to the conviction that modern life can be treated on the stage in the poetic mediums, and adequately presented only in that way."[32] This conviction he had held ever since he had first become interested in the theater, and it was not diminished by the fact that his initial attempts to write both *The Faith Healer* and *The Great Divide* in verse never materialized.

His idea of applying the resources of dramatic verse to a contemporary subject matter and speech idiom has continued to attract many American writers since Moody's time, though up to now few have come much closer than he did to mastering the difficult but worth-while challenge. Moody's death was a serious loss to the theater in general, but one which may be felt with particular keenness by those who share his belief in the chance for a renaissance of verse drama rooted in twentieth-century American life and language. For—given his indubitable theatrical talent and know-how; his fine ear for contemporary speech as exhibited in both prose plays; his ability, as manifested

in *The Fire-Bringer* and *The Death of Eve,* to write verse dialogue that is no less actable for all its literary merit; and a reputation, built up by the success of *The Great Divide,* which had
given him an "in" with theater managers and producers, as well
as with the theater-going public, such as no poet had ever before enjoyed in America—Moody was better equipped, and in
a better position, to establish such a renaissance than any other
American writer of his time. Had he ever realized his hopes of
fusing the best qualities of his prose plays with the best qualities of his verse plays, he might have contributed something
yet more momentous to the modern drama than anything we
can envision in even a completed and revised text of *The
Death of Eve.*[33]

But, to quote Eliot's *Burnt Norton* again, "What might have
been is an abstraction/Remaining a perpetual possibility/Only
in a world of speculation." All such conjectures as to what
Moody might have done had he lived longer are meaningful
only insofar as they constitute a commentary on what he did do
in the mere dozen-or-so years of his adult writing career, and on
the value which the products of that career can still have for
readers of today and tomorrow.

It is true enough that the particular kind of diction and
rhetoric which Moody employed in much of his verse may never
again be viable for American poetry; and that certain elements
of his thought—such as his melioristic view of history—may no
longer be palatable for most readers as literal ideology. But it
could be argued that the particular diction and rhetoric and the
literal ideology of any poet will become obsolescent as his epoch
recedes into the past; and this fact alone can hardly disqualify
Moody—any more than, say, Homer or Shakespeare or Whitman—
from reaching across natural barriers of time and change to
that part of the modern spirit which is also part of the universal
human spirit.

Half a century has often proved to be about the limit of
continuing vitality for literary movements like the one which
began shortly after Moody's death and which was, to some degree,
a reaction against the kind of sensibility and poetic techniques
he represented. We may be just about due, then, for a new
reaction of equal proportions—not, to be sure, a "return" to
Moody's kind of matter and manner, but perhaps a redefinition
of poetic virtue in terms which could again accommodate the
best in that matter and manner. With such a redefinition, the

manifest faults of Moody's non-dramatic verse—which have been so magnified since he first fell out of critical favor—may again be seen, as they were by critics of his own time and the decade following his death, to be outweighed and often redeemed by its manifest virtues.

Yet, considered in its totality, Moody's output of really first-rate non-dramatic verse—even if we include the best parts of *The Masque of Judgment*—was relatively small; and the revival which his reputation deserves must finally depend on his more significant and more wholly individualized accomplishment in the drama. *The Great Divide,* as well as its defective but sometimes impressive successor, *The Faith Healer,* has never quite lost footing in histories of the American drama. But Moody's verse plays have fallen into the same neglect as have his non-dramatic poems, and therein lies the biggest loss of all. For in *The Fire-Bringer* and *The Death of Eve* Moody reached his highest creative powers; and the philosophical vision expressed in these plays has durable value in terms not so much of any literal formulation as of the imaginative strength and maturity of its dramatic and poetic embodiment. Besides their intrinsic merits, the plays also continue to have value as a hope and example for writers concerned with the same fundamental issues—literary, theatrical, and philosophical—that concerned Moody more than half a century ago.

Notes and References

Chapter One

1. See especially G. B. Rose, "William Vaughn Moody," *Sewanee Review*, IX (1901), 332-36; William Morton Payne, "The Poetry of Mr. Moody," *The Dial*, XXX (1901), 365-69; Richard Watson Gilder's laudatory poem "A New Poet," *Atlantic Monthly*, XCV (1905), 748; and newspaper reviews of the 1906-8 New York production of *The Great Divide* cited in David D. Henry, *William Vaughn Moody: A Study* (Boston, 1934), pp. 173-74, 210.

2. The phrases are quoted from, respectively, reviews by Charleton M. Lewis, *Yale Review*, n.s. II (1913), 688; anonymous reviewer, *Atlantic Monthly*, CXI (1913), 719; Hermann Hagedorn, *The Independent*, LXXIV (1913), 316; and Payne, *The Dial*, LIII (1912), 484.

3. *American Poetry*, ed. Percy H. Boynton (New York, 1918), p. 697.

4. Gorham Munson, "The Limbo of American Literature," *Broom*, II (1922), 259-60. It is worth noting, however, that six years later, in his *Destinations: A Canvass of American Literature Since 1900* (New York, 1928), Munson neglected Moody altogether. Perhaps he changed his mind.

5. From reviews by an anonymous reviewer in the New York *Sun*, February 23, 1908; and by Emerson Hough in the Chicago *American*, April 17, 1906 (after the opening of the first version, *The Sabine Woman*). Quoted by Henry, pp. 173, 174.

6. In the 1948 *Literary History of the United States*, for instance, the only mention of Moody's poetry occurs in a brief reference to him as a probable influence on Edwin Arlington Robinson, but two full pages are allotted to Sculley Bradley's discussion of Moody's dramas, with particular emphasis on the prose plays (New York, II, 1013-15, 1157-58). This is in clear contrast to the 1917-21 *Cambridge History of American Literature;* there the poems and verse dramas receive far more prominent treatment than the prose plays (New York, III, 62-64, 290-91).

7. *A History of American Poetry, 1900-1940* (New York), p. 26.

8. See especially Howard Mumford Jones, *The Bright Medusa* (Urbana, 1952), pp. 46-64.

9. For example, in the first six editions of Louis Untermeyer's anthology *Modern American Poetry* (New York, 1919, 1921, 1925, 1930, 1936, and 1942), Moody was rather generously represented; but, in the seventh edition (1950), he was omitted altogether.

10. Princeton, 1961, p. 255.

11. See letter to R. W. Gilder, August 23, 1905, *Some Letters of William Vaughn Moody*, ed. Daniel Gregory Mason (Boston, 1913), p. 158.

12. Since Crane was a close friend of Moody's widow during his formative years (see footnote 20, below), it is more than probable that he knew Moody's poetry well and was influenced by it. Cf. the discussion of "The Moon-Moth" in Chapter VII.

13. Lewis, *Yale Review*, n.s. II, 698.

14. The prevailing poetic climate cannot be more graphically illustrated than by the early work of a man who has since come to represent everything antipathetical to it, William Carlos Williams. Here, for instance, are the opening lines of a sonnet called "July" from Williams' first volume, *Poems*, published in 1909 (Rutherford, New Jersey, no page numbers):

> Hot cheeked July, with lusty sinews primed
> For deeds of passion, hail! and halt afar!
> Thou wild incontinent, thy fiery star
> Hath sanctioned in thee dreams to naught atimed
> But thine own reckless humors. . . .

The lines are typical, in form, prosody, and language, of the entire volume. Williams has since, to be sure, repudiated this volume, and it is perhaps therefore ungracious even to remember it. But his earliest work is worth citing here as a not-too-extreme specimen of the age's poetry which, considering who wrote it, shows how much Moody's "old-fashioned" diction and rhetoric were part of a widespread phenomenon. Indeed, to compare verse like that of the young Williams with Moody's adult work (which was already finished by the time Williams published his first volume) is to see the difference between a poet helplessly constrained and driven to unrelieved banality by his traditional techniques, and a poet who could adapt such techniques to his own individual talent and make them serve rather than thwart that talent.

15. According to Lovett, in a letter to David D. Henry cited in the latter's book on Moody (pp. 41-42), Moody's part in the *History of English Literature* consisted of writing the chapters on the Anglo-Saxon period, the Norman-French period, the Age of Chaucer, Milton, and nineteenth-century literature exclusive of the novel.

16. Letter to Josephine Preston Peabody, November 25, 1900, *Selected Letters of Edwin Arlington Robinson*, ed. Ridgely Torrence (New York, 1940), p. 33.

17. *History of American Poetry*, p. 32.

18. "Philip Massinger," *Selected Essays, 1917-1932* (New York, 1932), p. 182.

19. Thomas Riggs, Jr., "Prometheus 1900," *American Literature*, XXII (1951), 399-423.

20. From the time of Moody's death to her own in 1932, Mrs. Moody continued to be a renowned hostess, at whose home many famous American writers and several famous foreign writers regularly gathered. Also something of a literary patroness, she was an important early supporter and encourager of Hart Crane. See Olivia Howard Dunbar, *A House in Chicago* (Chicago, 1947) for an interesting biography of Mrs. Moody and an account of her varied activities in the literary world both during and after Moody's own lifetime.

Chapter Two

1. *Poets of America* (Boston, 1885), pp. 456-61, 464, *et circa*.

2. Sonnet "Oh For a Poet—For a Beacon Bright," *Collected Poems of Edwin Arlington Robinson* (New York, 1961), p. 93. For another

expression of the same sentiment by Robinson in this period, see the sonnet "George Crabbe," p. 94.

3. On May 22, 1901, Robinson wrote to Moody: "There is not much more for me to say about your work, for you know what I think of it, how much faith I have always had in it, and how thoroughly I believe that you, with your extraordinary powers of expression, have it in you to give American literature a new meaning for the new century." (Quoted in Edwin S. Fussell, "Robinson to Moody: Ten Unpublished Letters," *American Literature*, XXIII [1951], 184.) In 1907, a letter of Stedman's to Percy MacKaye included Moody on a small list of current writers who were "absolutely poets" and who formed "a young, inspired phalanx of American poets, impelled by instinct and no less by conditions to composition in the highest of poetic forms." (Quoted in MacKaye's Introduction to Moody's *Letters to Harriet*, Boston, 1935, p. 38.)

4. "The Serf's Secret," *Harvard Monthly*, November, 1890. All these *Harvard Monthly* poems are quoted, either in full or in part, by Henry.

5. Quoted by Henry, p. 71, with the note: "Attributed by the New York *Times* of June 8, 1901, in which it was copied, to Moody's college verse. Not republished."

6. *Harvard Monthly*, July, 1894. Moody's interest in the visual arts, and his use of real or imaginary art objects as subjects or inspirations for his writings—as in this poem, the earlier sonnet "To the Niké of Paionios" (*Harvard Monthly*, June, 1890), the later "Faded Pictures," and some of the more graphic imagery of his verse dramas—reflect the fact that he was himself a painter as well as a writer. Trained early for a career in painting (see Chronology), he took the art up again several times in his later life; and a number of his friends have left comments on the excellence of his sketches and work in oils and pastels.

7. *Ibid.*, December, 1891.

8. *Ibid.*, May, 1892.

9. *Ibid.*, March, 1892.

10. To Josephine Preston Peabody, *Some Letters*, pp. 30-31.

11. *Harvard Monthly*, January, 1891.

12. *Some Letters*, p. 56.

13. This version, which appears under the title "Wilding Flower" in the May 16 letter (*Some Letters*, pp. 57-60), was a poem in thirteen six-line stanzas of alternating tetrameters and trimeters, rhyming *ababab*. Mason is quite right in stating that the revisions which Moody undertook partly at his suggestion did much to eliminate "obscurity of construction, turgidity of thought," and "intemperance of language" (*Ibid.*, p. xvii). Yet it is questionable whether the poet's substitution of rather skipping four-teener tercets for the original ballad-like stanzas constituted a prosodic improvement.

14. The same theme is treated in still more frankly personal terms, though less ably, in a little poem entitled "Dawn Parley," which Moody decided to omit from the 1901 volume, but which Mason published in *Some Letters*, pp. 71-72.

15. *The Nation*, LXXIII (1901), 154. Though the review was unsigned, it has been attributed by Lovett (Introduction to *Selected Poems of William Vaughn Moody*, Boston, 1931, p. lxx) to Professor Lewis Gates of Harvard, under whom Moody studied and later taught during his

year as an instructor of sophomore composition; and who, according to Lovett (*Ibid.*, pp. lxviii-lxix), first introduced Moody to the work of Francis Thompson.

16. *Some Letters*, pp. 52-53.

17. According to Mason (*Ibid.*, p. 27), Moody made the first sketch of "Jetsam" on a rainy afternoon at Caen shortly after the Chartres incident. Moody himself identified the original inspiration with that incident in a letter to Mason of December 1, 1895 (*Ibid.*, p. 41), in which he remarked that he was again taking up the poem. No certain evidence of its date of completion is available, and it is quite possible that Moody revised it several times before the 1901 volume. But in all essentials, the poem seems a product of the early Chicago period, prior to his return to Europe in the spring of 1897.

18. "Modern Symbolism and Maurice Maeterlinck," *The Plays of Maurice Maeterlinck* (New York, 1894), pp. 5-6.

19. René Taupin, in *L'Influence du Symbolisme Français sur la Poésie Américaine* (Paris, 1929), has claimed that Hovey and those American poets, such as Bliss Carman, whom he associated with himself as members of the new American Symbolist movement, never really applied the methods of the French Symbolists to their own poetry in any significant way. In fact, the French critic goes so far as to state that the American Symbolist school of the 1890's *"n'exista que dans l'imagination de Richard Hovey"* (p. 52). Even Moody, he argues, came much closer in his *"manière allégorique"* to the more systematic and non-suggestive methods of the French Parnassian poets than to the spirit and technique of the *Symbolistes* (p. 53). But Taupin was admittedly thinking chiefly of later allegorical poems like "The Brute," "The Quarry," and "The Menagerie," and not of poems like "Jetsam," which he seems to ignore, and which really does embody Hovey's theories to a far greater extent than any of Hovey's own works, apart from the translations, ever did. See the discussion of *The Fire-Bringer*, below, for a reference to the only passage in Moody's work which Taupin was willing to admit had genuine *Symboliste* qualities.

20. John M. Manly, Introduction to *The Poems and Plays of William Vaughn Moody* (Boston, 1912), I, p. xi.

21. For example, Bruce Weirick, in *From Whitman to Sandburg in American Poetry* (New York, 1924, p. 134), calls "Good Friday Night" "one of Moody's most perfect, if not the most perfect of his poems."

22. In a much-quoted letter to Mason dated May 24, 1896 (*Some Letters*, p. 63), Moody defended himself against the charges of overwriting with which he was, and would continue to be, familiar: "I think you are not tolerant enough of the instinct for conquest in language, the attempt to push out its boundaries, to win for it continually some new swiftness, some rare compression, to distill from it a more opaline drop. Isn't it possible, too, to be pedantic in the demand for simplicity? It's a cry which, if I notice aright, nature has a jaunty way of disregarding. Command a rosebush in the stress of June to purge itself; coerce a convolvulus out of the paths of catachresis. Amen!"

23. William Chislett, Jr., "William Vaughn Moody and William Blake," *The Dial*, LIX (1915), 142; Lovett, p. 1; Henry, p. 61.

24. Manly, p. xi, and Lovett, p. xxxix.

25. One of Robinson's remarks on the poem is quoted below; another

which is worth citing is his reference to Moody in a letter to Mrs. Laura E. Richards dated January 18, 1902, as "Von Moody, the pessimist man-child who branded himself the best of living poets with 'The Daguerreo-type'" (*Selected Letters,* p. 49). Manly (p. ix) praised the poem as "so deep of thought, so full of poignant feeling and clairvoyant vision, so wrought of passionate beauty that I know not where to look for another tribute from any poet to his mother that equals it." And the most intel-ligent of the reviewers of the 1912 *Poems and Plays,* Charleton Lewis, called it "a great achievement" (*Yale Review,* n.s. II, 701).

26. *History of American Poetry,* p. 27.

27. Ludwig Lewisohn, *Expression in America* (New York, 1932), pp. 308-9.

28. See note 15, above. Critics have also compared the poem favor-ably with attempts to treat a comparable subject in Cowper's "Lines to His Mother," Verlaine's lines *"Qu'as tu fait, toi qui voilà, De ta jeunesse,"* and, perhaps most pointedly, to Rossetti's sonnet "Inclusiveness" in which the poet thinks "as his own mother kissed his eyes/Of what her kiss was when her father wooed." See Lewis, *Yale Review,* n.s. II, 701; Paul Shorey, "The Poetry of William Vaughn Moody," *University of Chicago Record,* n.s. XIII (1927), 182; and Nash O. Barr and Charles H. Caffin, "William Vaughn Moody," *The Drama,* I (1911), 182.

29. Letter of May 22, 1901, Fussell, *American Literature,* XXIII, 184-85.

30. In a letter to Mason dated December 1, 1895, Moody had remarked: "I am losing sleep over a project for a play, dealing with a character and a situation which seem to me intensely significant and eloquent, that of Slatter [*sic*], the 'New Mexico Messiah,' who has been doing things in Denver of late" (*Some Letters,* p. 41). According to Manly (pp. xvi-xvii), he was planning the blank-verse treatment of the subject by 1898. By the following year, however, he had abandoned this for a prose treatment, which he completed during the summer of 1900. See Chapter VIII for discussion of Moody's subsequent work on *The Faith Healer.*

31. *Expression in America,* p. 306.

32. The last line is paraphrased from the words of the father who has come to have his defective child's illness cured by Jesus: "Lord, I believe; help thou mine unbelief" (*Mark,* 9:24). The same words appear, exactly quoted, in Bayard Taylor's blank-verse closet drama *The Prophet* (1875) as a refrain in the song of the hero David. (See *The Dramatic Works of Bayard Taylor,* Boston, 1880, pp. 5-6.) The influence of this play on *The Faith Healer* will be discussed below, as will the somewhat more important influence of Taylor's other closet dramas on *The Masque of Judgment* and on *The Fire-Bringer.*

33. Manly (p. ix) finds in this poem a "veiled but illuminating refer-ence" to Moody's mother, and therefore considers "Faded Pictures" a sort of companion piece to "The Daguerreotype." But in this he seems to be mistaken. "Faded Pictures" is quite explicitly about an ancient painting, and thus the portrait described could hardly be one of Moody's mother. It is true, however, that in its concentration on the permanent force of the eyes in the painting, the poem resembles "The Daguerreotype." Yet the very personal meanings of the longer poem give way here to a rather impersonal Browningesque meditation, with a strong atmosphere of the museum.

Notes and References

Chapter Three

1. *Some Letters,* p. 87.

2. Taylor's *Masque* depicts allegorically the evolution in human religious thought from the earliest worship of crude natural forces through various Pagan, Oriental, Semitic, and Christian theologies, toward some final, remotely envisioned apprehension of the true nameless Deity beyond them all. Unlike Moody's *Masque,* however, it is largely an apology for orthodox Christianity, since at the conclusion the "Voice from Space" which represents the true God assures Immanuel, who represents Christianity, that because of his doctrine of Love, his comes closest of all religions to realizing the ineffable truth: "Thou art my one begotten Son, in whom/I am well pleased" (*Dramatic Works,* p. 188).

3. Introduction to Moody, *Selected Poems,* pp. xl, xlii-xliii.

4. *The Complete Poetical Works of John Milton* (Boston, 1899), pp. xiv, xvi.

5. "The Marriage of Heaven and Hell," *Poetical Works* (Oxford Edition, 1958), p. 249. Cf. Moody's comment, p. 99: "The theology and the politics of the poet are at variance, and this fact introduces into much of the poem an unconscious insincerity. The words of the rebel angel have an intense eloquence, and the account of his doings and of his domain a persuasive vividness and majesty, which contrasts oddly with the pedantic woodenness of many of the passages consecrated to the Deity. It was largely in the attempt to overcome this paradox by which his villain insisted upon being his hero, that Milton lost himself in those long disquisitions that make some of the later books of the poem rather dreary reading."

6. Moody was a lifelong devotee of Wagnerian opera. One of his earliest published poems was a turgid sonnet inspired by the composer's work entitled "A Chorus of Wagner" (*Harvard Monthly,* April, 1890); and several of his letters, both early and late, speak of his enthusiasm for, and his frequent attendance at performances of, Wagner operas. See, for instance, *Some Letters,* p. 8, and *Letters to Harriet,* pp. 171, 181-82, 210, 254-55. These operas probably had an indirect but a telling influence on the *Masque,* as well as on Moody's later verse dramas.

7. *University of Chicago Record,* n.s. XIII, 178.

8. The entire episode is reminiscent, in substance and spirit if not in style, of Euripides' *The Bacchae,* which Shorey (p. 193) says was "Moody's favorite Greek play." See also Manly, pp. xxx-xxxi.

9. *Some Letters,* pp. 133-34.

10. For an excellent analysis of Moody's intellectual relations with the Transcendentalists and with nineteenth-century optimism in general, see Frederick W. Conner, *Cosmic Optimism: A Study of the Interpretation of Evolution by American Poets from Emerson to Robinson* (Gainesville, 1949), pp. 314-31.

11. It is not certain whether the "dark Antagonist" is man or Satan. The very ambiguity, however, points up Moody's emphasis on the "Worm that Dieth not" as the one true enemy of God. References to Satan and to the Fallen Angels are few in the *Masque,* but it is clear that Moody tends to associate them with humanity as representatives of a kind of evil

that is ultimately to God's benefit rather than absolutely and eternally opposed to him, as is the Worm.

12. Some of the early reviewers of the *Masque*, as well as Henry (pp. 126-27), pointed out the many recondite and rare obsolete words which Moody employs. In all fairness to Moody, however, it must be said that several of the words singled out by these critics (e.g. *sibilance, antinomy, nadir, rondure,* and *chrysalid*) are not nearly so recondite or obsolete as they intimate. Yet their lists do contain enough valid choices to indicate the degree of strain that is often apparent in the diction of the *Masque.*

13. It is such general stylistic devices, rather than specific borrowings, which constitute the real Miltonic influence on the *Masque.* The only instance of a direct echo of Milton's phrasing that I have been able to find occurs in a description of a nightingale's song by a "Girl's Voice" in Act Four, where the phrase "amorous dim delay" recalls Milton's description of the love-making habits of Adam and Eve: "...sweet reluctant amorous delay" (*Paradise Lost,* IV, 311).

14. For a listing of some of the fainter echoes of poets like Shelley, Keats, Tennyson, Swinburne, and Fitzgerald (*Omar Khayyam*) which occur in the *Masque,* see Shorey, *University of Chicago Record,* n.s. XIII, 180, 191-94. None of these is, however, nearly so direct as the echoes of Blake and Marlowe.

15. The striking image in the last three lines recurs more fully later in the *Masque* when Moody, with a real dramatic touch, has Raphael, the Spirit of the Lamp, and later Uriel discuss the crucifixion at the start of Act Two while gathered closely around the lamp which the Spirit carries, in order to shield its flame from the raging storm resulting from the catastrophe of the crucifixion.

16. Lovett, pp. xli, xliii.

17. Even R. P. Blackmur, in a generally unfavorable review of the *Selected Poems* ("Moody in Retrospect," *Poetry,* XXXVIII [1931], 331-37), saw fit to single out this passage as worthy of special praise. Of course, in the *Selected Poems* the lyric appears out of context—a fact which further enhances the quality of suggestiveness already present in its language.

18. G. B. Rose, "Two Poets," *Sewanee Review,* IX (1901), 332, 333.

19. See Robinson's letter to Josephine Preston Peabody, November 25, 1900, *Selected Letters,* pp. 32-33.

20. *Ibid.,* pp. 37-38.

21. Letter of August 27, 1899, *American Literature* XXIII, 175.

Chapter Four

1. Both Robinson and Mason had been advising Moody to direct his work more toward the contemporary scene, and he himself had recently passed on their advice to Josephine Preston Peabody. In a letter to her dated January 8, 1899, he had praised her first volume of poems but had remarked that there were passages he "could have wished a little nearer the every day speech;" and had added: "What we expect of you now is . . . to take hold of the common experience and common idiom and glorify it" (*Some Letters,* pp. 105-6).

2. For fuller discussions of the political backgrounds of the "Ode" and

literary responses by Moody's contemporaries to the Spanish-American War and the annexation of the Philippines, see Fred H. Harrington, "Literary Aspects of American Anti-Imperialism, 1898-1902," *New England Quarterly,* X (1937), 650-67; and Francis J. and Adaline Glasheen, "Moody's 'An Ode in Time of Hesitation,'" *College English,* V (1943), 121-29.

3. Lovett, pp. xliii-xliv.

4. Henry, p. 52. See also Frederick Eckman, "Moody's Ode: The Collapse of the Heroic," *Texas Studies in English,* XXXVI (1957), 86.

5. For a close study of parallels between this oration and Moody's imagery in the sixth strophe, see Glasheen, pp. 121-27.

6. Letter to Mason, September 26, 1901, *Selected Letters,* p. 44.

7. See Claude G. Bowers, *Beveridge and the Progressive Era* (Boston, 1932), pp. 68-69; and Glasheen, 128-29.

8. The passage in the *Areopagitica* to which Moody is referring reads: "Methinks I see in my mind a noble and puissant nation rousing herself like a strong man after sleep, and shaking her invincible locks. Methinks I see her as an eagle mewing her mighty youth, and kindling her undazzled eyes at the full midday beam; purging and unscaling her long-abused sight at the fountain itself of heavenly radiance...."

9. See *Life Studies* (New York, 1959), pp. 85-86. In his *Texas Studies* essay, Eckman compares the "Ode" to yet another latter-day poem on the subject, John Berryman's "Boston Common" (*The Dispossessed,* New York, 1948); and he makes this comparison the basis of his treatment of Moody's poem as "a memorial to the collapse of the Romantic grand manner in America" (p. 85). Eckman's essay appeared before Robert Lowell's poem, which is in many ways a stronger illustration of his thesis than Berryman's.

10. Letter to Moody, May 22, 1901, *American Literature,* XXIII, 185. Robinson did add, however, that he considered the last two lines of the poem "prodigious."

11. The one poem of the period which we know he did recite in public was a rather commonplace "Anniversary Ode" written at the invitation of Harvard University for Moody's appearance as guest poet at the 1900 commencement. The poem, which commemorates the 125th anniversary of Washington's assumption of command over the American army, was published in the *Harvard Monthly* in October, 1900, but never again reprinted.

12. Payne, *The Dial,* XXX, 369.

13. The exact date of "The Quarry" is uncertain, and it is therefore uncertain whether the Boxer Rebellion of the summer of 1900 figures at all in the poem's references. In putting down this bloody uprising against the reactionary government of China and the foreign nationals located within the country, the imperialist powers had again sought to exploit their capture of the capital in Peking for the purpose of looting the Chinese economy and taking over military control of the country. There is no direct indication in Moody's poem of any attempt to refer to this episode or to America's role in again discouraging the foreign nations from making capital of the resulting chaos. But it is not impossible that he may have had the Boxer Rebellion and its aftermath, as well as the original "Open Door Policy," in mind when he wrote the poem.

14. Moody had been a personal friend of both Fuller and Garland since his removal to Chicago, and through the latter he quite probably came to know the work of George, to whom Garland was something of a disciple (See Lovett, pp. xlv, xlvii-xlviii.). The enormous popularity at this time of Edwin Markham's poem of social protest, "The Man with the Hoe," may also have had some effect on Moody's didactic pieces—though in later letters he was to speak of Markham's most famous poem with something less than admiration (See *Letters to Harriet*, pp. 218, 235.).

15. Manly (p. xxxii) remarks that "Gloucester Moors" was "a favorite poem with workers in the slums."

16. Henry, p. 59; Shorey, 176. Analogues to the pessimistic passages in "The Brute" can, of course, be found in contemporaries of Moody like Frank Norris and Henry Adams. But it is not until Hart Crane's *The Bridge* that we find an important analogue in American poetry to the poem's optimistic contents.

17. In his September 26, 1901, letter to Mason (*Selected Letters*, p. 45), Robinson had written of the 1901 volume: "From the twenty or so who have spoken to me of the book I have heard nothing but praise with a big P. All, however, make an exception of the The Menagerie—not because they do not like it in itself but because it seems to be hopelessly out of place. I have a notion that I shall agree with them by and by, but the thing is so confoundedly clever that I hate to see it go."

Chapter Five

1. E.g., December 5, 1901: "This soul-destroying work makes me feel like a turnip in the head and a rotten walnut in the—well, not in the heart, I guess, let me say the sensorium. I keep boring away in the dark, like a captive tunnelling his way under the prison flags to daylight and fresh air"; or December 27, 1901: "Think of me as one who has been human and may in the fullness of time be so again, but who is at present a maker of textbooks and an offence to the sunlight" (*Letters to Harriet*, pp. 84, 87).

2. All reports of Moody's academic activities at Chicago show him to have been an excellent and very conscientious teacher. Yet his own feelings about his work were summed up in a reply to Professor Manly's request that he retain at least a part-time position on the university's English faculty: "I cannot do it; I feel that at every lecture I slay a poet" (Manly, p. xvi). His scholarly activities, on the other hand, did not come to an end with the publication of *A History of English Literature:* in 1904 he collaborated again with Lovett on a revised and condensed version of the *History* entitled *A First View of English Literature* (published in 1905); in 1909 he published an edition of DeQuincey in the Lake English Classics Series, with an introduction largely distilled from the chapter on that writer in the *History*.

3. E.g., May 20, 1902: "I have just finished the *Oedipus at Colonus,* and am perfectly bowled over by it. It is, for one thing, so *un*classical. A more romantic conception than the coming of Oedipus to Colonus, and his passing into death in the grove of the Eumenides, does not exist in poetry"; or June 2, 1902: "I told you I was much struck with the 'unclassical quality of the *Oedipus at Colonus.* The *Agamemnon,* both in con-

ception and execution, is romantic *à outrance.* I wonder how Messrs. Pope, Boileau and Co. ever succeeded in foisting into the canons of art that absurd category of classicism, anyhow?" (*Letters to Harriet,* pp. 112, 120). With the last remark Cf. Moody's introduction to his own edition of Pope's *Iliad* in the Lake Series (1900), p. 38.

4. See *The Poems of Trumbull Stickney,* ed. George Cabot Lodge, Moody, and John Ellerton Lodge (Boston, 1905), p. 105.

5. See Henry, pp. 149-60; and Barr and Caffin, *The Drama,* I, 188-89.

6. Letter of May 30, 1902, *Letters to Harriet,* p. 118.

7. Moody had, of course, known *The Bacchae* in translation—presumably Gilbert Murray's—since at least the time of the *Masque.* But when he and Stickney read the play in the original Greek, his enthusiasm for it became even greater than before. On July 30, 1902, he wrote to Harriet: "Can't you possibly contrive to get hold of a good translation of the *Bacchantes* of Euripides? It is my latest discovery and rapturously good. I myself know of no translation which is not worse than a caricature, but there must be such. Otherwise I shall have to make you one myself, for you must read it" (*Ibid.,* p. 139). The inspiration of Euripides' play is most manifest in the Dionysian spirit of several passages in Act Three. That of the *Agamemnon* and *Oedipus at Colonus* is less direct—though, as we shall see later, the latter play seems to have had a profound influence on *The Death of Eve.*

8. Letter to Mason, April 8, 1898, *Some Letters,* p. 100.

9. See *Letters to Harriet,* pp. 90, 157-58. Yeats was a personal friend of Harriet, who admired him and endeavored to have him meet Moody during his 1904 visit to America; but the meeting never occurred. Moody's attitudes toward Yeats's earlier plays, and particularly toward his "thesis about folk-poetry and the folk-spirit" as it affected those plays, was not entirely favorable (*Ibid.,* pp. 157-58, 180-81, 188, 223-24); nevertheless, his strong interest in the Irish poet's dramatic experiments is evident in the fact that he took advantage of every opportunity to attend performances of the plays when they appeared on American stages.

10. January 5, 1902, *Some Letters,* p. 143.

11. See Letter to R. W. Gilder, February 5, 1906, *Ibid.,* pp. 160-61; and Arthur Hobson Quinn, *A History of the American Drama from the Civil War to the Present Day* (New York, 1927), II, 10.

12. As Henry (p. 153) has pointed out, Moody's play, unlike the standard version of the original myth as represented by Aeschylus, "presumes that Man had fire before the flood and that the Promethean theft was a restoration." This emphasis on a *restoration* is important in the light of the play's psychological themes, suggesting as it does that physical and spiritual vigor is a natural human birthright, a norm, and that its absence represents an abnormality.

13. It is only in Taylor's play that Pandora is explicitly Prometheus' beloved. As Moody remarked in an article on Stickney ("The Poems of Trumbull Stickney," *North American Review,* CLXXXIII [1906], 1005-1018), the later poet's Pandora, besides being depicted as with child by Zeus, remains largely "a mysterious voice, singing in her travail songs of mystic meaning, whose bearing upon the action is poignantly vague" (p. 1016). Stickney does not specify any lovers' relation between Prometheus and this "mysterious voice."

14. Henry, by way of supporting his own thesis that *The Fire-Bringer* is dramatically deficient, singles out this passage to illustrate the "too obviously expository" quality of the opening scene, and complains that "*Pyrrha* rehearses the whole story of the past action to *Deukalion* who knows it as well as she" (p. 134). Yet a reading of the scene will show how the device of the question-and-answer pattern gives credibility to this rehearsal.

15. The idea of an initial unsuccessful attempt by Prometheus to steal fire from Heaven has no source in Aeschylus, Shelley, Taylor, or Stickney.

16. Charleton Lewis (*Yale Review*, n.s. II, 694) cited this outcry by the Woman's Voice as containing "the supreme touch of authentic Symbolism, ... the Symbolism of Mallarmé and Symons." Later, Taupin echoed this view by singling these lines out as one of the *"rare"* instances in Moody's work of verses *"vraiment symbolistes,"* and even added that they *"ne seraient pas déplacées dans une pièce de Maeterlinck"* (*L'Influence du Symbolisme Français*, p. 54). Actually, the entire series of outcries introduced by the Woman's Voice has something of the true Symbolist quality which Taupin denies is characteristic of Moody's work.

17. See Manly, p. xxxviii; Lewis, *op. cit.*, 692; and Jones, *The Bright Medusa*, p. 58.

18. There is in this assertion of Apollo's supremacy something of the spirit of Keats's *Hyperion*, which also seems to have influenced Moody's blank-verse style in places. See Martha Hale Shackford, "Moody's *The Fire-Bringer* for To-day," *Sewanee Review*, XXVI (1918), 407-16, for a study of the specific influence of *Hyperion* on the passage in Act Two where Pyrrha describes the coming of light after Prometheus' theft of fire.

19. New York, 1902, p. 290.

20. *Letters to Harriet*, pp. 131, 134.

21. See especially Riggs, "Prometheus 1900," *American Literature*, XXII, 399-423. The key phrases in Riggs's attack have been quoted in Chapter One.

22. Payne, *The Dial*, LIII, 485.

23. Letter of August 4, 1903, *Letters to Harriet*, p. 159.

24. Manly, pp. xxxvii-xxxviii.

Chapter Six

1. See *Poetry and Drama* (Cambridge, 1951). The central similarity between Moody's and Eliot's views lies in their common search for a metrical pattern which can be uniformly maintained throughout a play and within which every gradation of poetic intensity, from the most relaxed and prose-like to the most heightened and compressed, can cohere. The one major difference is that Eliot summarily rejects blank verse as a workable norm for the modern drama.

2. Letter of February 6, 1904, *Letters to Harriet*, p. 185.

3. See, for instance, p. 24, footnote 1; p. 189, footnote 1; and p. 248, footnote 2.

4. Lovett, p. liv; and Quinn, p. 11.

5. New York, 1931, pp. 87-94.

6. Letter of August 19, 1901, *Letters to Harriet*, p. 78.

7. Letter of August 29, 1901, *Ibid.*, pp. 81-82; and Letter to Mason, August 30, 1901, *Some Letters*, pp. 140-41.

8. Letter of March 31, 1904, *Letters to Harriet*, p. 190.

9. Quoted in MacKaye, Introduction to *Ibid.*, p. 18.

10. Until the publication of the *Letters to Harriet* had clarified the matter of dates, Moody's critics mistakenly assumed that the trip to Arizona took place in the spring of 1905 rather than in 1904. Hence Lovett himself plays down the influence of the excursion on *The Great Divide*, since he thought that by this time "the play was already practically finished" (p. liv).

11. See especially Lovett, pp. lv-lvii; Henry, pp. 170-80; and MacKaye, pp. 40-48.

12. Quinn, p. 11.

13. "William Vaughn Moody," *The Harvard Graduates Magazine*, XIX (1910), 261.

14. Henry, p. 189.

15. Moody himself confirmed this intent in a later newspaper interview quoted by Henry (pp. 183-84) from an unidentified clipping among Harriet's papers: "I had hoped to suggest that Ruth doesn't kill Ghent because she already felt the influence of the man. She has talked with him, a human relationship has been established between them, and it is impossible for her to shoot him in cold blood. Although she is scarcely conscious of it, the bond which is to unite their lives has been formed, and she cannot break it."

16. On February 1, 1909, after Miss Anglin had been replaced in the American cast by Mary Lawton, and while preparations were being made for the coming London production, Moody wrote to Henry Miller: "Please, please persuade whoever plays Ruth in London to put love into Act II. Miss Lawton plays it without one hint of tenderness and smothered affection (or rather affection battling with pride), and in consequence her yielding to Ghent at the close of the play seems unconvincing" (*Some Letters*, p. 167).

17. The double reversal was not in the first version of the play when it was presented in Chicago as *The Sabine Woman*, and the addition was surely the most important revision Moody made. See *Letters to Harriet*, pp. 280, 282-83, for a running account of his thought-processes while reconceiving the role of Zona (the heroine's original name) so as to make her in the end "the active, petitioner and pleader for the thing she has rejected many times from the hands of her lover."

18. In this connection, *The Great Divide* might be considered an interesting epilogue to the history of earlier developments in the American image of the West studied in Henry Nash Smith's *Virgin Land: The American West as Symbol and Myth* (Cambridge, 1950). The play quite clearly embodies the two "paired but contradictory ideas of nature and civilization" which Smith shows underlying nineteenth-century literary and historical interpretations of the American frontier. Yet by the end, while these ideas remain "paired," Moody obviously endeavors to resolve the inherent contradiction between them in terms of his progressive doctrine, whereby the union of Ghent and Ruth represents the hope for an ultimate union of nature and civilization.

19. Moody's evident desire to give the New England spirit fair and serious treatment is shown, on the other hand, by his strenuous objection to any attempt at making Philip a similar object of satire. After seeing

the road-company's production of the play in Detroit on January 23, 1909, he wrote to Miller: "... I am forced to protest against the way in which the character of Philip has been gradually, but at last in the end *totally*, changed, both in spirit and significance. It is now played as a comedy part, and the whole effort is spent upon the attempt to wring the words and action, willy-nilly, into the guise of comic relief. I need hardly point out to you that this is to deprive the play of an essential element and to very seriously damage it thereby" (*Some Letters*, p. 163).

20. Alfred Kreymborg, *Our Singing Strength: An Outline of American Poetry (1620-1930)* (New York, 1929), p. 287.

21. See Henry, pp. 173-74, 210.

22. Walter Prichard Eaton, *The Drama in English* (New York, 1930), p. 312.

Chapter Seven

1. "Old Pourquoi" (in its first and longer version) was published in *The Reader* for December, 1904; "Second Coming" in *Century*, December, 1905; "Musa Meretrix" in *The Reader*, May, 1906; "Thammuz" in *Scribner's Magazine*, October, 1906; "The Death of Eve" in *Century*, December, 1906; and "The Counting Man" in *St. Nicholas*, August, 1909. In addition, "I Am the Woman" appeared posthumously in the first issue of Harriet Monroe's new magazine *Poetry* in 1912.

2. Lovett (p. lxxxi) says that "The great bulk of his writing up to the time of his death was experimental, and as such was destroyed." There is, however, no mention in Moody's letters from 1901 on of his working at any poems other than those which appear in the posthumous volume.

3. Quoted by Henry, pp. 216-17. The journal is unidentified.

4. Letter of May 22, 1906, *Letters to Harriet*, p. 272.

5. In connection with the strong mystical element in poems like "The Moon-Moth," "Second Coming," and "Thammuz," it is worth mentioning that Moody insisted on seeing such mysticism as central to the Greek Romantic spirit. See, for instance, his letter of May 28, 1902 (*Ibid.*, p. 117), where he singles out "the Orphic poets, the teachers of the Dionysiac cult and the hierophants of Demeter at Eleusis" as propounders of "a doctrine of mystic regeneration, to be achieved ... not through denial of this life but by a complete entering into it."

6. *Yale Review*, n.s. II, 700.

7. Letter to Harriet (then Mrs. Moody), August 27, 1911, *Selected Letters*, p. 73.

8. *The Education of Henry Adams* (Modern Library Edition), p. 383 *et circa*.

9. *History of American Poetry*, p. 26.

10. Riggs, *American Literature*, XXII, 415.

11. *Selected Letters*, p. 73. Yet Robinson did, in the same letter, name "I Am the Woman," along with "Second Coming" and "Old Pourquoi," as the three best poems in the posthumous group. Generally, however, Robinson's enthusiasm for Moody's later verse was not nearly as great as it had been for the earlier poems. This probably reflected a change in his own general literary attitudes as he grew older.

12. Mason quotes this diary entry in his introduction to *Some Letters*, p. 28.

13. In the earlier version of the poem published in the December, 1904 *Reader* (and reproduced by Henry, pp. 257-61), this kind of humor is much more prevalent and much more heavy-handed. Moody's revisions consisted chiefly in some severe cutting; and the passages he omitted, including the original first four stanzas, were mostly taken up with rather drawn-out accounts of his relation with Mason, which take up only a small part of the later version.

14. Adams, *Op. cit.*, p. 472. Since this is the second time Adams has been cited in this chapter, it is perhaps necessary to remark that the first private printing of the *Education* did not occur until 1907; and it is improbable that Moody would have been acquainted with *Mont-Saint-Michel and Chartres*, which was privately printed in a limited edition for Adams' closest friends in 1904.

15. "The Magi," *The Collected Poems of W. B. Yeats* (New York, 1958), p. 124.

16. p. 1. Cf. Henry, p. 61.

17. Letter to R. W. Gilder, August 23, 1905, *Some Letters*, p. 159.

18. While he was working on "The Fountain," Moody remarked to Harriet, "My chief fear about it is it is too 'picturesque,' that the reader will take it at its face value and feel no uneasiness" (Letter of September 18, 1904, *Letters to Harriet*, p. 207). Judging from the final appearance of the poem, it is possible that he cut down on the "picturesque" elements, in order to insure that his allegorical aims would come through more clearly.

19. Chislett, "The Sources of William Vaughn Moody's 'Thammuz,'" *The Dial*, LX (1916), 370.

20. Lovett, p. lxxxviii.

Chapter Eight

1. From an unidentified newspaper interview after the New York opening, quoted by Henry, p. 218. Though Moody added that "By that I mean poetic feeling. I tried to put that feeling into 'The Great Divide,'" his more usual tendency was to identify "poetry" with *verse* rather than "poetic prose." Lovett reports (p. lxii) that near the very end of his life he confided to Ferdinand Schevill "his constant regret that he had given so much of his last precious time to prose, which he, like Milton, reckoned to be but 'the work of his left hand.'"

2. See Letter of July 26, 1906, *Letters to Harriet,* p. 294.

3. See Letter of October 7, 1906, *Ibid.*, p. 306.

4. *Ibid.*, p. 334.

5. Letter of October 3, 1907, *Ibid.*, p. 341.

6. For Moody's own account of the production, its reception, and his dissatisfaction with the script, see the letter to his sister Charlotte dated April 30, 1909, and quoted by MacKaye in the Introduction to the *Letters to Harriet,* pp. 62-63. See also Henry, p. 198, and the listing of newspaper reviews in Henry's bibliography, pp. 271-72.

7. Letter to Charlotte, MacKaye, p. 63.

8. The 1910 edition was intended to supersede an edition which Houghton Mifflin had published the preceding year of the four-act version used in the St. Louis production. According to Henry (p. 198), Moody had had this 1909 edition published at his own expense, but "So dis-

pleased was he with the stage results that he not only did not distribute the printed edition but he attempted to recall the few copies that he knew to be circulating." See Henry, pp. 198-99, for a summary of the principal changes Moody made in the 1910 edition.

9. See the listing of newspaper reviews in Henry's bibliography (p. 271). Moody was not present at the New York opening: by January, 1910, he was already very seriously ill and suffering from recurrent attacks of blindness; and he and Harriet (whom he had married in May, 1909) were in Southern California trying desperately to restore his health. See the excerpts from Harriet's diary for this period, quoted by MacKaye (pp. 389-90), for descriptions of Moody's reactions to the play's failure and to the somewhat more successful production it received at Harvard University on January 24.

10. The most sympathetic commentators have been Quinn (pp. 14-16) and Sculley Bradley (*Lit. Hist. of U.S.*, II, 1014-15). For representative examples of unsympathetic criticism, see Thomas H. Dickinson, *Playwrights of the New American Theater* (New York, 1925), p. 144; Henry, pp. 202-14; and Grant C. Knight, *The Strenuous Age in American Literature* (Chapel Hill, 1954), p. 208.

11. See Chapter Two, footnotes 30 and 32.

12. This was the original name of Moody's protagonist. In November, 1908, he decided to change the name because of a fear that its closeness to that of the actual Schlatter would give offense to some. The name he finally adopted in its place, Ulrich Michaelis, he had found in the New York City Directory. See Letter of November 22, 1908, *Letters to Harriet,* pp. 369-70.

13. *Ibid.*, pp. 318-19.

14. See especially the section of *The Varieties of Religious Experience* which deals with the contemporary "Mind-cure movement" (Modern Library Edition, pp. 92-124).

15. "Upon being asked in interview by a reporter if the play was an exposition of Christian Science, he [Moody] answered: 'What I wanted to point out in "The Faith Healer" is the power of the soul over the body—a doctrine not new with the Christian Scientists. . . .' " (Henry, p. 205).

16. Henry, pp. 203-4. See also Lovett, p. lix. Though Lovett states that there are "three versions extant" of *The Faith Healer,* the 1900 version is contained in none of the three public collections of Moody manuscripts —those in the University of Chicago, Princeton University, and Huntington Libraries. If the manuscript has survived, it is probably in a private collection. We do know from Moody's letters, however, that he made several false starts and revised his original purpose several times between the time he first began trying to write the play in verse in 1898 and the time he completed the 1900 version. See especially the letters to Mason dated January 17, 1899, and December 2, 1899 (*Some Letters,* pp. 107-8, 118).

17. *Independent,* LXXIV, 315.

18. *On Poetry in Drama* (London, 1937), p. 34.

19. Quinn, p. 10.

20. *Poetic Drama: An Anthology of Plays in Verse from the Ancient*

Greek to the Modern American (New York, 1941), p. 806. The play appears on pp. 807-17.

21. See the letter of May 1, 1907, quoted at the start of this chapter. The exact prophecy they had in mind was probably that in Revelation 21:1: "And I saw a new heaven and a new earth: for the first heaven and the first earth were passed away."

22. See Genesis, 4:15. Actually, the idea that the sign was set in his forehead as a memento of the murder of Abel is Moody's own elaboration. In Genesis its purpose is to protect Cain "lest any finding him should kill him."

23. Hagedorn, *Independent*, LXXIV, 316.

24. *Yale Review*, n.s. II, 699.

25. *Op. cit.*, pp. 16, 33-34.

26. According to Manly (p. xl), Moody had intended to add a final lyric "sung by Jubal as he leads . . . Abdera" up to the city gate. Lovett reports Harriet as claiming that this lyric would have been a duet (See Henry, p. 119). In any case, it was never written; and though it might have proved a very effective ending if it were anywhere near as good a lyric as some of those in the *Masque* and particularly *The Fire-Bringer,* its absence does not really detract from the sense of esthetic completeness we receive from the ending as it stands.

27. See *Poems and Dramas of George Cabot Lodge* (Boston, 1911), I, 229-339. In Lodge's drama, it is Cain rather than Eve who is really the arch-rebel; and in his rebellion he comes rather close to anticipating later existentialist ideas. His motive in killing Abel is fear that his weaker younger brother may procreate a race of cowards afraid to accept the idea of human freedom independent of God. Throughout the drama, as throughout Moody's, Abel is identified with Adam as the obedient, penitent servant of God. Cain is identified with Eve as the impenitent rebel who would make man independent through greater and greater knowledge. In this, of course, Lodge and Moody part company, since the theme of *The Death of Eve* is man's need not to accept and affirm his estrangement from God but to overcome that estrangement. Quite possibly there was a reciprocal influence in Lodge's and Moody's dramas, since the first version of Moody's own poem "The Death of Eve" was written a year before *Cain* appeared.

28. Lewis, *op. cit.*, pp. 695-96. See also Taupin, p. 55; and Henry pp. 167-68.

29. Manly, p. xl.

30. Quoted by Henry, p. 119, from a note of Lovett's based on Harriet's account of Moody's plans for completing the play.

31. Letter of October 7, 1906, *Letters to Harriet*, p. 306.

32. Letter of August 5, 1904, *Some Letters*, p. 148.

33. On February 17, 1909, while in the midst of his discouraging labors on the second complete version of *The Faith Healer,* Moody wrote to the wife of his one-time Harvard professor C. H. Toy: "The thing I have most at heart just now is a poetic—I mean a *verse*—play. I have got a grand idea, and keep feeling my muscle to see if I am up to doing it, thus far with rather discouraging responses from my system. Also, I am torn between the ideal aspect of the theme and the stage necessities— the old, old problem. Perhaps in the end I will let the stage go to ballyhoo,

and write the thing as I see it, for that justly lighted and managed stage of the mind, where there are no bad actors and where the peanut-eating of the public is reduced to a discreet minimum. But this–after all–is an uncourageous compromise..." (*Some Letters,* p. 169). Undoubtedly, however, the idea of lapsing back into closet drama would have seemed more than "uncourageous" to Moody in his less dejected moods. Whether the new verse play he refers to was *The Death of Eve,* a drama about St. Paul which Henry (p. 215) finds hinted at in MacKaye's elegy *Uriel,* or one on those contemporary materials he wanted so much to treat in verse, there is no way of knowing. If he was not referring to *The Death of Eve* but to a new play, it was one he never began. For the revision of *The Faith Healer,* which he wrote after the St. Louis production that March, was Moody's last creative endeavor.

Selected Bibliography

PRIMARY SOURCES

(*In Chronological Order*)

(*For a listing of magazine publications of Moody's poems, including both the early ones rejected for his volumes and later ones republished in the volumes, see Henry, pp. 264-65.*)

Editor, *The Pilgrim's Progress,* by John Bunyan. Boston: Houghton Mifflin Co., 1897.

Editor, *The Rime of the Ancient Mariner,* by Samuel Taylor Coleridge, and *The Vision of Sir Launfal,* by James Russell Lowell (one volume). Chicago: Scott, Foresman, and Co. (Lake English Classics Series), 1898.

Editor, *The Complete Poetical Works of John Milton.* Boston: Houghton Mifflin Co., 1899.

Editor, *The Lay of the Last Minstrel,* by Sir Walter Scott. Chicago: Scott, Foresman, and Co. (Lake English Classics Series), 1899.

Editor, *Marmion,* by Sir Walter Scott. Chicago: Scott, Foresman, and Co. (Lake English Classics Series), 1899.

Editor, *The Lady of the Lake,* by Sir Walter Scott. Chicago: Scott, Foresman, and Co. (Lake English Classics Series), 1900.

Co-editor, with W. W. Cressy, *The Iliad of Homer, Books I, VI, XXII, XXIV.* Trans. by Alexander Pope. Chicago: Scott, Foresman, and Co. (Lake English Classics Series), 1900.

The Masque of Judgment. Boston: Small, Maynard, and Co., 1900.

Poems. Boston: Houghton Mifflin Co., 1901. (Republished as *Gloucester Moors and Other Poems.*)

With Robert Morss Lovett, *A History of English Literature.* New York: Charles Scribner's Sons, 1902.

The Fire-Bringer. Boston: Houghton Mifflin Co., 1904.

With Robert Morss Lovett, *A First View of English Literature.* New York: Charles Scribner's Sons, 1905.

Co-editor, with George Cabot Lodge and John Ellerton Lodge, *The Poems of Trumbull Stickney.* Boston: Houghton Mifflin Co., 1905.

"The Poems of Trumbull Stickney," *North American Review,* CLXXXIII (November 16, 1906), 1005-18.

The Faith Healer (four-act version). Boston: Houghton Mifflin Co., 1909.

Editor, *Selections from DeQuincey.* Chicago: Scott, Foresman, and Co. (Lake English Classics Series), 1909.

The Faith Healer (three-act version). New York: The Macmillan Co., 1910.

The Great Divide. New York: The Macmillan Co., 1911.

The Poems and Plays of William Vaughn Moody, ed. John M. Manly, 2 vols. Boston: Houghton Mifflin Co., 1912.

Some Letters of William Vaughn Moody, ed. Daniel Gregory Mason. Boston: Houghton Mifflin Co., 1913.

Selected Poems of William Vaughn Moody, ed. Robert Morss Lovett. Boston: Houghton Mifflin Co., 1931.

Letters to Harriet, ed. Percy MacKaye. Boston: Houghton Mifflin Co., 1935.

SECONDARY SOURCES

The one book-length study is Henry, David D., *William Vaughn Moody: A Study*. Boston: Bruce Humphries, 1934. Valuable for biographical and bibliographical data and as a summation of earlier Moody criticism (on which Henry draws quite heavily throughout), this work contains some good original comments on the prose plays; but the criticism on the poetry and verse plays is generally thin and unoriginal.

The reader is referred to Henry's bibliography, pp. 266-72, for a fairly complete listing of books and articles dealing with Moody from 1900 to the time Henry's study appeared, and especially for a listing of contemporary newspaper and periodical reviews, preserved among Mrs. Moody's papers, of the various works published during Moody's lifetime and the first productions of his plays. The following list of books and articles includes only the most significant among those published before Henry's book, or those which contain important critical material not cited or assimilated by Henry. Works published after Henry's book, though fewer in number, are represented more liberally.

BARR, NASH O., and CHARLES H. CAFFIN. "William Vaughn Moody: A Study," *The Drama: A Quarterly Review*, I (1911), 177-211. One of the more incisive early appraisals of the lyric poems and verse dramas, with some helpful suggestions regarding their literary sources (Barr). Caffin's contribution on the prose plays is briefer and less important.

BRADLEY, SCULLEY. "The Emergence of the Modern Drama," *Literary History of the United States*. New York: The Macmillan Co., 1948. Contains (pp. 1013-15) a brief but perceptive discussion of the central moral theme which animates all Moody's plays, in verse and prose.

CONNER, FREDERICK WILLIAM. *Cosmic Optimism: A study of the Interpretation of Evolution by American Poets from Emerson to Robinson*. Gainesville: University of Florida Press, 1949. Valuable both for its illumination of the general intellectual backgrounds of Moody's progressive ideas, and for the specific discussion of Moody (Chapter XIII, "The Paradox of the 'Genteel Tradition': Hovey, Lodge, and Moody," pp. 314-31) as "the last important figure in American poetry who can be called . . . a bona fide 'cosmic optimist.'"

DICKINSON, THOMAS H. *Playwrights of the New American Theater*. New York: The Macmillan Co., 1925. Unsympathetic to both the verse dramas and *The Faith Healer*, but worth reading for its enthusiastic and suggestive, if sometimes oversimplified, analysis of *The Great Divide*.

ECKMAN, FREDERICK. "Moody's Ode: The Collapse of the Heroic," *Texas Studies in English*, XXXVI (1957), 80-92. Centered on a comparison between "An Ode in Time of Hesitation" and John Berryman's poem

"Boston Common," the article is in the main an unsympathetic study of the "Ode" as "a memorial to the collapse of the Romantic grand manner in America."

FUSSELL, EDWIN S. "Robinson to Moody: Ten Unpublished Letters," *American Literature*, XXIII (1951) 173-87. A valuable supplement to the critical materials in Edwin Arlington Robinson's *Selected Letters*.

GLASHEEN, FRANCIS J. and ADALINE. "Moody's 'An Ode in Time of Hesition,'" *College English*, V (1943), 121-29. An informative study of the political and literary backgrounds of Moody's "Ode."

JONES, HOWARD MUMFORD. *The Bright Medusa*. Urbana: University of Illinois Press, 1952. An eloquent latter-day defense of Moody as a chief figure in the half-forgotten but significant "poetic renaissance" that began at Harvard near the turn of the century, and also included Stickney, Lodge, and Santayana. The main critical emphasis is on Moody's trilogy as a major humanist document.

KNIGHT, GRANT C. *The Strenuous Age in American Literature*. Chapel Hill: University of North Carolina Press, 1954. A more or less year-by-year account of American literary activity during the first decade of the twentieth century, with some general but occasionally incisive comments on Moody's poems and plays as they related to the period as a whole.

LEWIS, CHARLETON M. "William Vaughn Moody," *Yale Review*, n.s. II (1913), 688-703. Probably the most sensitive and informed of all the early articles on Moody. Enthusiastic but not uncritical. Particularly valuable for its discussion of Moody's relations to French poetry of the later nineteenth century.

LEWISOHN, LUDWIG. *Expression in America*. New York: Harper and Brothers, 1932. A consideration of Moody as "the symbolical transition figure between the polite age and the modern period in American culture," with chief emphasis on the social and political poems. Ambivalent in its evaluations, but with occasional good insights into both Moody's virtues and shortcomings.

LOVETT, ROBERT MORSS. Introduction to Moody's *Selected Poems*. Boston: Houghton Mifflin Co., 1931. Contains important biographical material and some intelligent critical comments on the poems and verse dramas.

MACKAYE, PERCY. Introduction, Conclusion, and Notes to Moody's *Letters to Harriet*. Boston: Houghton Mifflin Co., 1935. The fullest source of biographical information about Moody's later years and especially about his theater activities. Also contains a bibliography, pp. 439-43, which sometimes supplements that in Henry's book.

MANLY, JOHN M. Introduction to Moody's *Poems and Plays*. Boston: Houghton Mifflin Co., 1912, Vol. I. The first extended biographical sketch of Moody, with some good interpretive and evaluative remarks on the poems and verse dramas.

MATTHIESSEN, F. O. *The Responsibilities of the Critic* (A collection of Matthiessen's essays and reviews selected by John Rackliffe). New York: Oxford University Press, 1952. Contains a brief study of Moody's poetry and verse plays reprinted from a review of the 1931 *Selected Poems* which originally appeared in the *New England Quarterly*. For all its brevity, worth reading for an indication of attitudes toward Moody by one of the century's finest literary historians. Though critical of

Moody's verse techniques, Matthiessen displays considerable respect for the "solid quality" of his ideas and for "the range and energy of his conception of life."

QUINN, ARTHUR HOBSON. *A History of the American Drama from the Civil War to the Present Day.* 2 Vols. New York: Harper and Brothers, 1927. Vol. II. One of the best and most sympathetic appraisals of Moody's place in the history of the drama. Gives serious attention to the theatrical values of *The Fire-Bringer* and *The Death of Eve,* as well as of the prose plays.

RIGGS, THOMAS, JR. "Prometheus 1900," *American Literature,* XXII (1951), 399-423. A comparison of uses of the Promethean theme in *The Fire-Bringer,* Stickney's *Prometheus Pyrphoros,* and Lodge's *Cain* and *Heracles,* set against the contemporary philosophical climate represented chiefly by Henry Adams. An intelligent article, but weakened by a rather narrow thesis which causes the author to underrate Moody's drama simply because its final optimistic outlook runs contrary to Adams' pessimistic interpretation of modern scientific discoveries.

ROBINSON, EDWIN ARLINGTON. *Selected Letters.* Ed. Ridgely Torrence. New York: The Macmillan Co., 1940. Contains excellent critical insights into the work of his friend Moody, particularly during the period from 1899 to 1901.

SHACKFORD, MARTHA HALE. "Moody's *The Fire-Bringer* for To-day," *Sewanee Review,* XXVI (1918), 407-16. A laudatory essay on the universal significances of Moody's drama. Though fairly brief, one of the best earlier critical studies of *The Fire-Bringer;* shows good insights into Moody's general philosophical outlook.

SHOREY, PAUL. "The Poetry of William Vaughn Moody," *University of Chicago Record,* n.s. XIII (1927), 172-200. An enthusiastic study of the poems and verse dramas, emphasizing the "modernity" of their contents and defending the traditional modes Moody chose as vehicles for those contents. The most valuable section is the one where Shorey traces sources for some of the lines and phrases in which Moody owed a direct "debt to other singers."

Index